Writers of Wales

EDITORS

MEIC STEPHENS R. BRINLEY JONES

GWASG PRIFYSGOL CYMRU MCMXXII

GEORGE EWART EVANS

1909–1988

(Photograph reproduced by kind permission of David Gentleman)

Gareth Williams

GEORGE EWART EVANS

University of Wales Press
on behalf of the Welsh Arts Council

1991

It is important, I agree, for a writer to place himself in the main stream of culture from the past. It is also important for him to interpret correctly the impact of the present; most important of all to give artistic expression to the unformed, inarticulate desires and strivings of a people in a rapidly changing world.

George Ewart Evans in WALES, August 1939, p. 225.

I

The achievement of George Ewart Evans is rich in range, humanity and paradox. Born in 1909 in a mining village in industrial Glamorgan, he had by the time of his death in 1988 established a lasting reputation as the unrivalled interpreter of rural East Anglia. Conditioned by personal experience and the inspiration of the miners' inter-war struggle to a lifelong commitment to the left in politics and culture, he became the trusted confidant and sympathetic recorder of the notoriously taciturn, apolitical, deferential farm-workers of the unremittingly flat landscape of Suffolk. Compelled by deafness to abandon teaching, he became a pioneer of oral history, of getting history from the people by listening to them. What he discovered from his oldest informants, born in the last century, was an entire, disappearing world of rural memories, language, customs and folklore, a *prior culture* under sentence of death from the internal combustion engine, the displacement of the horse by the tractor and the triumph of mechanization. Ironically, it was the acquisition in 1950 of two pieces of precision technology, the tape recorder and the hearing-aid, that enabled him to provide that *prior culture* with its fullest obituary in a sheaf of books with evocative titles like THE PATTERN UNDER THE PLOUGH, WHERE BEARDS WAG ALL, THE DAYS THAT WE HAVE SEEN and FROM MOUTHS OF MEN, in a sequence that followed the first of his studies of the oral tradition, ASK THE FELLOWS WHO CUT THE HAY, which has been reprinted eight times since its publication in 1956 and has attained the status of a classic. A Classics graduate himself, he became an anthropologist, folklorist and ethnographer, and in the process redirected the study of history; he was much in demand as a lecturer to university extension, Workers' Educational Association and Continuing Education classes, and was in addition a versatile author, producing a constant stream of fiction and verse as well as radio and film scripts. For George Ewart Evans was first and last *a writer* and he never wrote anything of significance that did not owe its inspiration to the environment, culture and community of the south Wales that nurtured him:

My upbringing in a mining valley made it almost inevitable that my writing should take a certain slant, and should be coloured and deepened by living in a community that was in crisis.

(SPOKEN HISTORY, p. 213)

That community was Abercynon.

II

It is only one of the many paradoxes surrounding the life and work of George Ewart Evans that the historian of the *prior culture* should have come from anywhere as recent as Abercynon, a mining settlement fifteen miles north of Cardiff, thrown up by the final wave of industrialization that broke over south Wales in the second half of the nineteenth century. So recent was it compared with what he later called *my second academy*, the Suffolk village of Blaxhall which was older than Domesday, that only in 1893 did the residents of the new township at the confluence of the Tâf and Cynon Rivers decide to call it Abercynon in preference to the proffered suggestions of Navigation, Aberdare Junction, Cynonvale and the tongue-twisting though topographically accurate Abertafachynon.

Until the first pits were sunk in 1889 it had been a rural village of fewer than fifty cottages and farms. But once coal began to be raised, from 1894, it became overnight a human coral reef on which life began urgently to cluster. Its population soared to 6,000 by 1901 and to nearly 10,000 by 1911. Amenities and facilities sprang up: streets like Glancynon Terrace, containing shops such as William Evans's grocery in Bristol House, and next door to it Calfaria Welsh Baptist Chapel, built in 1894, where William Evans became a deacon and superintendent of the Sunday school in 1907; schools like Abertâf Elementary, attended by William Evans's eleven children; as well as public houses and the imposing Workmen's Hall, opened in the year that really ushered Wales into the twentieth century, 1905. Water and gas had to be laid on and roads widened to meet the requirements of increased traffic. Although the first motor car was seen in Abercynon in 1904, it got no further than Cilfynydd Common and had to be hauled back by horse, the primary mode of transport during the boyhood of young Ewart, the third son of William Evans, and the first born to his second wife Janet, née Hitchings, of Maesteg.

In later life George Ewart Evans, an amalgam of his mother's energy and his father's sensitivity, would proclaim *the strength of the hills*, the title he eventually gave his autobiography—*the Glamorgan Hills spoke to me as no other scene has spoken to me since* (THE STRENGTH OF THE HILLS, p. 45)—but his earliest memories were of two dramatic events on the floor of the valleys below. In 1913 occurred the Cilfynydd cyclone (or, according to one's village chauvinism, the Treharris tornado) that killed two people, and on 14 October, in neighbouring Senghennydd, the horrific explosion at the Universal Colliery that killed 439. The next day the four-year-old Ewart saw, unforgettably, hundreds of colliers in their Sunday black streaming over the mountain to the stricken village, *girding it as if with an emblematic mourning ribbon.*

If Abercynon itself was of recent origin, the surrounding older industrial districts had for decades, in the years between 1860 and 1900 especially, been areas of considerable literary activity. A circle known as 'Clic y Bont' was only the best-known of the several coteries of bibulous bards and versifiers that met in the long room of the Ynysybwl Inn, the Carw Coch at Aberdare, the Stag at Trecynon and the New Inn at Abercynon. They included locally acclaimed figures like 'Morien', 'Myfyr Morgannwg', 'Brynfab', 'Dewi Wyn o Essyllt', 'Tawenog' and 'Carnelian', though not 'Mabwyson', the bardic name of W. H. Dyer who gave this clique of literary comets its derisive appellation because of the eisteddfodic closed shop it operated. Dyer himself, a notably unkempt individual who lived in a shack—he was the likely model for the ragman Dando Hamer in George Ewart Evans's much-anthologized story 'Possessions'—had been baptized by the equally hirsute and even more legendary William Price of Llantrisant who, when he saw 'Mabwyson' coming out of the water, thought he had baptized the devil himself. Some of the tales about Dr Price, frequently recounted to his numerous offspring by William Evans who had known the famous cremationist in his native Pentyrch, are creatively recycled in George Ewart Evans's 1947 novel, THE VOICES OF THE CHILDREN, where the young Willie Pritchard and his friends are held spellbound by the yarns spun by Jack Ragtime at the Mason's Arms.

Another source of local lore and legend that George Ewart Evans frequently referred to later was the history of the parish which included Abercynon, LLANWYNNO (1888) by 'Glanffrwd'. In assembling his description of the community on the eve of the transforming economic changes of the late nineteenth century, 'Glanffrwd' (Revd William Thomas, 1843–1900) drew on the oral recollections of the oldest inhabitants, some of whom were in their eighties, and his chapters on 'Traditional Sayings' and 'Old Characters' find an echo in ASK THE FELLOWS WHO CUT THE HAY, except that there the 'Village Legends, Superstitions and Customs' and 'Old Words and Sayings' are not those of south Wales, but of Suffolk. An inveterate collector of oral tradition, 'Glanffrwd' was and remains one of the best sources of the stories surrounding, for instance, the fleet-footed Guto Nyth Brân, chaser of hares and victor over his English rivals, who died young in 1732 and was buried in Llanwynno churchyard. George Ewart Evans recounts Guto's fatal last race sensitively, economically and with firm impersonal observation in a short story called 'Folk Tale', first published in THE WELSH REVIEW in 1939 and later included in his 1975 collection LET DOGS DELIGHT.

Ewart Evans, at least over the short sprint, was no mean Guto himself, a considerable athlete on track in the summer and on the wing on the rugby field in winter. The year he left Mountain Ash County School (1927) he ran professionally and played for 'The Old Firm', the name popularly given to Mountain Ash Rugby Club, by then enjoying a somewhat fading reputation as one of the leading Welsh sides, in the immediate post-war period studded with international players and trialists. If the fortunes of the club took a sharp downward turn in the late twenties this was due more to the prevailing economic climate than to Ewart Evans's performance on the wing.

To assist his path financially to University College, Cardiff, at a time of great domestic difficulty as the Depression pushed the family grocery business ever closer to bankruptcy, he decided to run for his money as professional sprinter and coach. This is one of the several aspects of life in inter-war south Wales on which he casts real illumination in his THE STRENGTH OF THE HILLS, which evokes quite remarkably the upbringing of a working-class county schoolboy in the south Wales valleys between the wars. Against a backcloth of deepening economic crisis and personal hardship, the burning desire on the part of financially crippled parents, especially mothers, for their children's betterment, the fecklessness of others, the critical role played by caring, book-lending teachers, the long summer of 1926, the collective music-making, the anthropology of chapel society and the courtship rituals of the Sunday evening parade by groups of young men and women—these are all seen through a wryly affectionate lens whose focus is undimmed by sentiment.

It is in the discussion of sport that the connections between local and national identity, social class and popular culture are particularly well handled. For in the Valleys the amateur–professional link was relatively meaningless, whereas the coastal towns followed the English middle-class model of segregated grammar schools which fostered an amateur outlook. Professional running along old railway tracks and tramways was long established in the Valleys before the annual race-meeting for professional runners, the so-called 'Welsh Powderhall', was inaugurated in 1903 just lower down the valley from Abercynon at Pontypridd where George Ewart Evans himself ran, though his most important win was in a handicap race at Merthyr Vale which earned him fifteen pounds, *over seven weeks' wages for a collier in 1927, and for me a small fortune*, as he later recalled. Running was more than a matter of monetary reward or even physical stimulation; it was mentally exhilarating too, inducing in him *a subjective oneness of mind and body bound together in harmonious order*, a kinaesthetic sensation that *my mind appeared to be as much in my muscles as in my head.* The 'oneness' of things would always exert a particular fascination for him.

Several of his short stories are set against a background of professional running. 'The Powder Monkey' (Wales, VII, 1948) is one of them. It is about eight-year-old Johnny Edwards who has inherited a running muscle from his father Luther, himself once renowned in four or five valleys for his prowess on the wing and on the track. Seeing himself in his son, Luther takes him to be coached by Rhondda Parry who starts him with a gun and calls him his 'powder monkey' because he is small and quick and lives in the old Powder House where colliery explosives were once stored before being moved further up the mountain, away from the encroaching village; it is also, of course, a play on 'Powderhall' running. After several training sessions with Rhondda and his assistant Walter *('Put the wool up, will you, Walter?')* he is entered for a meeting where some of the back markers—this is handicap racing—were older, bigger boys, *as big as men*, and Johnny is beaten in the semi by one of them, a lanky boy called Raker *who came from another valley and who used to chase after small boys as if he'd eat them.* Undeterred, Johnny continues to practise, building up his speed as his father becomes increasingly crippled. For all Luther's entreaties to enter Johnny immediately in upcoming races, Rhondda holds him back until a Bank Holiday meeting for twenty pounds. Raker is in the same race and attracts the money while Rhondda and Walter back Johnny, who wins. Arriving back Johnny passes his friend Davey John who is making a tent with bracken just behind his garden wall, the mountain a symbol of innocence in an adult world where professional running brings money to an impoverished household. In the Edwards home, Rhondda places all the winnings under the caddy on the mantelpiece, though Luther attempts to refuse it. It is Johnny who hands his mother the money, before asking, *'Can I go out and play with Davey John?'*

We cannot miss, in this story, Ewart Evans's careful re-creation of time and place, the juxtaposition of the ferny hillside and scarred industrial village, the felt experiences of childhood, the keen ear for valley speech and the other deft touches that indicate that he was writing from within a world he knew intimately. Through his very attentiveness to the peripheries of working-class life he is able to illustrate something of the universal humanity at its core.

III

George Ewart Evans the writer emerged in the 1930s during that literary renaissance in Wales which led, outside it, to what Keidrych Rhys called *a revival of interest in the disagreeable Welsh.* The Anglo-Welsh writers of the late thirties and forties grew out of a set of by now familiar circumstances. Ewart Evans himself had no doubt that it arose as a form of literary social protest against the human despoliation of the Depression. The product of a society that could not afford professional writers, least of all those with the money or time to devote to more sustained kinds of writing, he emerged from what Glyn Jones, who was a part of it, has described as 'the talent belt' of politically radical, religiously Nonconformist families whose Welsh-speaking *fathers*, for the most part teachers, shopkeepers or preachers, began speaking English at home. There were, too, historically longer-term factors which left their mark on Ewart Evans's writing, like the numerical decline but continuing emotional appeal of religious Nonconformity, the coming to maturity of the Welsh secondary schools (like Mountain Ash County School, opened in 1907), the emergence of the non-Welsh-speaking population as a clear majority within Wales, and the forum provided by the 'little magazines', the Dublin Review, Keidrych Rhys's Wales, Gwyn Jones's Welsh Review, Robert Herring's Life and Letters Today which was virtually hijacked by the Anglo-Welsh and, for the politically committed, Edgell Rickword's LEFT REVIEW.

It was the indebtedness which engulfed the family business and his own fruitless search for employment in the early thirties that drove Ewart Evans to take up a position on the political left which he never abandoned. Though the miners' difficulties only compounded those of his family, his support for them never wavered: *in years to come,* he wrote in 1937, *the Miners' Struggle will acquire an almost legendary character . . . for the present no book has adequately translated the epic quality of their resistance.* Jack Jones's autobiographical UNFINISHED JOURNEY, in Ewart Evans's eyes when he reviewed it, certainly fell short of that requirement. After mercilessly castigating the author's indecent anxiety to disown his former travelling companions and forget he had ever been a miners' representative, *one finally comes away with the impression of Mr Jones meticulously wiping his feet in readiness to tread the Ithacan carpet of respectable people like Mr Lloyd George who writes the preface* (WALES, Autumn 1937, pp. 128–30). In the circumstances of the thirties it was an unforgivable betrayal.

His savage contempt for the monied class, the leisured capitalists he held responsible for the economic and political crisis of the thirties, is equally blistering in his pre-war poem 'At The Seaside':

Froth on the lip of a crescent sea
proudly preening on promenade
assault of sea on windy rock awaring
the moments sporting as with splash of spray.

there snatches wrinkled-neck grey-suited
paper that tells him if his money-cakes are burning.
flat-slippered shuffles to deck chairs facing sun
the weight of years and paunches bearing down
ineffectual gaze at flesh that flaunts it by.
high-conscious they sit behind the hydro sunglass
at ease to view with vague forebodings.
coming to tea with honey and sun-burned arms.
What comes after this? where turns the wheel?
no longer hold our corner of the sun?
. . . Fear is left with sugar at the bottom.

(WALES, March 1939)

His opposition in this decade to what he called *the present war-ridden bourgeois rotten reality* disposed him to find an ideologically congenial outlet for his work. He found it in LEFT REVIEW, a Communist literary journal founded in 1934 out of dissatisfaction with the contemporary state of publishing in order to encourage *literature that expressed and reflected the actual strength of the downtrodden . . . or could convey by realistic treatment their natural conditions of work and communicate their humanity and the plight of their position.* LEFT REVIEW expressly encouraged working-class authors and did unearth a few, notably Lewis Jones and some East-End Jewish writers. The thirties saw new concepts constructed around 'the people' and 'culture', chiefly in the realm of literary criticism, and the search for an organic popular culture found common ground among both the SCRUTINY faithful and Marxist critics like Alick West and Christopher Caudwell. But whereas to the Scrutineers the crisis of modern civilization was to be resolved through the study of literature and the preservation of traditional values, radical left writers inverted this élitism by celebrating the culture of the people whose creative strengths needed to be tapped and released. Eventually it was oral history that, from the 1950s, became for George Ewart Evans a means of releasing that creativity as he developed a way of giving history back to the people in their own words. In recording the unforced rhythms and unadorned speech of his often unlettered informants, he believed he was restoring to people a heightened sense of their own worth, making history a democratic activity. With *his* background he did not need to be taught this, any more than in the 1930s he needed to be told by middle-class intellectuals that literature was political.

Under the robust editorship of Rickword and then Randall Swingler, LEFT REVIEW was never an internal Party organ but a national review. Though it included non-Communists among its contributors, and some birds of passage like C. Day Lewis and Stephen Spender, the solid majority retained a lifetime of commitment to the left: these included historians like A. L. Morton and Dona Torr, scientists like J. D. Bernal and Thomas Hodgkin, musicians like Alan Bush and A. L. Lloyd, and writers like James Hanley and George Ewart Evans. 'Red Coal' by George Geraint, a pseudonym Ewart Evans adopted to protect his by then hard-won teaching post in Cambridgeshire, appeared in the February 1937 number of LEFT REVIEW. It is a mining story strong on social realism and a sense of the experience of work, even down to what working people wear, in this case the new boots which Dai Morgan proudly and noisily wears to work after three years' unemployment, only to be killed on his first day back by a rock fall; the only visible part of him on the stretcher is his boots.

In George Ewart Evans's second published story 'Pause for Conversation' (WALES, April 1937), apparel serves the dual purpose of social signifier and *the suggestive symbol which in a short story serves as a small lens opening to a wide and implied tract of country* (LIFE AND LETTERS TODAY, no. 145, 1949, p. 265). Joe, half-blind with the nystagmus that has made him redundant, his old shabby overcoat drawn together by two buttons supplemented by pieces of string, is in Pete the Italian's café discussing the needless death, through managerial negligence, of two brothers in an industrial accident. At the top of the street an Easter *Cymanfa Ganu* (hymn-singing festival) is in full swing *to thank Who-was or What-ever-May-Be for a happy, if shortened, release from starving.*

However, *not everyone who was idle that day wanted to sing, and many were debarred from doing so, since they did not possess the suit of 'best clothes' which was the unofficial though none the less binding pass to the Sanctum. 'Fancy singing* Messiah *in a muffler. Never been heard of . . .'* This year it is the *Elijah* and the sound of the great chorus 'Thanks be to God, He laveth the thirsty land' reaches even into Pete's café. *'They're 'avin a gran' time up there' ventured Pete tonelessly . . . Joe silently raised his stick in salute and stepped on to the pavement.* Lacking a respectable suit himself in the thirties, George Ewart Evans flung off faith but bore the impress of his chapel upbringing throughout his life. It had given him, he reckoned, *a code of social conduct that was a buttress to the thoughtlessness and instability, the waverings of adolescence.* Later he advocated its inclusion as a proper subject for the oral historian since *it should be recognised as the current form of what we now classify as myths.* But it was never an avenue he chose to explore himself, preferring to concentrate on what he believed to be the central historical topic of work.

It is the social consequence of the lack of work that constitutes the underlying theme of another story set in the south Wales of the Depression, 'Theirs is the Kingdom' (LIFE AND LETTERS TODAY, No. 22, 1939) which begins:

Shwni Thomas, Tophouse, hadn't been to Chapel for a long time. He hadn't bothered again since the last big Strike. Most of the Boys stayed away when their bowler hats became dented, and the seats of their chapel pants began to shine, and Shwni, like the rest of them, spent most Sundays up on the mountain.

This is where George Ewart Evans himself spent long formative hours *tiring the sun with talk* in the period after leaving University College, Cardiff, in 1931 with a second-class degree in Classics, a teaching certificate and the prospect of long-term unemployment because of a ten-per-cent cut-back in teachers, especially of Classics, a decision which George Ewart Evans viewed as the beginning of the long decline of Classics in schools. *It was then [in 1931] that I made my decision to become a writer,* even if his initial satisfaction came from translating classical authors into English verse. *I like to think both Catullus and Virgil were Celts,* he wrote to a friend in 1986, and his first published piece was a prize-winning translation of Catullus in the SUNDAY REFEREE in 1934.

It was in 1934, too, that his career took a new turn when, on the strength of his ability to teach athletics, he secured a position at an experimental community college at Sawston in Cambridgeshire. It was his first experience of East Anglia, and

for a long time I had no bearings at all. I had moved from hills to a draughty plain with no recognizable landmarks. But there were compensations, especially the uninterrupted view of the sunrise and sunset. Some were unforgettable. For the first time in my life I knew what the Greeks meant by their image of the inverted bowl of the sky. On clear nights the sky was an arch of praise.

(RINGERS AND SINGERS, BBC Radio talk, March 1969)

Sawston Village College was a secondary school and community centre combined, a response in educational and recreational terms to both the depressed state of East Anglian farming and the 1926 Hadow Report. Sawston, opened in 1930, was the first of several such colleges that were the brainchild of the county's Director of Education, Henry Morris, to George Ewart Evans *one of the unsung cultural architects of our time*, an enlightened educationalist who stressed the value of extramural and continuing education in rural as well as urban areas, the need for vocational and practical instruction alongside the conventional academic syllabus, and the need to revitalize village community life. Evans always bore the imprint of Morris's influence, whether in his wide-ranging commitment to adult education and the WEA, or his conscious attempt to reinvigorate the village community at Blaxhall; from Morris, too, he acquired an informed appreciation of art and design, another source of inspiration later. And at Sawston he met Florence Ellen Knappett, a rather proper London history graduate whose wide reading and sharp mind were a foil to the athletic, good-looking, literary-minded and politically committed Welshman; they married in 1938 after a courtship in which she tried to civilize him with Jane Austen. He countered by foisting Palme Dutt on her, for by this time he was the secretary of a Cambridge group of Communist party members whose well-intentioned, but to him academic, idealism was a world away from the harsh realities of working-class exploitation and human distress he knew at home. The contrast was personified by the pseudo-conspiratorial Communism of middle-class university intellectuals like Hugh Sykes Davies, one of the Cambridge Apostles, on the one hand, and at grass-roots level the uncompromising social analysis pungently dispensed by his self-educated Communist friend Jim Adlam, a well-informed, critical, unemployed miner of acute political insight. On the hills above Abercynon, in the shade of a dry-stone wall on Graig-yr-hydd, Adlam and his companions brought an abrasive scientific rationalism to bear on current problems and George Ewart Evans deliberately sought out their company as often as he could in the 1930s. Adlam's Communist perspective (he appears in the short story 'Ben Knowledge' as free-thinking

Jim Adams: *He was a collier, too, but he knew books . . . he'd even caught up with philosophy and had a go at wringing its lean and scraggy neck*) permanently influenced George Ewart Evans's social thought. He never renounced or disguised his lasting attachment to the political left, and occasionally it catches the reader by surprise, as in the concluding paragraphs of ASK THE FELLOWS, when the serene mood of tranquil reflection is suddenly punctured by a kick at the *rococo facade of British democracy.*

The miners on the mountainside above Abercynon *talked about everything under the sun from Marx, Feuerbach, Engels, Plekhanov, and some of them had actually read them.* George Ewart Evans listened and drew them further into conversation to acquire background to the fiction he hoped to write; he also went down a pit on two occasions in the thirties to get an accurate idea of the actual working conditions. Only from the later perspective of Suffolk did he finally grasp the historical significance of what his companions had been telling him about their work, their tools and the skills of their craft. But even at the time he learned that *the older men had in their keeping the past of their people, and I got from them a lively sense of the scene before the opening up of the deep mines fifty or sixty years before . . . of the valley as it was then and had been for centuries.*

The hills were therefore of two-fold significance in the development of George Ewart Evans. From the miners squatting by the dry-stone wall he learnt something of the relationship between history, economics and social structure, and the assumption of equality in conversation with working people, who were worth listening to.

At the same time it was brought home to him that the recent industrial development was only a modern overlay on a much older culture. As a boy he had delivered groceries by pony and trap to hillside farms where the primitive *car-llusg* (slide-car) was still in use by old farmers like John Evans of Pen-y-graig who whitewashed the walls of his buildings to ward off evil spirits. Only later was he struck by the full impact of this juxtaposition of the present and the past.

As he told a conference at the South Wales Miners' Library in Swansea in 1980:

On the hills the Middle Ages were still alive. On its material side the slide-car instead of the cart and wheels; and on the traditional side, the full belief in an order that was really pre-Christian. In the valleys the newness, the vigour . . . of the Industrial Revolution . . . and on the hills and the moor-lands barely half-hour's climb away the ancient pastoral culture that had hardly changed for centuries.

(THE SOUTH WALES MINERS AND THEIR INHERITANCE, 1980, p. 14)

IV

These two elements, of social crisis in the valley and immemorial survivals in the hills—tension and tradition—shaped not merely the personal outlook of George Ewart Evans; they explained, in his view, the development of the Welsh short story. While it was

no accident that the writers who had the greatest influence on its direction grew up during the twenties and thirties in industrial South Wales, chiefly in those valley and coastal towns that were so devastated by social and economic crises,

at the same time

the very nature of the Welsh tradition made it almost inevitable that the Welsh writers of the last thirty years should choose either the short story or lyric verse . . . For though most of them were writing in English they had grown out of the same cultural seed-bed as their compatriots who were using the older language. This tradition gave them strength and, in many respects, a favoured start.

(WELSH SHORT STORIES, 1959, Introduction, pp. 10–11)

Early Welsh verse and THE MABINOGION, by whose mythic elements he was always fascinated, exemplified in his view the restraint and taut economy of statement demanded by the short story, which ought properly to be

regarded as the first statement of a development that should continue in the mind of the reader after the actual story has finished.

There are several noteworthy aspects concerning this anthology of Welsh short stories George Ewart Evans edited for Faber in 1959 apart from his highlighting of tradition, especially oral tradition, in his introduction to it. It was the fourth such anthology, following the anonymously edited first Faber collection of 1937 and Gwyn Jones's (Penguin) and 1956 (OUP World's Classics) anthologies. Whereas the contributors to the 1956 collection had, almost without exception, all been the wrong side of forty, George Ewart Evans deliberately sought out younger writers, not all of whom, admittedly, went on to consolidate their initial promise. Nor was he the first anthologist to include translations from the Welsh. Tegla Davies, Kate Roberts and R. Hughes Williams were included in 1937, for instance, and Tegla Davies, Kate Roberts, W. J. Gruffydd and D. J. Williams in 1940. Ewart Evans included Islwyn Ffowc Elis as well as the established Kate Roberts and D. J. Williams in his 1959 anthology, primarily on grounds of quality but also because, as someone who had through his own efforts converted the tenuous, chapel-familiar Welsh of his youth into a language he now read with fluency and, later, spoke and wrote with increasing confidence, he believed that

any Welsh writer who is using English should make himself familiar with the Welsh language. He's at a great disadvantage if he knows nothing of it or of the literature. But I also believe that if you have been brought up in Wales you

absorb the social attitudes and the rhythms of the language, to a certain degree, by a kind of cultural osmosis . . . Welsh writers have the weight of the whole tradition behind them.
(The First Fifty Years: Anglo-Welsh Short-Story Writers, BBC Radio talk, November 1968)

Consequently, although a story by Alun Lewis—Lewis, Dylan Thomas and Glyn Jones he regarded as the three greatest influences on the development of the modern Welsh short story in English—was written in India and not Welsh in any specific sense, he justified its inclusion

on the principle that a writer's way of looking at things is chiefly conditioned by the culture and environment in which he spent his early years, adding with autobiographical feeling, *however far a writer travels he takes the country of his boyhood and youth along with him: for it is in this country that his true poetic fibre has been nourished.*
(Welsh Short Stories, Introduction, p. 14)

In 1975 his readers were reminded that George Ewart Evans, though by now an established East Anglian writer, had taken the country of *his* boyhood and youth along with him with the publication of a collection of his own short stories, Let Dogs Delight. In the absence of any prefatory or editorial matter its underlying principle can perhaps be inferred from his review of Roland Mathias's The Eleven Men of Eppynt, where he expresses his belief that collected stories ought not to be printed in the order of their composition since this is merely to invite attempts at tracing the writer's development, if any. Every story sets a new problem and each time the writer must solve it anew. More importantly

> *if the collection is a good one the reader perseveres to the end; but only with the greatest difficulty is he able to differentiate one story from another. All [should] seem to coalesce into a formless* mood *and rarely does one story stand out memorably from the others.*
>
> (DOCK LEAVES, Summer 1957, p. 64)

This is an exact description of the stories collected in LET DOGS DELIGHT. Written between 1937 and 1954, these are folk or fairy tales whose elements are fantasy and humour; they are written, too, in the tradition of the teller of tales and embellished with characters and incidents known personally to his listeners. It is a technique which lapses occasionally into a buttonholing style of the 'Now if you can spare a minute or two' variety which can become irksome. Nor are these any folk-tales of the *modern* Welsh: Victoria Row, Llwyncelyn, is not Gwyn Thomas's Meadow Prospect, and Wil Slag, Twm Mufti, Eic Caneuon and Wil Flagons lack the Runyonesque individuality of Cynlais Coleman the Comet, Edwin Pugh the Pang and that lover of the head voice, Mathew Sewell the *sotto voce.*

Eight of the twelve stories are concerned with relationships between men and animals, their setting an impoverished industrial Welsh valley that still shows the traces of a pastoral community where people live in a poverty alleviated only by luck or sorcery—a peasant poverty. Only in the story entitled 'Gold Key', a talisman which retains its powers only so long as people believe in it, is there a direct reference to pit closures and social hardship; for the most part the poor are reconciled to a world beyond their control by taking as their heroes not the rich and powerful but the cunning and elusive, like the uncatchable dog of the title story. There is a relaxed geniality and sly humour in the delineation of characters like Ben Knowledge who had a nodding acquaintance with the philosophy of Bishop Berkeley, Wil Slag whose pig was mortgaged up to his nose ring, and Ianto Parry, who revived his wife's interest in life by taking his pony upstairs to her sick bed, a Welsh practitioner of the horse-whispering techniques that feature so prominently in his books on Suffolk.

While some of the stories are undoubtedly circumscribed by an excessively knowing, eyes-a-twinkle way of introducing them (of the 'Well if you knew Wil Slag you'd agree with Ianto Parry' variety), there is one, 'Possessions', which, crafted as a tale rather than a yarn, is worth all the rest put together. A story about the choice a family fallen on hard times has to make between their donkey and their piano, it explores the relationship between possession and love with a delicacy that invites comparison with some of D. H. Lawrence's early stories. It shows what George Ewart Evans *could* achieve as a story-writer when he stopped trying so hard to be entertaining, a weakness he recognized in a diary entry of 1941 (20 August):

I have been compromising with 'Reality', sentimentalising it to a certain extent, sidestepping the big important themes in contemporary Welsh life.

He called them 'dialect stories', and they reveal his keen ear for the characteristic speech rhythms of south Wales *(There is he going like hell, quietly, across the field. But now just he pulls up sudden like)* and the literal translation of Welsh syntax, as in *Tonypandy Annie was live fire on the skin of the bookmakers,* where the Welsh idiom *tân ar groen* is translated into the demotic English that is still to be heard among the older residents of the Valleys even today.

The same ear, and the same roguish ability to turn predicament to advantage, are recognizable in a fictional East Anglian context in the twelve short stories collected together as ACKY (1974), to which LET DOGS DELIGHT was a companion volume. Akerman Flatt is a retired horseman living in the imaginary Suffolk village of Fenhall. A rural Andy Capp with more winsome ways, he spends his time talking about the past, thinking up ways of adding to the hoard of banknotes (hidden in the mattress) which he occasionally smoothes out with a flat iron, engaging in a running battle of wits with the WI's formidable Mrs Horringer, and generally being less solicitous of his wife than he is of his pig. This is a light, easy-going collection which illustrates in fictional form his fascination with dialect and the spoken word in an East Anglian setting.

The irony of this, and of George Ewart Evans's larger achievement as an oral historian, is that from the early 1940s he was diagnosed as suffering from otosclerosis, a hereditary softening of the bones of the inner ear which made him increasingly deaf. Ultimately the means by which he found his true vocation (once he had acquired in the early fifties a hearing-aid and a tape recorder which enabled him to play conversations back loudly), in the immediate term it downgraded him in the RAF to mundane tasks whose banality affronted him but which at least allowed him the time for bursts of concentrated writing in the form of short stories and verse. He had toyed with writing poetry since the early thirties, if only, at that stage, in translation. In 1939 he won first prize at the Denbigh National Eisteddfod for a verse play for radio in English about a mining disaster, called 'Something After Death'. Called up in October 1941, for the next four and a half years that he was in blue uniform *(a colour I was never partial to)* he vented his anguish at his hearing disability and his mounting frustration at long absences from his young family, as he was shunted endlessly around the country, in over-rhetorical and rather old-fashioned poems through which he attempted to salvage some self-respect in the face of the absurdity, boredom and damage to selfhood which the conscript is particularly prone to.

So all the slow growth,
Love of the fugue, delight in the skilled act,
Reached the asphalt
Where sameness is the highest god,
Where aeons of cunning neutral paths
Are slacked and murdered by a loud command,
And he must wait the belling of a voice,
Like Pavlov's dog . . .
('The Recruit', WALES, July 1943)

In one of his wartime letters to his wife, he uses

a phrase from a poem by Allen Tate, 'the animated dead'.

That's what a soldier is—the bomb or a bullet doesn't wholly kill him, he's already half killed by the training. Because the training—in this Army and Air Force of a reactionary state —is designed to kill the alive part of a man and to bring him down to a level only inches above the soil which will eventually claim him.

He found the kind of discipline he was forced to observe particularly irritating; it consisted, in his view, of *all nerve and barking* and was *founded on mutual distrust and fear*, creating a rift that was *another face of the class struggle*. To his diary he confided that *the only difference between being in the RAF and being in prison is that in prison one's relatives can pay one a visit ... And when you're in prison you know how long you're in for*. Impatient of release he found himself imitating the incantatory style of the preachers of his youth:

O God of intricate works, O God of transportation,
O God of drill and wide disposition,
Of hard-lying and strategic withdrawal
Of moving forward and of dying ...
O lord, O well-braided one, O one in many, O high
prince of strategy ...
O god look benevolently upon us
O God help us all if thou camest fully into thy kingdom!
('Airman at a Railway Terminus', WALES,
Summer 1945)

What was already a bad war for George Ewart Evans worsened in 1942 with the death of his father in February and, in September, the loss at sea of his brother Roy, news of which reached him while he was serving in a coastal aerodrome in Lincolnshire and which he transmuted into a story about two airmen killed when their plane goes down 'Beyond The Trees':

They had died quickly. Their flame was out before the fire started. It was perhaps a better death than the slow death of the sea.

Although he never reconciled himself to being in uniform, these were the years of his autobiographical novel of a valley childhood, THE VOICES OF THE CHILDREN, written in 1943–4 and dedicated 'For Roy', which the Penmark Press published in 1947. *Trying to be as objective as I can,* he looked back on it thirty years later:

I think it has the merit of being sincere and of giving an authentic picture of valley life with glimpses of the old traditional community on the hills. But it certainly cannot be considered as a novel ... Autobiographical fiction would be the category that would fit it most nearly. On the negative side, this book bears the mark of its origins. I wrote it while I was in the RAF and had to work whenever I could: under hedges, in rooms where the light was so dim (owing to black-out regulations) I could hardly see what I'd written, or in NAAFI bars where the light was passable but the noise and interruptions were not conducive to good writing. But its main defect—its episodic nature—is due to my being suddenly posted from one station to another and having to take up my scraps of paper and sort them out and start again in an entirely new setting.

(Letter to Iorwerth Peate, 3 January 1979)

Viewed through the eyes of the narrator, young

Willie Pritchard, the characters in The Voices of the Children are seen large and clear as a child would see them, and as a child would notice but accept the quirkiness of older people like Jack Ragtime, who warmed his knife in the tea before spreading the butter and who kept a corner of the Kaiser's moustache in his wallet. Thus, as Gwyn Jones remarked, *it has the immediacy of things lived through and people lived with* and the childhood portrayed is one still easily recognizable to many from a similar background—this family, these aunts and uncles,

> *the river bank, the mountain road, the little grocer's shop, the grimy majesty of the industrial village . . . and boys quite amazingly like the boys one knew in other valleys and on other hills.*
>
> (Welsh Anvil, 1949, p. 62)

The response of English reviewers was generally positive, too, even if, like Pamela Hansford Johnson, they were over-inclined to dwell on *that good, singing prose that our Welsh writers seem to find comes as natural to their pens as figures to an accountant.* (John O'London's, 17 October 1947). The Manchester Guardian's reviewer (10 October 1947) found its *caressing tones* and *musical prose that lulls and engrosses* a relief from the harsh staccato of the book he was incongruously asked to notice at the same time, Chester Himes's If He Hollers Let Him Go. In the Daily Worker (27 November 1947) Allen Hutt applauded the mastery of atmosphere but not the apparent lack of point and purpose of a story that wanted *a beginning and (even more) an end.* Glyn Jones, however, writing in the WELSH REVIEW (VI, 1947), recognized immediately that this was precisely its virtue:

To the writer about children the important thing is not that he should remember *in the sense of being able to recall events but that he should retain the power to* feel *himself back into the life-mode of childhood, still to know in his solar-plexus what it is to be passionate, perpetually bewildered and four feet high.*

Among the several striking vignettes in THE VOICES OF THE CHILDREN—the sharply visualized topography of the shop (in effect, Bristol House), the theatricality of the preacher working up a *hwyl (it was better than the pictures)*, and Uncle Tom's impassioned defence of the miners—there is a portent of things to come in an account of Davies the Blacksmith shoeing a horse:

We watched Davies bending his strength over the hoof: taking out the old nails with his sharp pincers, levelling off the horn, fitting the new shoe, nailing it and paring the hoof with his curved knife and filing it when he had finished. He worked quickly and smoothly, speaking to the pony in a language he could understand. It was all so interesting that I hardly breathed and my mouth got dry through watching. Davies straightened up occasionally to answer Uncle Tom's questions—they were talking about the pits—or to give his opinion; and it was only then that we became aware of what he was saying. While the blacksmith worked all our interest was on his movements: the dull blow of the hammer on the nail as it was driven home, the rasp of the file, and the knife showing the mottled whiteness of the hoof.

(THE VOICES OF THE CHILDREN, pp. 41–2)

George Ewart Evans's writing changed direction

after moving with his family to Suffolk in 1948, but the signposts were already in place. There was nothing he later wrote that was not already anticipated in the fictional and imaginative re-creation of his own lived experience. He had made a modest, by no means insignificant, contribution to the twentieth-century Anglo-Welsh literary movement, but his reputation rests on what he achieved not as a writer of fiction and verse but as a historian. It is to a consideration of that greater achievement we must now turn.

V

The gloomy introspection and self-pity of George Ewart Evans's diaries between 1940 and 1948 indicate that for all the serenity of his fiction he was throughout these years hounded, like his *bête noire* Winston Churchill, by 'black dog' moods of deep intensity. The uncharacteristic and shockingly violent ending of his grim, Caradocian short story of 1940, 'Be Master', more truly indicates his temper at this time:

He became dead-calm; the furious pulsing in his head ceased and all his confusion fell away. He got up slowly on to his knees, looking sideways under his half-open eyelids at the woman, who still sat the table. Then, Jehu, he rose up.

She screamed when she saw him. His face was changed; distorted. She made towards the door but he slid across the table and caught her by the hair. Then he pressed her head against the seat of a chair, until she knelt on the floor. Taking off his belt with its heavy metal buckle, he began to beat her with all his strength. She screamed, but he drowned her cries with his shouting:

'Jezebel. Thou Jezebel. Master in my house. Cursed woman. The prophets of the Lord. Master in my house. The prophet of the Lord.'

And her scream became a quiet whimpering. He dragged her out through the back door and threw her down the steps on to the little area below, shouting all the while, 'Throw her down. Throw her down.'

Then he jumped from the door down on top of her with his heavy boots. When she was still he dragged her into the coal-shed and locked the door.

Throughout the 1940s he was subject to frequent bouts of depression that he believed were threatening him with total demoralization. *I felt I should have gone berserk*, he later recalled of these years, *were it not for my writing*.

Forced to leave Sawston and the college to which he had briefly returned in May 1945 because of the impossibility of finding an affordable house in the area, for the next three years he and his family moved to his wife's family's home at Enfield while he found, and soon became increasingly overwhelmed by, a teaching post in Edmonton. *What a devastating prospect it seems*, he wrote in his diary on 15 August 1945, *an overcrowded house, a difficult time at school, and stuck with the writing*. It got worse: domestically the strain took its toll on family relationships; his writing stalled as he tried his hand with children's stories, rejection slips accumulated, and THE VOICES sold painfully slowly. School was *like a mad house*, and he was too preoccupied with the urgency of getting out of it to take heart from the experience of others. *Had a letter from Glyn Jones, Cardiff, yesterday: 'school is like a menagerie. The staff will have to be issued with Tommy guns shortly'* (Diary, 10 March 1948). These were years when he viewed life, literature and himself with a high seriousness. His frequently reiterated motto at this time was Aschenbach's 'Hold fast' from DEATH IN VENICE. *It may 'be good for my genius', as Henry James said, to have such a period of hell as this, but it cannot be good to be almost annihilated* (Diary, 1 March 1942). *I need to find strength from somewhere* (5 May).

A profoundly depressing sequence of diary

entries comes to an abrupt end with that for 19 July 1948: *E* [his wife Ellen] *has accepted the job and the house at Blaxhall, Suffolk*, and George Ewart Evans's two autobiographical volumes of the 1980s themselves divide at this apparently natural caesura. In reality the next eight years were to prove little less difficult than the previous eight for a struggling writer coping with increasing deafness and trying to bring up four notably active young children while his wife earned what regular income they had as a village schoolmistress. It was here in Blaxhall, however, that his writing career radically changed direction, here that *I began to learn the technique of what became later known as oral history.*

Blaxhall lies six miles from the Suffolk coast, half-way between Woodbridge and Aldeburgh in the light soil of the Sandlings. When the Evans family arrived there in 1948 it was a scattered, straggling village of four hundred people with the nearest railway station three miles away and one bus a week to the nearest big town of 'Ipsidge' as the local people called, and still call, Ipswich. Occupied by the Romans in the second century, mentioned in Domesday Book in the eleventh, Blaxhall to the new arrivals seemed totally historic; that *it was still in the oil-lamp, well and bucket-sanitation stage* only intensified Ewart Evans's sense of domestic crisis.

Though he had known East Anglia since the mid-1930s, he was still unreconciled to the stark contrast between his native Wales with its pastoral farming on the hills above the bustling, politically conscious, industrially turbulent valley and the flat, arable, politically conservative, hierarchically ordered Suffolk landscape relatively untouched by the industrial changes of the previous century. While the notion that cultural differences are partly the product of environmental ones is as old as at least the seventeenth century, it was the great nineteenth-century agriculturalist James Caird who first drew a distinction between the kind of agriculture practised in the mainly pastoral north and west of England on the one hand, and that of the predominantly arable south and east on the other. By the time a much later generation of social and agrarian historians like Alan Everitt and Joan Thirsk came to elaborate on this division in terms of a relatively free, mobile, dissenting pastoral area as against a more static and subservient arable zone, George Ewart Evans had independently concluded that this must have affected the organization and conditions of life in the two regions and that the arable farming that predominated in East Anglia extended well beyond the farming itself: *it permeated the whole community and therefore helped to condition it.* He had an unerring sense of place which enabled him to detect subtle differences among even neighbouring villages within the arable zone, and they were invariably differences that proved, on closer inspection, to be socio-economic in nature.

As he came to appreciate how wide the class division in the eastern part of England between the farmer and the hired agricultural worker was, he learned too that the reticence of the latter was not an illustration of Marx's 'rural idiocy'—for throughout the first half of the nineteenth century the East Anglian countryside was in an uproar of radical, often violent, protest—but a direct consequence of the insecurity created by agricultural depression, unemployment, the lack of effective trade unions and the constant threat of victimization which taught people to hold their tongue. Furthermore, he attributed the lack of any organized desire to study the old rural community in England (which increasingly irritated him when his applications for grants-in-aid were rejected) and the contrastingly better support for the study of folk life in the Celtic countries, to the inferior status of the low-paid, downtrodden farmworker at the bottom of the rigidly ordered social structure of southern England generally and of East Anglia in particular. We might speculate that in England, ever since the late-medieval tripartite division of the countryside into landlords, tenant farmers and agricultural labourers, just as there was not an independent peasantry—as in, say, France, Poland, or Wales—so there was a tradition of the pastoral, but no folk museums; what still mostly pass for folk museums in England are country houses and heritage centres.

In contrast, too, to the fierce urge for education and self-improvement George Ewart Evans had known among his own people in Wales, what struck him in this part of rural England was the apparent anti-intellectualism of countrymen and women. Mrs Celia Jay, for instance, born in 1885 and one of his first Blaxhall informants, was a highly intelligent woman who won a book prize at school, but when her mother caught her reading it in her bedroom it was taken from her and she never saw it again: Mrs Jay senior was one of those parents who thought reading made children dissatisfied with their station in life. He was also critical, initially, of the apparent lack of musicality among the East Anglians; he missed the spontaneous singing in harmony he remembered *in chapel, after playing rugby, in long walks on the hills, in almost any social occasion. I missed this almost as much as I missed the hills.* But he found in time that the people of East Anglia were not at all unmusical; it was merely that their musicality took an entirely different form from the collective music-making he had known in Wales. In Suffolk he discovered a vigorous tradition of folk-song and bell-ringing, and, as in Wales, it arose directly from the people. There was still a difference, for all that: whereas in Wales singing enjoyed immense social acclaim, in East Anglia neither folk-singing nor bell-ringing had the same status. It was to confer dignity on rural campanology as an art and on Henry Puttock the ringer that George Ewart Evans devoted a chapter to the method and mathematics of bell-ringing in ASK THE FELLOWS WHO CUT THE HAY.

So perhaps south Wales and Suffolk were not so dissimilar after all. This was certainly true of the farm-workers, who had been the largest single work-force in the country after the miners in 1914: both were primary producers of fuel—food and coal—necessary for energy, both were undervalued and underpaid. More significantly, in East Anglia as in upland Glamorgan there were survivals of a former culture. What George Ewart Evans did, in fact, was to transpose to Suffolk his already considerable knowledge of *the prior culture* of the lower Cynon Valley in whose history, archaeology and antiquities he had long been avidly interested: *What I should have liked to do (this came to me when I was ten years of age) was to go about examining castles and ruins—anything to do with the past,* he wrote later. Glamorgan's loss was East Anglia's gain.

This lay in the future. In the late 1940s his intention was still to continue writing fiction, but this presented problems. *My writing about Wales was a product of the Twenties and Thirties; the country had changed during the intervening generation.* In any case he felt Keidrych Rhys's WALES had become *windy, flatulent and adipose*, an opinion shared by his wife who had for some years thought it had *a* fin de siècle *atmosphere about it*, and that *the Welsh Renaissance was wearing a bit thin.* About this time, too, his friend Glyn Jones was urging a change of literary direction. Believing Ewart Evans's *true line of development* lay with stories of feeling and human emotion like 'Beyond the Trees' *rather than knockabout clowning of the Rhys Davies type of story*, he posed the question

Don't you feel we must—as Anglo-Welsh writers I mean—make a new start, get away from the subjects, attitudes and styles we have been using? . . . to get out of the wood that is beginning to grow up around us.

(Letter from Glyn Jones, 31 August 1949)

Glyn Jones could hardly have envisaged the new start that George Ewart Evans was unconsciously already making. Although *my natural and deepest allegiance was to my own country and I felt resentment at being weaned from it . . . writing about England was a kind of betrayal*, he resolved to continue writing fiction, albeit now in an East Anglian context. From his conversations with his neighbours he hoped to acquire background for his stories in the same way as he had spent hours with the unemployed miners of his youth, but he came to realize that what the retired shepherd Robert Savage and his wife Prissy were telling him was immeasurably more important than anything he himself could hope to write. Their conversation was laced with archaic words and obsolete linguistic forms used in the identical sense that Chaucer and Shakespeare had used them, the same words as those employed by the sixteenth-century farmer Thomas Tusser, and talking of the same methods of minding sheep as those described in Spenser's SHEPHEARDES CALENDAR. This fortified his conviction that the unlettered were often better talkers than the formally educated, and he embarked on a remarkable sequence of books that were eventually to establish him as an authority on the folk-life and material culture of East Anglia. In so doing he pioneered the trail of oral history before the first settlers arrived.

In actual fact, *oral history* was never a term he cared much for; it reminded him, he said, of *the filing cabinet of a well-equipped dentist.* And he told his friend Peter du Sautoy of Faber and Faber when his reputation was already secure, *There's nothing I should like less than to be embalmed as one of the potentates of oral history* (letter of 12 December 1971). There was a nice coincidence about the reluctant potentate's arrival in Suffolk, even beyond the mildly intriguing fact that he was unwittingly following in the footsteps of an earlier Welsh exile who wrote on Suffolk, Robert Reyce, perhaps Rice, author of the first detailed description of the county (THE BREVIARY OF SUFFOLK, 1618), who believed his forerunners had come there from Wales with the Tudors in 1485. For coincidentally with the Evans family's arrival at Blaxhall in 1948, in New York that year the Columbia University historian Allan Nevins launched his Oral History Project aimed at recording the reminiscences of 'significant' Americans. By the time the British Oral History Society was founded at York in 1973, George Ewart Evans could claim to feel like Molière's M. Jourdain who had been speaking prose for most of his life without knowing it. Although he established a close intellectual rapport and warm personal friendship with the foremost members of the younger generation of British oral historians like Paul and Thea Thompson of the University of Essex, he confessed to being

a bit disillusioned with oral history as it has developed in Britain and have lost any enthusiasm I had for the movement. I find that when I go to conferences they hold . . . I'm not really in sympathy with them, probably through an inability to tune into their wavelength. I sometimes feel I must be an odd person—something like Dai Bach y Sowldiwr from the Rhondda whose mother saw his company marching and called out proudly 'Look! Look! Our Dai! He's the only one in step.'

(Letter to Iorwerth Peate, 10 November 1976)

What he did know was that oral history was the first kind of history, was indeed as old as history itself, with a lineage extending from the Bible and the Greek historians via the medieval chroniclers and the chorographers of Tudor and Stuart

England down to the social surveys of Mayhew, Rowntree and Booth. As we have seen, it was in the Wales of the 1930s that his interest in oral history had, however unconsciously, been awakened and where he *had come to recognize that a sizeable residue of the history of the people remained in transmissible form in the community itself, the customs, the myths, the nation's language and—most of all—the deeply ingrained communal responses.*

If George Ewart Evans had a technique, he never theorized about it, preferring instead to stress the need for patience, courtesy and humility. The interview he regarded as a friendly talk, insisting that it was less a technique than a human relationship, for *no amount of technique can compensate for absolute sympathy with the people being interviewed.* Perhaps his hearing-aid gave him a slight air of vulnerability which made people more relaxed and forthcoming in his company. Certainly he spoke to initially faintly suspicious people in a way that was, to them, unfamiliar; it took him a whole winter of visits to get information out of one old horseman. He read extensively for background information and researched manuscript and printed sources painstakingly in libraries and record offices, for he was only too aware that oral testimony of itself does not constitute reality and that the oral historian needs access to other sources if he is not to be ensnared by the mental categories of his informants. And not only documentary sources: like the renowned historian of the English landscape, W. G. Hoskins, for whom he had great respect, he was a great believer in *a dose of boots* as a useful antidote to a diet of too much parchment and paper. But as one who learned more from talking than from walking, he recognized that what he was getting from the conversation of old people was often more accurate than the printed sources and frequently a corrective to official records, which are

merely a version of what happened as compiled by the winning side . . . the title deeds for an authority to rule.
(FROM MOUTHS OF MEN, p. 174)

His were *flesh and blood archives*, but while many of his older informants were *books that walked*, he insisted on a proper recognition of their human dignity: they could not be opened at random or their pages turned at will. They were rich repositories of information on a whole range of topics, on dialect, farming processes and tools which could be traced back to fourteenth-century documents; but, he claimed,

we interview mainly in order to bring back man into history —not man mediated through trends, movements, distribution maps and statistics but men and women in the flesh . . . to give the feel of history, the sense of the past which is such an essential ingredient of the best historical writing . . . not for the historical information but that little bit extra—that enlightenment, a trace element of imagination, a little supererogatory grace, a sense of history.
(ORAL HISTORY JOURNAL, I, No. 4, 1972, p. 71)

George Ewart Evans's sense of history, inspired by the conviction that *once you have lost sight of people, as a historian you are lost, for history is first and last a humanity*, prevented him from claiming too much for the oral method. He never wanted to see it elevated into a specialism with boundary fences and an esoteric vocabulary to deter the uninitiated. One of the reasons he disliked the term 'oral history' was that it implied a misleading analogy with the way in which history, a corporate discipline, had already been excessively fragmented into its economic, agricultural, legal, medical aspects, and so on, whereas in fact it should be thought of not as a *new discipline* but as a *new technique* to be used in any branch of the old discipline of the study of the past. What he advocated was a less restrictive approach which encouraged an awareness of the interrelatedness of historical phenomena where *everything tied in.*

He had, as we can see, a profoundly democratic view of the accessibility of learning and of history in particular, for he firmly believed it was within the reach of everybody to preserve the past, since *historical truth is not the monopoly of the library or the muniment room.* His view of academic specialists was shot through with ambivalence. While possessing a characteristically Welsh respect for 'professors', he was sufficiently confident in the value of his own work to declare that academics *are naturally resistant to any different treatment by someone who does not accept unquestioningly the received way of interpreting the distant past.* He was, however, prepared to make a notable exception in the case of the great French historian Marc Bloch (1886–1944), whose work he knew and admired, and whose authority he liked to invoke, not only on the characteristics of rural society but on academic conservatism: *too often we see the dismal and wasteful spectacle of scholarship running complacently in neutral gear.* Both in the broad sweep of his own knowledge of English agrarian history from the Middle Ages and in his readiness to draw on disciplines as diverse as archaeology, folklore, geography, technology and aerial photography, George Ewart Evans was following in Bloch's footsteps. For Bloch too was something of an outsider, a believer in 'a wider and more human history' who was able to look beyond the legal and institutional framework of agrarian systems and who *had no patience with historians who thought agricultural practices below their dignity or held their noses when they passed by dunghills* (Keith Thomas in THE OBSERVER, 14 January 1990). Bloch too was a historian who believed that a prerequisite for a proper understanding of the *past* was a knowledge of the *present*.

George Ewart Evans's own disdain for entrenched academic frontiers which demarcated history from anthropology, and both from folklore, was as much a consequence of the fact that in the fifties and early sixties he had little or no contact with academics, as of his historical and intellectual intuitiveness. This ambivalence enabled him to discover an unlikely ally in the person of the then Regius Professor of History at Oxford, Hugh Trevor-Roper, who famously asserted that

> *historical revolutions are not made by historians . . . Those who have directed the course of history have almost all been non-historians or at most amateur historians: Machiavelli, Montesquieu, Herder, Hegel, Marx. And Sir Walter Scott . . .*
>
> (H. R. Trevor-Roper, THE ROMANTIC MOVEMENT AND THE STUDY OF HISTORY, 1968, p. 13)

What Evans particularly liked about Scott was his use of vernacular speech, so that even though some of the narrative passages read woodenly today, *the dialect comes off the page as fresh as ever.*

VI

Yet for all the subtlety and epigrammatic verve with which George Ewart Evans argues the case for 'spoken history'—occasionally at some length (*Evans must try not to become a bore*, protested one exasperated reviewer of THE DAYS THAT WE HAVE SEEN)—doubts still linger. We commend his reluctance to make exaggerated claims on behalf of oral history and his consciousness of its limitations (*only very occasionally, in my experience, does it uncover new areas altogether*); we entirely agree that it is good at *supplying extra sources for conventional history by salvaging the sort of material that tends to slip between the meshes of print or documentation*; we take his point that *the higher up the social scale you go the more wary the informant who has a persona to protect, which is another reason for favouring ordinary people*. Despite his provision of striking individual examples of recourse to documentary sources that merely confirm oral testimony, we occasionally wonder whether George Ewart Evans still allows enough for the fact that memory is a notoriously fallible medium, a selective as much as a recording mechanism, and like any other mechanism prone to fault and failure. In the words of one of the leading practitioners in the field, *oral materials are not so much windows on the past as prisms* (David Henige, ORAL HISTORIOGRAPHY, 1982, p. 5). Then, exemplary in sympathy and unobtrusiveness though his tape recordings show him to be, we wonder, too, whether he fully recognizes the guiding role played, even unwittingly, by the interviewer as director and organizer of the testimony, recognizes, in other words, the extent to which the historical discourse remains in the hands of the interviewer.

Another difficulty arises from the apparent ease with which he interchanges *oral history* and *oral tradition*, for they are not synonymous. Essentially the difference is that while oral history is the study of the recent past by means of personal recollections, oral tradition consists of wisdom handed down by word of mouth for generations beyond one life span. So when George Ewart Evans tells us that the older miners of Abercynon on whom he relied for eye-witness testimony of work practices also *had in their keeping the past of their people*, he is conflating the two meanings. At the same time he is clearly aware that just as, in the words of Alessandro Portelli (HISTORY WORKSHOP, 12, 1981, p. 100), *the credibility of oral sources is a* different *credibility*, so has oral tradition, the oldest form of recording known to man, its own logic, which often resides in objects as well as words. Not for nothing did he take with him in Blaxhall a serrated sickle, as he had taken a pair of yorks or a tommy-box to the dry-stone wall above Abercynon, to initiate and focus the conversation.

George Ewart Evans always believed, too, that there were powerful Celtic inducements to attaching a high valuation to oral tradition as the embodiment of *the wisdom of the tribe*, the mechanism by which primitive (basic, rather than backward) societies operate as well-balanced, complex entities. He learned a great deal about tapping the social memory from state-supported folklore specialists in Ireland where a professional class of remembrancers, memorizers, poets and story-tellers were the repositories and transmitters of oral tradition. The Welsh equivalent of these guardians of the communal memory was the *cyfarwydd*, the teller and writer of tales whose artistry and restraint George Ewart Evans identified as one of the most durable elements in the Welsh literary tradition.

Through a combination of both oral testimony and oral tradition supported by a wide but discriminating reading of primary and secondary sources—they were never mutually exclusive—George Ewart Evans developed his organizing concept of *the prior culture*. His older Blaxhall informants, he believed, *represented the last generation of a line that had extended from Biblical times right to the threshold of the twentieth century*; but what sounded the death-knell of *the prior culture* was the arrival on the land of oil- and petrol-driven machines, so that

> *the date 1485 is of comparatively little significance: from a narrowly political standpoint it was the beginning of the end of the Middle Ages; but it can be stated with equal force that, as far as agriculture and the countryside are concerned, the true end of the Middle Ages is not the accession of the Tudors but the introduction of the internal combustion engine.*
> (THE HORSE IN THE FURROW, p. 126)

This, he believed, brought to an end a period that had lasted well over two thousand years, and it was to be the remainder of his life's work to record and interpret the memories of people who *were living in a historical environment that was being subjected to cataclysmic change . . . the last generation in a continuous line since farming began.*

Now whether continuity of tradition in quite this way is historically plausible is a matter for conjecture. It does not necessarily follow that practices and conditions recollected by the elderly must themselves be of great antiquity. While it is not impossible that certain beliefs or tools *have* survived since Roman or pre-Christian times, it is improbable that their context will not have changed. It is difficult to conceive of a period before change began and agrarian historians tell us that it is likely that many of the agricultural practices of the late nineteenth century were different even from those of the middle of the century, without going back two millennia. In fairness, George Ewart Evans himself concedes this—*the village has never stood still; it has never been constant* (ASK THE FELLOWS, p. 238). He was too imaginative a historian not to recognize that East Anglian society can never have been entirely static, least of all in the century after 1815 which saw Britain transformed by industrial and urban growth, mass production, the rise of democracy and the implementation of legislation which affected the countryman in varying ways from employment to education, and ushered in changes of the most complex kind, even in rural Suffolk.

For all that, he never wavered from his conviction that East Anglia's relative isolation, poor communications and absence of any close, large-scale industry inured the region to significant change until after the Second World War, and preserved a remarkable degree of stability which reinforced the resistance to new ideas of its inhabitants, particularly shepherds like Robert Savage. To a certain extent he was surely right. *The modern landscape of Suffolk is still essentially a medieval one*, writes Norman Scarfe (THE SUFFOLK LANDSCAPE, 1972, revised ed., 1987, p. 192), while mechanization's impact was delayed in many parts of the country until well into the twentieth century, certainly later than the period before the First World War recalled by George Ewart Evans's older informants. Even if manufacturers of agricultural machinery like Ransomes were in business in Ipswich from the 1860s, for much of East Anglia human and animal muscle was still crucial to most tasks about the farm. Victoria's reign was, after all, 'the apogee of the horse world' and some aspects of *the prior culture* survived well into that reign in the form of herbal cures, protective remedies and assorted rituals that George Ewart Evans reveals in their abundant profusion in, especially, THE PATTERN UNDER THE PLOUGH (1966). The point here is that while he interprets these as indications of an enduring awareness of pagan deities and supernatural spirits, one significant way in which *the prior culture* surely *had* changed was that these were no longer objects of worship.

A possible reluctance on George Ewart Evans's part to concede that long-familiar rituals might still undergo adaptation to changing circumstances was highlighted by the historian E. P. Thompson in replying to Evans's query about some aspects of 'rough music', the cacophonous, shaming sanction by which the pre-industrial village policed itself and which is accorded a chapter called 'The Rough Band' in THE PATTERN UNDER THE PLOUGH:

Lévi Strauss says noise signals some lack of regularity in the material or human universe. The trouble of course, as always with the study of folk ritual, is that derivations are not necessarily the same as functions at some other historical period and in some other social context. I don't like having to take the first and original derivation for a ritual as being the dominant one through all contexts, since it seems to me to deny the continuous creative process by which men have modified rituals and appropriated the old rituals to new functions.

(Letter from Edward Thompson, 13 September 1972)

The objection might also be raised that an interpretation of the past that derives from the experience and consciousness of individuals necessarily tends towards a static 'before' and 'after' model. To a historian as—thankfully—unconventional as George Ewart Evans such reservations seemed literally academic. His rejoinder to one university critic who accused him of lacking 'a sense of history' was robustly unrepentant:

Whose history? or what history? If I had not emerged from the strong sense of history as it existed thirty years ago I should never have escaped from its rigid encasing and it would still be hanging around my neck like a millstone. There is not one history . . . [but] *an amalgam of partial histories.*

(ENCOUNTER, November 1976, p. 72)

VII

For all his notion of a *prior culture* receiving its sudden quietus from the internal combustion engine, George Ewart Evans was far too honest and realistic to dabble in that rural nostalgia which Suffolk, particularly, seems to attract, from the misleading paintings of Constable and Gainsborough in the eighteenth century to the literary evocations of Adrian Bell and Ronald Blythe in the twentieth. Yet it was as a rural romantic from the Leavis 'organic community' stable that George Ewart Evans's compatriot in East Anglian exile, Raymond Williams, perceived him after fastening on to an unguarded remark in THE PATTERN UNDER THE PLOUGH about *a way of life that has come down to us from the days of Virgil.* Raymond Williams *(. . . from Virgil? Here?)* found it *deeply saddening* that Ewart Evans was *one of those writers I share so much with in experience and memory* [who] *are in an instant of allusion, of a different way of seeing history, the strangers they ought not to be* (Raymond Williams, THE COUNTRY AND THE CITY, 1973, p. 17).

In fact the idea that George Ewart Evans subscribed to the notion of a vanished, golden rural world will not withstand close scrutiny. For one thing, he knew of the great advantages which the machine had brought to the countryside by taking the back-breaking and debasing toil out of farming, providing for better working conditions for the farm labourer, and admitting the old village to a larger environment (ASK THE

FELLOWS, p. 239). For another, his view of the organic community was too clear-sighted to be distorted by those images of a vast arcadian idyll conjured up by the words 'rural England':

To imply that the old village that has been displaced . . . formed an organic unit is not to sentimentalize it. The organism was in fact far from being healthy. There was intense poverty in it.

(THE FARM AND THE VILLAGE, p. 154)

For all Raymond Williams's strictures—*If there is one thing certain about 'the organic community', it is that it has always gone* (CULTURE AND SOCIETY, p. 253)—George Ewart Evans believed it to be an exact figure of speech; not a literary value-judgement, but an accurate description of a community where co-operation and interrelatedness were a stark economic necessity. It was far from being one

where the supposed high-mindedness of its prevailing mores made it neighbourly and cosy to live in since most organic communities were woefully uncosy *for many of their members.*

(MIDLAND HISTORY, Autumn 1973, p. 130)

Nor was this a belated realization. George Ewart Evans never had been an apologist for the world we have lost for he was only too well aware of the less congenial reality behind it. The homeward-plodding ploughman was not so happy in his rustic poverty as the deeply embedded English tradition of rural retrospect continues to make out. It was particularly inapplicable to Suffolk, notoriously a low-wage county and throughout the second half of the nineteenth century one of the poorest and most insanitary areas in England, its rural underclass poorly housed and ill fed. *I think we ought to see the past quite clearly. There was nothing romantic about it,* he wrote in his early ASK THE FELLOWS, where home-brewed ale and the bacon curing in the chimney corner are accompanied by leaking thatch, streaming walls, aching muscles and sodden clothes. '*Don't tell me about the good old times. They were wicked old times,*' he is told by one of his informants. '*Good old times indeed? The squire and the farmer ruled the villages. The worker was a slave.*' '*That was a hard life and I wouldn't like to see it over no more,*' says another who had not known any land of lost content. *Self-sufficient the rural community may have been, but this is not to imply that this part of England was particularly merrie: for the majority of people it appears to have been exactly otherwise.*

That the hierarchical, authoritarian social system of the old dispensation still survived into the second half of the twentieth century in at least parts of Suffolk, Florence and George Ewart Evans discovered for themselves when they moved in 1962 to the paternalistic, closed, model village of Helmingham, built and owned by the Tollemache family. The Evanses found here few echoes of the poet Gray's description of Grasmere (*This little unsuspected paradise, where all is peace, rusticity and happy poverty*). What they *did* encounter was a cowed population and a smouldering resentment among the older inhabitants not found in any written record: '*You were under and dussn't say anything.*' They were better housed but more subservient. A girl who failed to curtsy to her

Ladyship was likely to be caned the next day at the village school, which had separate entrances for farmers' and tradesmen's children (Upper School) and for labourers' progeny (Lower School), a division which was social not academic. Cottage leases in Helmingham contained obligations concerning regular attendance at church (WHERE BEARDS WAG ALL, Chaps. 11, 18 and 19).

George Ewart Evans's Suffolk, then, is peopled neither by clod-hopping, intermarrying half-wits nor by Ovaltine milkmaids waving from every five-barred gate. Nor was his oral history ever in danger of lapsing into floral history, a flowery, indulgent nostalgia perpetuating the calendar and chocolate-box image of a timelessly tranquil countryside. The village was an occupational community, not a setting for smock and straw whimsy. For this reason the acclaim accorded Ronald Blythe's portrait of an east Suffolk village, AKENFIELD (1969), given the soft-focus treatment in an equally famous film by Peter Hall, raised George Ewart Evans to a pitch of indignation. The absence of realism in Hall's filmed idyll was not entirely lost on other critics. Gavin Millar noted that its appeal was to the WATERSHIP DOWN constituency, though *the rural world in* WATERSHIP DOWN, *albeit rabbity, is a tougher place than any observed in* AKENFIELD.

George Ewart Evans reserved his fire for the book itself, and directed such a fusillade of criticism at it (in THE LISTENER, 13 February 1975) that Blythe *(I thought stoning to death went out with Lockhart)* felt obliged to enlist the support in the next issue of his vicar, to testify publicly to his good character. *I didn't propose to take on the Church and the Anglican saints,* wrote Evans to Iorwerth Peate (letter, 15 March 1975). AKENFIELD: PORTRAIT OF AN ENGLISH VILLAGE was based on interviews with the pseudonymous residents of an imaginary, in fact composite, village in east Suffolk. *It is like giving us cellophane-covered pap as a substitute for good, coarse, wholemeal bread,* protested George Ewart Evans. In his view this *specious kind of country writing with Mr Blythe as its Ossian-Macpherson* was *not history of any known category* since it was *shot through with fantasy and fiction.* What he found particularly culpable was the almost total expunging of the dialect, an unforgivable violation of the integrity of the original speech of the informants, for which and for whom he always held the greatest respect.

Reputable exponents of the oral history methods that George Ewart Evans had pioneered, like Raphael Samuel of Ruskin College, Oxford, were quick to recognize the difference between the varnished speech of Blythe's interviewees, their grammatical idiosyncrasies and dialect expressions eliminated, and that of Evans's farmworkers, ragged at the edges maybe but twisting, turning, coiling around *so that you actually hear them ruminating.* Evans dismissed what he regarded as Blythe's opportunistic piece of 'faction' with the expressive phrase of the Suffolk countryman, *just a load o' squit.*

VIII

The expressiveness of the language of the Suffolk countryman was a source of endless fascination to George Ewart Evans, partly because of the intrinsic literary interest and historical overtones of words like *well-happed* for fortunate, *page* (an apprentice to a shepherd) and *mavis* (a thrush)—*words that I was familiar with in the early poets like Chaucer, Spenser and Shakespeare, without ever expecting to hear them in ordinary discourse*—partly too because of its freshness, especially when spoken by a labourer who was so tired *'it was uphill work coming home afterwards, and if I'd ha' hit a cobweb I'd ha' fallen back'uds'*. The language attracted him also as a necessary purgative of the *abstract gas that gets into ordinary speech through our listening to the effusions of the mass media* (this is Ewart Evans the grammar-school stickler for the correct use of English, whose pleasure in 1967 at the adoption by the syndics of the Cambridge Examination Board of ASK THE FELLOWS as an A-level text stemmed from far more than mere self-interest). The sinewy texture and concrete, tactile imagery of rural speech were perfectly embodied by the farmer who tested the readiness of the soil for sowing by dropping his trousers and taking its temperature with his bare backside (THE FARM AND THE VILLAGE, p. 143).

There were still deeper reasons for George Ewart Evans's attention to spoken language. He believed dialect words and phrases ought to be related to the context of their use, that language was conditioned by its environment. Thus the clear, unadorned speech of the East Anglian countryman had persisted because the material culture remained intact. *The culture of a language reflects in some degree the culture of which it is a part;* as the technology changed, so did the language. Robert and Prissy Savage, George Rope, Henry Puttock and Katie Ling

had followed their jobs, kept up the customs and used the tools exactly as their ancestors had done for centuries, and they could describe their activities accurately in all their detail in language possessing in itself countless reverberations from the past.

(THE DAYS THAT WE HAVE SEEN, p. 16)

They were nearly all brought up in contact with the land, and used language that was steeped in centuries of continuous usage . . . It was as if their work, the work of their hands, had fashioned their tongue and moulded their speech to economical and often memorable utterance.

(SPOKEN HISTORY, p. 123)

George Ewart Evans was himself the product of a work culture and in Suffolk he found further confirmation *that in tackling the main work of a community we identify the central historical topic. His work is the centre of a man's life* (ibid., p. 148). George Bourne (Sturt), writing in the early years of this century in direct opposition to the great mass of affected country literature even then already in vogue, had intended his books like THE WHEELWRIGHT'S SHOP (1923) to be less reminiscence than accounts of a way of life centred on one kind of productive activity. George Ewart Evans went further; by according work its necessary centrality he was able not only to structure his conversational approach but to recover and gain access to that disappearing *prior culture. The common phrase 'working class'*, he wrote, *is at once a vindicator of the main province of oral history and an actual pointer to one of the most fruitful areas of exercising* [it]. Continuity with *the prior culture* was established in the work, customs, tools and processes his informants recounted to him with such detail and precision. After all,

> *To a man who has spent his life at a certain work or craft it is a point of honour to describe its details fully and without distortion: the work has become a part of him, and to give a wrong description or to make an error of fact would be like an offence against his person . . . In his work his standard is the highest and this carried over into his recounting of it.*
>
> (WHERE BEARDS WAG ALL, p. 27)

In comparison with the sophisticated interpretations proposed by more recent historians and social scientists of the values and meanings of the experience of 'work' and of the language in which those meanings are expressed, George Ewart Evans's notion of its fundamental continuity can look rather one-dimensional. But once again he was identifying early a topic which has since become the subject of lively debate among professional academics. His sense of the past sufficiently suffused his perception of the present for him to realize that, in a rural no less than in a mining community, the biggest factor in determining its character, *the greatest social determinant,* was its work. George Ewart Evans wrote with keen insight on occupational subcultures, the distinction, for instance, between the kind of aloof independence maintained by shepherds who by the nature of their job usually worked alone, and the more gregarious ploughmen or, as they were known in Suffolk, horsemen. There were hierarchies of precedence *within* occupations, too; Ewart Evans describes particularly well the ritualistic atmosphere of 'turning-out', the order in which horsemen departed for and returned from the fields:

The head horseman or first baiter went first; then came the first baiter's mate; then the second baiter who was followed by his mate. If the horseman, either through perversity or absent-mindedness, took his team out of the stable before his turn in the ordered procession there was a true disturbance,

and an erring groom was rated with a peremptory *'Don't you know where your place is?'*

The same precedence was carefully observed at the end of the day when the teams had completed their work in the field. If a second horseman, for instance, happened to finish ploughing somewhere near the gate, it would not do for him to proceed out. He had to 'hold to one side', draw his horses away from the gate until the first horseman and his mate had passed through. Only then could he move his team into the procession that both horses and men had looked forward to, at least during the latter hours of their long task in the field.
(THE HORSE IN THE FURROW, pp. 28–9)

The Suffolk horseman possessed other skills in addition to the management of horses; he was required to be equally adept at ploughing, drilling and cultivating land with a team of horses. His work was often a vehicle of status-enhancement, when the test of his skill as a craftsman was formalized in semi-eisteddfodic ploughing competitions where a quarter-inch deviation of furrow was subjected to the critical appraisal of peers in the field and later in the taproom.

To the ploughman the straight furrow is an end in itself, calling for all a man's skill, a kind of quest after the mathematically unattainable: skill and craft carried to the point where the straight furrow becomes utility's tribute to art.
(ASK THE FELLOWS, p. 128)

George Ewart Evans listened closely to his neighbours' descriptive accounts of their old hand-tools like the sickle, flail, weed-hook, dock-chisel and corn-cradle as, earlier, he had observed the use of the miners' mandril, pick and hand boring-set. He listened and recorded, never losing sight of the fact that it was the tape rather than the transcript that was the actual historical document.

This kind of material, of course, was tailor-made for broadcasting, given that so much of it was in the form of conversations and recollections recorded on magnetic tape; given, too, that George Ewart Evans saw himself as a communicator in the tradition of the activist writer and teacher. There were reciprocal gains in that the recording equipment lent him by the BBC was technically far superior to the battery-driven (batteries being vital in unelectrified Blaxhall) Marconi Midget with which he had begun accumulating oral material in the early fifties.

In the fifties and sixties the BBC employed imaginative producers who were permitted to invest resources in feature-length programmes for the old Third Programme and the regional services, and even allowed to recruit such blithe spirits as poets and folklorists to help make them. Among his several other accomplishments George Ewart Evans was a prolific writer of radio scripts based on his own recordings, though the irony of the title of one such series, THROUGH EAST ANGLIAN EYES, was a source of wry amusement to him. Two producers with whom he enjoyed a particularly close rapport, because of the emphasis they attached to the actuality of speech and their vigorous combination of history, literature and politics, were David Thomson, with whom he later wrote THE LEAPING HARE, and Charles Parker, whose famous Radio Ballads acquired for him an international reputation. Their encouragement coloured, even helped to structure, George Ewart Evans's whole approach in the critical sixties when, in the absence of any monitoring academic contact, he struck out into uncharted territory.

By the end of that decade Thomson and Parker and the kinds of programmes they made had become victims of Broadcasting House's capitulation to the new imperatives of cost-efficiency and commercialism, a change of policy that cut the Third Programme to the quick and George Ewart Evans's income as a writer by a third. The last time he saw Charles Parker before the latter's death in 1980 was at the South Wales Miners' Library in Swansea in 1975 when Ewart Evans as lecturer was chaired by Parker, that year the holder of a Fellowship at the Library. He believed that Parker was a casualty of *the recently revived doctrine of private enterprise*, an apparently Victorian value that *in its modern context has become a euphemism for one of the most deplorable of the medieval Seven Deadly Sins—Greed, which Charles Parker as a caring man, a champion of the working-class, spent all his energy in resisting*. Historians of the post-war years, in Ewart Evans's view, would bless Charles Parker for *the cultural gold* he had so patiently accumulated. He had made enemies, certainly,

> *but what pioneer gets an undisturbed passage? He had a wide and absorbing vision which, by and large, embraced a celebration of the common man. He attempted to live up to it . . . He had numerous rebuffs but he rode them all, confident that he was doing a socially valuable service not only to his coevals but also to men and women in the generations to come.*
>
> (SPOKEN HISTORY, pp. 149–50)

These words are particularly applicable to George Ewart Evans himself; he had written his own obituary.

IX

That time was not yet, though. He was listening, recording, interpreting and writing throughout the 1970s, in terms of his published output his most productive decade. His historical books had by now acquired a special ambience with the illustrations drawn by his son-in-law David Gentleman: the matching of the textual and the pictorial was something to which George Ewart Evans devoted a great deal of care, having chosen for Ask the Fellows decorations by the nineteenth-century artist Thomas Bewick and persuaded the renowned Anglesey-based Charles Tunnicliffe, who was much impressed by Evans's work, to illustrate The Horse in the Furrow. His reputation was secure as the first to devote to rural life the loving care which Richard Hoggart, Peter Townsend and the whole contemporary studies industry were lavishing on urban communities.

The decade began with the publication of his fifth book of oral history, Where Beards Wag All, its title taken from Thomas Tusser, its epigraph from a fourteenth-century *cywydd* by Iolo Goch, Y Llafurwr *(The Farm Worker)*. Written in constantly supple prose—for George Ewart Evans was a literary craftsman of a high order—it contains, in addition to careful descriptions of modes of speech, riveting elucidations of work routines and social hierarchies now dissolved, of occupations now extinct like the whitening-roll maker and the geographically isolated marshmen, and of labour migrations long since forgotten, like the seasonal movement of young Suffolk farm-workers to the breweries of Burton-on-Trent, an activity unknown to economic historians before George Ewart Evans, latching on to a chance remark by one of his respondents, tenaciously researched it. These lively accounts, noted Angus Wilson (in THE OBSERVER, 10 January 1971), represent *rich contributions to the hinterland of fiction and poetry*, a timely reminder that George Ewart Evans always regarded *himself* as primarily a writer. *History*, he wrote, *is not merely the mechanical acquisition of knowledge about the past: it is more than anything else the imaginative construction of it. 'Fiction', it has been said, 'is history's fourth dimension'* (ASK THE FELLOWS, p. 16). He was a didact, too. Thirty years before educationalists sought to enshrine 'empathy' as a desideratum of meaningful historical study, he was stressing that the historian's proper objective is *not so much to know the past as to feel it*. In his advocacy, via regular contributions in the 1950s to THE TIMES EDUCATIONAL SUPPLEMENT, of family history projects for schoolchildren and the educative role of museums in stimulating a lasting historical curiosity and awareness, he was well in advance of current thinking.

He anticipated some of the themes that professional historians would later more thoroughly explore too. In THE DAYS THAT WE HAVE SEEN (1975)—the title he had originally proposed for his first East Anglian book twenty years earlier, until he came across Ezra Pound's translation of a Chinese poem with its haunting refrain, 'Ask the fellows who cut the hay'—he examined the role of the public house as an early labour exchange just when the history of the English alehouse was about to become a serious historical subject, as well as the organization of the all-important hay trade, and the close links between agriculture and the sea, a theme he pursues in the context of the herring industry and maritime sayings and superstitions.

The focus of FROM MOUTHS OF MEN (1976), by contrast, is urban rather than rural, and on commerce and industry rather than farming. In some respects less satisfying than some of his other works it confirms that George Ewart Evans's real achievement lay in the sublimating of his storytelling gifts to the process of listening to the reminiscences of others. The relatively unedited transcripts of recorded conversation can make for occasionally clumsy reading, and we sense an absence of that historical weight which underpins his rural work, but for all its impressionism FROM MOUTHS OF MEN is still enlivened by some startling images: a Suffolk bank counter piled high at Christmas with rabbit and game left by local farmers, a cart-driver left high and dry in Ipswich main street when his horse was unceremoniously requisitioned during the Great War. There is another image here too: of a fourteen-year-old boy miner, Hywel Jeffries, sick every time he reached the fresh air after inhaling gases all day underground. For in this book George Ewart Evans returns to Wales, not, except briefly, to the deep-mining, steam-coal area of his native east Glamorgan, but to the drift-mining, anthracite field of the Dulais Valley further west. He reverts, too, to a familiar theme, the impact of mechanization on craft skills, on the work experience and the social relationships surrounding them. Even by 1930, the miners on Graig-yr-hydd had told him, the old tools which the men, knowing them by feel alone, had no need to label, had been displaced by the mechanical cutter and conveyor which altered traditional work practices and customs, and severed the men's holistic relationship with nature—for *everything tied in* just as much beneath the ground as on it—as in their ability to notice the warning signs of a trickle of dust or creak of timbers that precede a roof-fall. As Uncle Tom protested:

Twenty years ago they mined coal. There was an art in it. Now they drag it out like a clumsy midwife bringing on a delivery. Get it out. Get it out at all costs; let the devil take care of the consequences. And he nearly always does . . .

(THE VOICES OF THE CHILDREN, p. 119)

Social relationships also were altered as coal-face mechanization undermined the craftsman's status, dissolved the close protective (perhaps also exploitative?) bonds of the stall system, and diminished the respect of younger men for seniority. A mark of a civilized society, in George Ewart Evans's view, was its respect for its aged.

In FROM MOUTHS OF MEN he also takes a further perceptive look at the role of dress, that *essential part of social history* he had first drawn attention to in THE HORSE IN THE FURROW as a means of social affirmation and sending signals. In his recognition that *dress is an integral part of the history of any society* he was again blazing a trail followed by others, especially those who, since the early

1960s, had advocated a closer relationship between history and anthropology. It was a development that George Ewart Evans warmly welcomed, for he had been engaged at the interface of history, anthropology and ethnography ever since his THE PATTERN UNDER THE PLOUGH (1966), where he first makes the connections to which he returns with verve in his last published work, SPOKEN HISTORY (1987). Its flavour can be gauged from the account of his discovery in his half-timbered house in Needham Market, where the Evans family lived for six years after leaving Blaxhall in 1956, that walnut shells were packed between the joists. They were there, it appeared, for insulation. But George Ewart Evans, the former Classics student, remembered that walnuts were scattered at Roman weddings to protect the offspring. Had this some magical significance? Or do we settle for the insulation? This questioning is typical of a book that is throughout probing, suggestive and illuminated by frequent flashes of insight.

THE PATTERN UNDER THE PLOUGH's unorthodox amalgam of archaeology, anthropology, rural sociology and folklore so confused conventional categories that THE LISTENER (12 January 1967) reviewed it among its Travel Books. George Ewart Evans himself was under no such misapprehension. If anyone had asked him in the 1960s what he had been writing about, *I would have said it was an attempt at recording the folk-life of a community, or alternatively—to refer to it in more academic terms—social anthropology*. But if this is how he conceived of it himself, he arrived at that position from the study of folk-life and folklore.

X

Systematic folklore study began in nineteenth-century Scandinavia where from an early stage it included research into dialect, material culture and folk-life. It was in this Scandinavian, ethnographic sense that Ewart Evans himself conceived of the folk,

> *the people of country or region irrespective of class or creed; and the study of folk life implies not only a systematic examination of the material culture of a region but the relating to it of the region's beliefs, customs, language, myth, and social organization.*
>
> (THE PATTERN UNDER THE PLOUGH, p. 21)

It was the 1930s that saw a quickening of interest in the (pastoral) Celtic countries, as opposed to (arable) southern and eastern England, though it was in the 1960s that George Ewart Evans cultivated links with the Irish Folklore Commission in Dublin and, in the particular person of Iorwerth Peate, with the Welsh Folk Museum, St Fagans. At the same time his reading of Sir James Frazer's THE GOLDEN BOUGH, of Lewis H. Morgan (via Engels), and of Malinowski, Lévi-Strauss and E. E. Evans-Pritchard led him to the conclusion that the historian who supplemented the evidence of documents with oral testimony was in fact poaching on anthropology, using living people as sources. Like Claude Lévi-Strauss, George Ewart Evans distinguished between history, that organizes its data in relation to conscious expressions of social life, and anthropology, which proceeds by examining its unconscious foundations. George Ewart Evans's specific contribution was to show how the study of oral tradition could help at once the historian, the anthropologist and the folklorist, not to mention the student of dialect and the archaeologist. He professed puzzlement that most British social anthropologists chose to study abroad, when there was a rich harvest to be gathered in this country, and he believed that anthropology with its preoccupation with the unconscious element in the people it studies could in turn learn from folk-life specialists *how to study a culture from the inside*, just as oral testimony *enables you to get inside the heads of people*.

His close personal friendship with Iorwerth Peate emanated from mutual respect and conviction that the study of material culture should go hand in hand with that of oral tradition and dialect. It was *I Iorwerth a Nansi Peate* that Ewart Evans dedicated his HORSE POWER AND MAGIC (1979). This was hardly the first time he had written on this topic, for horse-myths and the secret lore of the horseman are recurrent themes in his work. His originality here lay in uncovering an 'inner ring' of horsemen, all born before 1900, who by the use of specifically prepared oils and powders, secret ceremonies and esoteric practices (like going to a stream at midnight during full moon and performing a rite with a bone from a dismembered frog) were able to immobilize a horse in any kind of circumstance. This apparently magical ability to 'jade' or arrest a horse was achieved by, for example, painting a gatepost with a concoction to which the horse's acute sense of smell violently reacted and it would refuse to pass through the gate until the smell had been neutralized. Evans found classical precedents for this, in the same way as he linked horse-whispering, by which a horse was controlled by blowing up its nostrils or through speaking to it in a low voice, to ancient totemic horse cults from which was descended, for instance, the Mari Lwyd, a well-known Glamorgan wassailing tradition still active in Abercynon when George Ewart Evans was born there in the early years of the twentieth century. His long-standing fascination for horse cults was partly to be explained by the fact that *both my parents came from districts where the myth of the Mari Lwyd was very much alive*—his father from Pentyrch, his mother from Maesteg—*so that one could say it was part of my inheritance.* Horse psychology features often in Ewart Evans's early fiction: Dan Thomas Hallier *was a proper man with hosses . . . brought up in the country he was before coming to the pits here and he could make a hoss do anything bar talk* ('He Saith Among the Trumpets Ha Ha', WALES, No. 5, 1938), and Ianto Parry took his horse upstairs to his ailing wife's bedside to speed her recovery.

The Mari Lwyd survival affirmed the resilience of the oral tradition and showed the remarkable tenacity of myth. Seen in the context of horse-lore from other parts of Britain (north-east Scotland) and Europe (according to Gibbon, horse magic was practised at the shrine of St Martin of Tours in the reign of Clovis), it reinforced George Ewart Evans's conviction that history is a continuum both in time and extent.

It was satisfying to him to discover that the legend of Guto Nyth Brân had its equivalent in many cultures world-wide. Oral tradition, seen from the vantage point of the Jungian psychology in which Ewart Evans had immersed himself during the war, was a means of finding the deep layers of symbolic meaning in the collective unconscious. The 'pattern' under the plough referred not only to the boundaries of long-forgotten prehistoric fields but to the pattern of primitive beliefs which still underlay the social memory of the Suffolk *gwerin*. There were therefore two main strands to oral history as George Ewart Evans conceived of it: it was a source not only of knowledge about craft skills and practical activities, but of folklore and myth as well. History, myths and traditions were all intermingled in the same complex of information his neighbours were giving him about their work.

Curiously, therefore, while George Ewart Evans can hardly be accused of being a misty-eyed romantic when it came to the history of the labouring past, when he allowed legend and even whimsy a free rein in the pursuit of horses' skulls, severed heads and hares, history and anthropology could sometimes come off second best—at least in the narrow academic sense, though much of Ewart Evans's strength and attractiveness is precisely that he so steadfastly scorned the restrictive assumption that *what does not come within the orbit of Jowettian knowledge is not knowledge at all.* His most imaginative excursion was the pursuit he undertook, jointly with David Thomson, of THE LEAPING HARE (1972). An engaging amalgam of folklore and anthropology blended with an

Aubreyesque pleasure in detailing legend and anecdote, it attempts to explain the frequency of hare myths in Britain and Ireland, and Welsh hares are hunted with zest. When the eminent anthropologist Edmund Leach damned with colossal condescension *this jumble of fantasy and mis-statement* and concluded that *scholarship apart . . . advocates of Robert Graves and his White Goddess may consider the whole enterprise more significant* than he had, he was doing more than merely reviving Ewart Evans's suspicions of the Cambridge intelligentsia he had been dubious of since the 1930s—he was identifying a potent element in Evans's whole approach.

Graves's celebrated study of Celtic mythology emphasized for Ewart Evans that primitive myths are expressions of symbolic truths intuitively apprehended, rather than what is commonly understood as scientific truth.

In myth the central core of meaning cannot be described in detail because . . . instead of pin-pointing the truth in exact referential terms, myth circumscribes an area where it is certain the truth lies.

(SPOKEN HISTORY, p. 215)

At this intersection of history, myth and legend George Ewart Evans shared common ground with Graves, whose encomium that *a single page of* THE PATTERN UNDER THE PLOUGH *is worth a wilderness of folk-motifs* so delighted him, and also, in particular, with the writer-artist David Jones who so powerfully integrated landscape, people, mythology and language in fusing the past and present of the Welsh. Evans especially admired the ANATHEMATA where artefacture is invested with mystical significance and where the actual and mythological coalesce. Like Graves, whose WHITE GODDESS was subtitled 'A Grammar of Poetic Thought', Jones sought to integrate anthropology, archaeology, comparative mythology and literature in a search for the ancient 'deposits'—a Jones keyword—in the Welsh-British social memory. It was comparable accretions, slow-moving historical silts and strata, that George Ewart Evans believed he was unearthing in his patient excavations of oral tradition. Certainly it was from the ANATHEMATA that he acquired his notion of the 'modern break' which brought *the prior culture* to an end, though David Jones seems to have meant by it the whole of the nineteenth century, whereas George Ewart Evans clearly uses the phrase to connote the disjunction of the First World War and its accompanying —or consequential (the relationship is not made clear)—technological impact, perhaps at the expense of the *truly* dramatic post-war change in land ownership, the *seigneurial* 'break'.

This deep-seated, romantic streak in George Ewart Evans brings us back to his non-historical writing (to say 'non-creative' is in his case a meaningless distinction). In 1949 he had contributed a poem, 'The Pursuit', to A NEW ROMANTIC ANTHOLOGY, edited by Henry Treece and Stefan Schimanski. Here he found his work keeping company with David Jones's IN PARENTHESIS. In this period, thanks particularly to Henry Morris and Sawston, George Ewart Evans, who had a strong visual sense, could be linked to the neo-Romantic movement of the forties and early fifties which attracted writers and artists to 'Celtic Britain'. Painters like Graham Sutherland and F. R. Konekamp had found sanctuary and inspiration since the mid-thirties in the Pembrokeshire of Celtic legend which was celebrated by Ewart Evans himself in a poem 'North from the Prescelly Mountains' that appeared in a 'David Jones number' of DOCK LEAVES in 1955. In 1951 the Festival of Britain gave George Ewart Evans the pretext for arranging a local exhibition in Blaxhall celebrating the history and work of the village, which elicited a treasure trove of tools and artefacts that in turn led to the writing of ASK THE FELLOWS. The 'Festival issue' of DOCK LEAVES that year commemorated an exhibition of contemporary Welsh painting by, among others, Sutherland, Ceri Richards and David Jones, and contained a poem by George Ewart Evans, 'The Two Birch Trees', in which his neo-Romantic mistrust of mechanization (an ambivalence which pervades even his later historical work) is clearly if rhetorically articulated:

Twin boles are defiant monument
To those who have hid the sun with stones;
And their marbled affirmation is louder than the street:
The force that split the rock will rend the city
And in this square will shout
Its old and leaping triumph over death . . .

In the same issue the exiled artist Konekamp, intuitively apprehending mysteries in the hills and mountains that could almost be physically touched *as a water diviner the floods underneath the soil*, lamented that *we in the West are losing the organic connection with the vital life around us . . . with the universal pattern* whose significance had been grasped *by Picasso and Henry Moore*. This was entirely consistent with George Ewart Evans's own thinking, as can be seen from the remarkably similar terms in which he expressed himself in the last book he wrote:

I have also been encouraged to take an unfashionable view of researching the past by the experience of modern artists. During this century they have gone back to early man for renewal . . . Artists like Picasso, Braque and Henry Moore recognized that tribal art had an atmosphere about its sculptures and artefacts . . . Artists have gone back to the primitive for inspiration and have found guidance.

(Spoken History, p. 217)

And by implication he included himself among those who found symbolized in the crafts values like use and permanence which were ultimately to be more highly regarded than profit, values which would help to counter *the waves of mechanization and depersonalizing that have engulfed many of our social artefacts.*

If David Jones was one of those who directed George Ewart Evans to the primitive for inspiration and guidance, he also may have provided him with an intellectual reinforcement of the visceral sense of Welshness which he never lost and which he asserted ever more stridently in his later years. *Even in the primary school* he recalled in his autobiography

I realized that Wales had been given Cain's portion. Right through its history Wales has had to fight for its existence as a nation; at first through direct physical assault, later through

having to resist the subtler appeal to its people to give up their nationhood and become 'English-like-us'. But Wales was the first of England's colonies and a Welshman cannot forget it.
(The Strength of the Hills, p. 98)

George Ewart Evans never did forget it, and his strenuous efforts in later life to perfect his command of written Welsh—he never lost the ability to read it, and his wartime notebooks contain his own potted history of Welsh literature from the seventh century to the twentieth—as borne out in his correspondence with Iorwerth Peate who would magisterially correct his friend's grammatical errors by return of mail, suggest he strongly endorsed what David Jones wrote (in Wales, No. 40, 1959) that

it is certainly no want of realism which makes one assert that the things of the Cymry are intricated in a rather special way with a historic language in an historic terrain . . . there is [in Wales] *the whole tie-up of very ancient duration with site and locality whereby terrain and nomenclature and the web of history are so intermixed as to be hardly patient of separation . . . an enclave harbouring a community of living men and women with a living language and tradition linking the Britain of now with that of the earliest deposits.*

The renegade Welsh Baptist George Ewart Evans, more truly in exile from his native Wales than the Anglo-Welsh, Catholic convert David Jones, who lived there only three years in the 1920s, ever was, came to a deeper appreciation of his own historical identity through his study of the oral tradition of East Anglia; for if the old dialect-speakers of Suffolk had in their keeping their *filtered gold of centuries* then even more so was this applicable to his *own* people and language. In his Presidential Address in 1971 he told Section H (Anthropology) of the British Association:

Welsh has all the ancient virtues of a language that has been used by a people who have lived close to the soil for at least a couple of thousand years; and the language has taken its sustenance from it. Yet someone will no doubt say 'But most of us no longer live in a peasant community. I grant you there's a point in recognizing the virtue of the language but why make all this fuss about keeping it alive?' Now, strange as it may seem, it needs saying yet again that Welsh is not simply a kind of regional language as so many opponents of a Welsh language policy appear to imply. It is the language of a separate people, a nation.

Having discovered in East Anglia that language is the expression of an underlying social structure, it followed that

if this organic theory is valid, a people that loses its language is not merely dropping an appendage or changing into a new garment, it is losing its very soul, the entity that alone ensures it will remain a nation.

That George Ewart Evans was a *Welsh* writer can hardly be doubted.

XI

George Ewart Evans, the uncommon celebrator of the common man, died on 11 January 1988 in the village of Brooke near Norwich. If *his* lasting regret was that circumstances conspired to prevent him from reversing the direction he had followed over fifty years before, *when the road to England was similar to the path to the lion's cave—the footprints all pointing one way*, our regret must be that he was so gratuitously denied the formal recognition in Wales that his achievement demanded. While the Universities of Essex and Keele conferred on him honorary doctorates, the University of Wales, of which he was a graduate, offered him in 1978 when his life's work was done, the honorary degree of *Magister in Artibus*. It was an offer he declined. He wrote:

If I had really wanted this award, I would have gone after it in the half century (nearly) since my initial degree. From the university's standpoint my writings have been almost entirely about the wrong country. But I have been reconciled to this anomalous position for some time, of being more or less an outsider in both countries.

(Letter to Iorwerth Peate, 16 March 1978)

It was his *outsider*'s perspective, just as he was on the *fringes* of academic life, that brought East Anglia into such sharply edged focus. But it was the time and place into which he was born and where he was brought up that shaped him, the valley and also the hills, those Welsh hills which *had always formed the clearest map in my mental topography that half a century of living in a flat landscape had failed to eradicate*. The days that he had seen contain the key to the paradox that a writer from Abercynon who aspired to be an interpreter of the coal-mining communities of his native Glamorgan instead achieved lasting fame in Suffolk by asking the fellows who cut the hay.

Bibliography

GEORGE EWART EVANS

George Ewart Evans wrote a considerable amount of published fiction and verse; as an oral historian and folklorist he was also a prolific contributor to periodicals, magazines and academic journals. What follows cannot pretend to be anything like a full bibliography, even if that were possible; but it does, I believe, convey something of his remarkably diverse output.

Section A adds to the preliminary list in Brynmor Jones (ed.), A BIBLIOGRAPHY OF ANGLO-WELSH LITERATURE 1900–1965 (Cardiff, 1970), and I have included in this section transcripts of George Ewart Evans's feature programmes for the BBC Welsh Home Service.

In Section C I have not included any of the far more numerous programmes he made about East Anglia, his radio scripts for children, nor his many articles and reviews for, in particular, THE TIMES EDUCATIONAL SUPPLEMENT. While this therefore is the fullest bibliography of the writings of George Ewart Evans so far compiled, it makes no claims to being exhaustive, merely representative.

A. Fiction and Poetry

Novel

THE VOICES OF THE CHILDREN (Penmark

Press, Cardiff, 1947). Two extracts appeared in THE WELSH REVIEW, IV, Nos. 3 and 4, 1945.

Collected Short Stories

Editor, WELSH SHORT STORIES (Faber and Faber, London, 1959), with Introduction and story 'The Medal'.

ACKY (Faber and Faber, London, 1974).

LET DOGS DELIGHT (Faber and Faber, London, 1975).

Individual Short Stories
(those included in LET DOGS DELIGHT are preceded by an asterisk *).

'Red Coal' (published under the pseudonym George Geraint), LEFT REVIEW, 3, No. 1 (February 1937).

'Pause for Conversation', WALES, No. 2 (April 1937).

'He Saith Among The Trumpets Ha Ha', WALES, No. 5 (Summer 1938).

*'Folk Tale', WELSH REVIEW, 1 (May 1939).

'Theirs is the Kingdom', LIFE AND LETTERS TODAY, No. 22 (1939).

'Be Master', LIFE AND LETTERS TODAY, No. 29 (1940).

*'Let Dogs Delight', LIFE AND LETTERS TODAY, No. 31 (1940), also included in TWENTY-FIVE WELSH SHORT STORIES, eds. Gwyn Jones and Islwyn Ffowc Elis (Oxford University Press, London, 1971).

*'Gold Key', ENGLISH STORY, First Series, eds. Woodrow and Susan Wyatt (Collins, London, 1941).

'Like a Lion', LIFE AND LETTERS TODAY, No. 48 (1941).

*'The Cow', LIFE AND LETTERS TODAY, No. 51 (1941).

'Beyond the Trees', WALES, New Series, I (July 1943).

'The Destination', BUGLE BLAST, Second Series, ed. Jack Aistrop and Reginald Moore (Allen and Unwin, London, 1941).

'You'd Cut Each Other's Throats', LILLIPUT (August 1944).

'The Singer', WALES, IV, No. 6 (Winter 1945).

'The Powder Monkey', WALES, VII, No. 28 (February–March 1948).

*'Ben Knowledge', WALES, IX, No. 31 (October 1949).

*'Feet and The Man', PICK OF TODAY'S SHORT STORIES, No. 3, ed. John Pudney (Odhams, London, 1952).

*'Possessions', WELSH SHORT STORIES, ed. Gwyn Jones (Oxford University Press, London, 1956), also included in THE GREEN BRIDGE, ed. John Davies (Severn Books, Bridgend, 1988).

'The Journey', WALES, New Series, No. 4 (December 1958).

'The Medal', WELSH SHORT STORIES, ed. George Ewart Evans (Faber and Faber, London, 1959).

Other Miscellaneous Prose

Answer to Questionnaire ('Do you consider yourself an Anglo-Welsh writer? For whom do you write?' etc.), WALES, No. 8/9 (August 1939).

'An emergent national literature', WALES, New Series, II (1943).

'The foils are poisoned so that the good may die' —a tribute to Alun Lewis, WALES, 4 (Summer 1944).

'Myddleton's Glory', LIFE AND LETTERS, No. 123 (1947).

'The Mabinogion', LIFE AND LETTERS, No. 138 (1949).

Radio Features (transcripts)

JOURNEY TO SOUTH WALES, BBC Welsh Home Service (February 1957).

The First Fifty Years: Anglo-Welsh Short-Story Writers, BBC Welsh Home Service (November 1968).

Poems

'At the Seaside', Wales, No. 6/7 (March 1939).

'Poem' *(Progress in the peaceable blue of a sky in summer . . .)*, Wales, No. 10 (October 1939).

'The Recruit', Wales, New Series, No. 1 (July 1943).

'The Clerk', Wales, New Series, No. 1 (July 1943).

'Winter 1939', in Modern Welsh Poetry, ed. Keidrych Rhys (Faber and Faber, London, 1944).

'Poem' *(To a flat sky is pinned the tilted moon . . .)*, Wales, New Series, No. 3 (1944).

'Ailsa Craig', Wales, V, No. 7 (Summer 1945).

'Airman at a Railway Terminus', Wales, V, No. 7 (Summer 1945).

'Seeing is Not Seeing', Anglo-Welsh Review, 11, No. 28 (Winter 1949).

'The Pursuit', in A New Romantic Anthology, eds. Stefan Schimanski and Henry Treece (Grey Walls Press, London, 1949).

'Richard Lewis (1900–1966), Miner: Once Mayor

of an English Town', ANGLO-WELSH REVIEW, 16, No. 38 (Winter 1967).

'Poem' *(Forty years in the world's turning . . .)*, DOCK LEAVES, 2, No. 4 (January 1951).

'The Two Birch Trees', DOCK LEAVES, 2, No. 5 (May 1951).

'The Statue', DOCK LEAVES, 4, No. 11 (Summer 1953).

'North from the Prescelly Mountains', DOCK LEAVES, 6, No. 16 (Spring 1955).

'The Golden Bird' (radio poem for five voices), DOCK LEAVES, 8, No. 22 (1957).

'The Dead Pheasant', WALES, No. 40 (1959).

Children's Fiction

THE TURNPIKE (Paxton Playlets for Juniors and Seniors) (Paxton, London, 1950).

THE FITTON FOUR-POSTER (Blackie, London, 1952).

Film scripts for the Children's Film Foundation (unpublished):

THE SHIP IN THE FOREST (1955).

THE CAT GANG (1958).

B. Autobiography

THE STRENGTH OF THE HILLS (Faber and Faber, London, 1983).

C. Oral History

Books (all published by Faber and Faber, London):

ASK THE FELLOWS WHO CUT THE HAY (1956). The references in the text are to the 1987 Faber paperback reprint of the second, 1965, edition.

THE HORSE IN THE FURROW (1960).

THE PATTERN UNDER THE PLOUGH (1966).

THE FARM AND THE VILLAGE (1969).

WHERE BEARDS WAG ALL (1970).

THE LEAPING HARE (with David Thomson) (1972).

THE DAYS THAT WE HAVE SEEN (1975).

FROM MOUTHS OF MEN (1976).

HORSE POWER AND MAGIC (1979).

SPOKEN HISTORY (1987).

Selected Articles

'The horse and magic', NEW SOCIETY (14 March 1963).

'Let your yeah be yeah', NEW SOCIETY (25 July 1963).

'Wart-charming', NEW SOCIETY (3 August 1963).

'The corn-harvest', NEW SOCIETY (19 September 1963).

'Christmas light and dark', NEW SOCIETY (22 December 1964).

'Flesh and blood archives', THE AUTHOR, 77 (June 1966).

'Folk life studies in East Anglia', in J. Geraint Jenkins (ed.), STUDIES IN FOLK LIFE: ESSAYS IN HONOUR OF IORWERTH C. PEATE (Routledge, London, 1969).

'Aspects of oral tradition', FOLK LIFE: JOURNAL OF THE SOCIETY FOR FOLK LIFE STUDIES, VII (1969).

'The relevance of oral tradition', PRESIDENTIAL ADDRESSES OF THE BRITISH ASSOCIATION, SWANSEA MEETING 1971, pp. 83–94.

'Using our museums', THE TIMES EDUCATIONAL SUPPLEMENT (26 February 1971).

'Flesh and blood archives: some early experiences', ORAL HISTORY JOURNAL, 1, No. 1 (1972).

'Approaches to interviewing', Oral History Journal, 1, No. 4 (1972).

'I am a tape recorder', Encounter (November 1976).

'The south Wales miners and their inheritance', Eighth Report of the South Wales Miners' Library (Swansea, 1982–3), pp. 13–18.

D. Evaluations and Obituaries

Iorwerth C. Peate, 'George Ewart Evans', Y Faner (27 Gorffennaf 1979).

Vincent H. Phillips, 'The historian of England's *gwerin*', Book News from Wales/Llais Llyfrau (Spring 1984).

Paul Thompson, The Voice of the Past (2nd ed.) (Oxford, 1988).

Alun Howkins, 'George Ewart Evans 1909–1988: an appreciation', Oral History Journal, 16, No. 2 (1988).

Alun Howkins, 'George Ewart Evans 1909–1987' [*sic*], History Workshop, 26 (Autumn 1988).

The Daily Telegraph (12 January 1988).

The Times (13 January 1988).

David Thomson, in the Guardian (15 January 1988).

Colin Ward, in the INDEPENDENT (18 January 1988).

Rheinallt Llwyd, 'George Ewart Evans—arloeswr hanes llafar', BARN (Hydref 1988).

Trefor M. Owen, 'George Ewart Evans', FOLKLORE, 99, No. II (1988).

Acknowledgements

I cannot claim to have known George Ewart Evans personally. I heard him lecture twice, met him once, and have two letters from him in his distinctive italic handwriting, one of them written in Welsh. Since he was never in his own lifetime accorded proper recognition by either the University of Wales or the Welsh Arts Council, I salute the Editors of the 'Writers of Wales' series for including him in a series published by the one body on behalf of the other. In preparing this posthumous but not uncritical tribute, my principal debts have been to George Ewart Evans's immediate family. His son and literary executor Matthew Evans allowed me complete freedom of access to all the materials I wished to consult. I am also indebted to George Ewart Evans's daughter Susan and her husband David Gentleman for being literally so accommodating and for many other kindnesses besides. I much enjoyed talking about him too with his daughter Jane Palmer, and with his brother Sydney. Among his many friends who were always ready to share with me their memories of George Ewart Evans, and who allowed me to quote from letters in their possession, I would like particularly to mention John Bodley, Alun Howkins, Glyn Jones, Gwyn Jones, Colin Richmond and Peter du Sautoy. For replying so helpfully to specific requests I am also grateful to Jim Davies, David Egan, Hywel Francis, Rheinallt Llwyd, Nick Mansfield and Havard Walters. I hope they recognize in these pages at least *something* of the man they regarded with such affection and admiration. The interpretation I offer here is mine alone, fortified by George Ewart Evans's own reminder in FROM MOUTHS OF MEN (p. 176) that *there is not one truth . . . but many truths.*

Acknowledgements are due to the University College of Wales for the grant of a Sir David Hughes Parry Award towards the costs of research and writing, to Dorothy Evans and Margaret Parry who word-processed the final draft so efficiently, to Ceinwen Jones of the University of Wales Press for her editorial vigilance, and to Faber and Faber Ltd. for permission to use quotations from George Ewart Evans's books.

This book is dedicated to
the memory of my beloved niece
Sophie Calvin (1974-90)

The Author

Gareth Wyn Williams is a native of Barry, South Glamorgan. He was born in 1945 and educated at Barry Boys' Grammar School and Balliol College, Oxford, where he read History. He did research at the London School of Economics and Political Science and at the University of Chicago where he was a University Fellow in 1967–8. After a brief period of schoolteaching, he was appointed in 1970 to a lectureship in History at the University College of Wales. He has written widely on the social history of Wales in the nineteenth and twentieth centuries, especially on popular beliefs, popular culture and the history of sport and recreation. He is the co-author of FIELDS OF PRAISE (University of Wales Press, 1980) which won a Welsh Arts Council Prize for Literature in 1981, and the author of YR YMGIPRYS AM Y GOGLEDD (Gwasg Prifysgol Cymru, 1985). Gareth Williams is a Fellow of the Royal Historical Society and Dean of the Faculty of Welsh-Medium Studies at University College of Wales, Aberystwyth, where he is a Senior Lecturer in History. He is married, with two sons.

The Author

This Edition
designed by Jeff Clements,
is set in Monotype Spectrum 12 Didot on 13 point
and printed on Basingwerk Parchment by
Qualitex Printing Limited, Cardiff

It is limited to 1000 copies of which this is

Copy No. 0357

British Library Cataloguing in Publication Data

Williams, Gareth 1945-

George Ewart Evans. — (Writers of Wales; 0141-5050).
1. Great Britain. Historiography. Evans, George Ewart
I. Title II. Series
941.007202

ISBN 0-7083-1093-1

EFFECTIVE PLANNING

in Training and Development

Leslie Rae

First published in 2000

Kogan Page Limited
120 Pentonville Road
London N1 9JN
UK

Stylus Publishing Inc.
22883 Quicksilver Drive
Sterling, VA 20166-2012
USA

British Library Cataloguing in Publication Data

A CIP record for this book is available from the British Library.

ISBN 0 7494 3359 0

Typeset by Jean Cussons Typesetting, Diss, Norfolk
Printed and bound in Great Britain by Clays Ltd, St Ives plc

Contents

Preface vii

Introduction 1

PART ONE: Programmes – Learners and Objectives 5

1. **Designing the Training and Development Programme** 7
The training cycle in planning – areas of responsibility, learner workshops, other learner approaches; Pre-course and on-course confirmation of content – pre-course questionnaires, on-course activities, identifying the key needs of the learners; Setting the scene

2. **Considering the Potential Participants** 21
Individual learner qualities; Kolb's Learning Cycle; An alternative learning model; Learning styles – the Learning Style Questionnaire; Learning preferences; The practical significance of learning models; Other learning influences – sensory learning; Barriers to learning – language and speech barriers, psychological barriers, barriers attributable to the trainer, environmental barriers, the learning attention span; Positive features of learning

3. **Setting Training Objectives** 45
The elements of objectives; Benefits of using 'SMART'; The advantages of objectives; The disadvantages of objectives; Writing training objectives; Clarify and agree the actionable training objectives; Establish priorities; Feasibility; An objectives action plan; The practical uses of objectives – prior to the programme, at the start of the programme, during and at the end of the programme

PART TWO: Planning and Designing On-the-job Training and Development 61

4. On-the-job Training and Development – 1 63
On-the-job training programme planning stages; Reference to the agreed objectives; Consider the target learning population – level of starting knowledge, location, timing; On-the-job training and development planning and design; A competences approach to programme material; Types of on-the-job training approaches; GAFO; Coaching – the uses of coaching, the basis for coaching; Benefits and disadvantages of coaching; Coaching practice

5. On-the-job Training and Development – 2 83
One-to-one instruction – criteria for effectiveness, the cycle of instruction, planning the instruction approach, planning instructional methods, designing training/instruction events; Project management; Mentoring; Team development – team roles; Delegation – barriers to delegation, the process of delegation; Alternative on-the-job training approaches

6. Alternative On-the-job Training Approaches 102
Secondments and job rotation; Action learning; Support groups; Quality circles; Books – patterned notetaking; Open learning packages – planning for open learning, text-based open learning; Multi-media open learning packages – audio cassettes, audio-visual packages, video and interactive video, trigger videos, interactive videos; Computer-assisted (CAT) and computer-based (CBT) training programs – Web- and Internet-based training, the benefits of CBT, the disadvantages of CBT, trainer attitudes, planning the use of CBT

PART THREE: Planning and Designing Off-the-job Training and Development 125

7. Off-the-job Training Approaches – 1 127
The off-the-job planning process; Objectives and the learning population; Training accommodation; Advantages and disadvantages of off-the-job training; Time – starting and finishing dates; A training programme planning guide – training programme design, guideline document for the training practitioners; Knowledge of training formats – training courses, workshops, conferences, seminars; Off-the-job training methods – trainer presentations, buzz groups, syndicates, discussions, demonstrations, question and answer sessions

8. Off-the-job Training Approaches – 2 **144**
Case studies and simulations; Role plays – variations, review and feedback, observing role plays, action summary; Activities – activity restraints, choosing activities, technological advances, action summary; Brainstorming; Videos; CAT, CBT and CD-i; Planning the training programme – summary

9. Planning the Training Sessions **157**
The stages in designing a learning session; Timing; Detailed session planning; The traditional text or vertical method format; The headline method; OHP slides as briefs; Horizontal planning – planning stages; Patterned notes planning

10. Planning Activity Sessions **176**
Planning questions – why?, how many?, which and what form of activity and where from?; Types of activity; The final choice; Resource activity listing; Technological advances – activities on the Internet, the Echelon learning library, the GAIA project, the Training Zone, other Internet sites, US sites; Using the resource collections; Planning the introduction of an activity; Observation and review

PART FOUR: Planning the Evaluation of Training and Development **189**

11. Planning the Evaluation of Training and Development Programmes **191**
Evaluation and validation; Reactionnaires; Planning evaluation – reasons for evaluation, reasons given for not evaluating; Who undertakes evaluation?; Planning the evaluation process; Other evaluation models; A limited evaluation plan – the four-stage evaluation process, recommended questionnaire, appropriate form of reactionnaire, post-training evaluation measures; Planning conclusion

Recommended and Further Reading **211**

Index **215**

Preface

Planning in training and development is as important as in any other form of performing services, tasks or other actions. Cases where the training has had little or no planning can quickly result in little or no learning; a confusing training programme for both the trainer and the learners; loss of trainer and training credibility with the learners and their managers, resulting in reduced use of the training; and so on. Planning does not necessarily guarantee fully effective training but, everything being equal, it is more likely to produce an effective, enjoyable, credible training programme.

The training process is a complex one and starts long before the actual programme, even as far back as the decision-making event when some form of training is proposed. Whatever the source of the requirement, in whatever form and for whatever reasons, the training from that stage must be planned as effectively as possible.

The objectives of this book are to describe the steps necessary in this planning and design process to prepare a training and development programme. Although the context emphasis is on direct training practices the techniques can be readily applied more widely to such approaches as open learning, interactive video and computer-based training programs, and Internet training programs.

The text of the book follows a logical pattern:

Part One – planning and designing training and development programmes – learners and objectives;
Part Two – planning and designing on-the-job training and development;
Part Three – planning and designing off-the-job training and development;
Part Four – planning the evaluation of training and development.

These parts cover three-quarters of the training process or cycle, the part omitted being the initial one of the identification and analysis of training needs. If action in that area shows that training will not fulfil the identified needs then the planning process stops there; otherwise TNIA (training needs identification and analysis) is an integral and preceding part of the planning process. There are a number of excellent sources of detailed descriptions and guidelines for TNIA – these are quoted in the recommended reading section at the end of this book.

Training and development is rich in 'technical' terms, frequently many for the same process or approach, equally frequently many that defy accurate definition. Throughout this book 'programme' is used to refer to a complete training process over a period of time, usually consisting of training courses, workshops, open learning programmes and so on. 'Session' refers to a specific and discrete event within a programme (such as a presentation or discussion), although nowadays sessions also include other activities, videos and the other tools of training. 'Workshop' is considered to be a relatively short programme at which participants (usually experienced in the workshop subject) meet to reinforce their learning, propose and agree back-at-work actions, or develop as a group or team. 'Activity' is a term I use that includes experiential pursuits, known severally as games, exercises and activities. The book stops at the actual presentation stage, as this is very personal to the training practitioner and again is a subject covered extensively in training and development literature.

Having myself practised the techniques described in this book, I hope that it will encourage training practitioners – managers, officers and programme designers – to look more closely at the effective requirements necessary when new or modified training is proposed. I accept that in many cases the time allowed for planning is limited – often because the training was required 'yesterday' – but this is no excuse for not attempting as much as possible, since a more effective approach will in fact reduce the time needed, as well as producing a more effective result.

I must thank Philip Mudd of Kogan Page for his continued interest in and support for my writing and the needs of training practitioners.

Introduction

When the policies and strategies of an organization include a commitment to training and the decision to provide appropriate and relevant training and development programmes, these need to be converted into practical action, usually by the training or HR department. Prior to this conversion or translation it is essential that a substantial amount of detailed planning takes place.

How the provision of the required training is planned will be determined by:

- the type of organization;
- the size of the organization;
- the distribution of individuals, work groups or teams;
- range of job roles and number of individual roles within this range;
- the needs of individuals at all levels;
- special initiatives such as commitment to quality management, priority customer service, and provision of higher and vocational education.

The planning and introduction of a required training and development pattern in an organization will depend on a number of factors that have to be considered and acted on before detailed planning of the programme can take place. This introductory activity will be a global outline planning that can include:

- the introduction of training and development into an organization as a new service;
- the modification and/or extension of an existing training and development programme as a result of changing or additional needs in the organization;

- the modification of an existing training and development programme as a result of the identification of individual needs;
- the introduction, extension or modification of new training aspects – eg new material courses or the extension of existing courses to include new material – into an existing programme;
- the introduction, extension or modification of individual sessions already existing in programmes;
- the introduction or extension of open learning, computer-assisted training (CAT), computer-based training (CBT), Internet-based training and other new technological issues.

Whichever requirement has been identified from this list, the first step will always be some form (the more extensive and intensive the better) of training needs identification and analysis (TNIA). The scale of this will obviously depend on the extent of the training and development visualized, as shown in the list above.

I have been involved as consultant in a number of organizations where a diversification of the existing training and development provisions became necessary and the senior management decided in each case that an improvement/change had to be investigated. As some of these organizations were large companies, with several sites throughout the country, nationwide TNIAs of the organization and the management structure were undertaken. These resulted in recommendations for the installation of much more up-to-date programmes, which also enabled growth as new requirements were identified.

Without the decision by the organizations to embark upon full TNIAs it is possible (as has been the case in other organizations of which I am aware) that training courses would just have been added on with little benefit to the organization. As a result of the TNIA in two cases, lengthy, expensive courses for all managers were replaced by a series of short modules, only the managers who required training in the subject attending them. The training function was not only improved, but the organization's costs were reduced through a more economical use of resources.

When a programme has been established for some time requirements can change, either subtly or grossly, and these can often necessitate the modification of a session or number of sessions in the programme. These require planning, albeit not to the same extent as in the events described above, but in as detailed and valid a manner as possible; and, of course, all the other aspects in between require planning or replanning to a greater or lesser extent. Failure to take this planning seriously or to the extent necessary will almost certainly result in the failure of the training, will demand replanning and, hence, the unnecessary use of time and resources that could have been prevented by earlier, effective planning.

PART ONE

Programmes – Learners and Objectives

1

Designing the Training and Development Programme

This chapter:

- discusses the training cycle and specifies the areas of planning and design;
- considers the range of responsibilities in planning and design;
- describes the information required immediately prior to the planning process;
- identifies the learning aspects, styles and preferences of learners;
- suggests a communication model and an alternative learning model;
- applies the learning models to practical situations;
- identifies and describes the barriers to training and learning.

THE TRAINING CYCLE IN PLANNING

Two important events will trigger the need for the planning and designing of a training and development programme:

1. the result of any investigation into needs based on suspicion of a problem;
2. the introduction of a new or revised operation or method of working.

Both these should (I would like to say 'will' but this would not be universally true) initiate a training needs analysis and investigation, which may be the precursor to the introduction of a training programme. The TNIA may, however, show that the problem can be solved by means other than training.

The TNIA forms the early part of the training cycle, as demonstrated in Figure 1.1. In this representation the part of the cycle described in this book is shown in italics.

It will be seen that the planning and design section appears to be a relatively small, unimportant area of the full cycle, but it is a crucially important area.

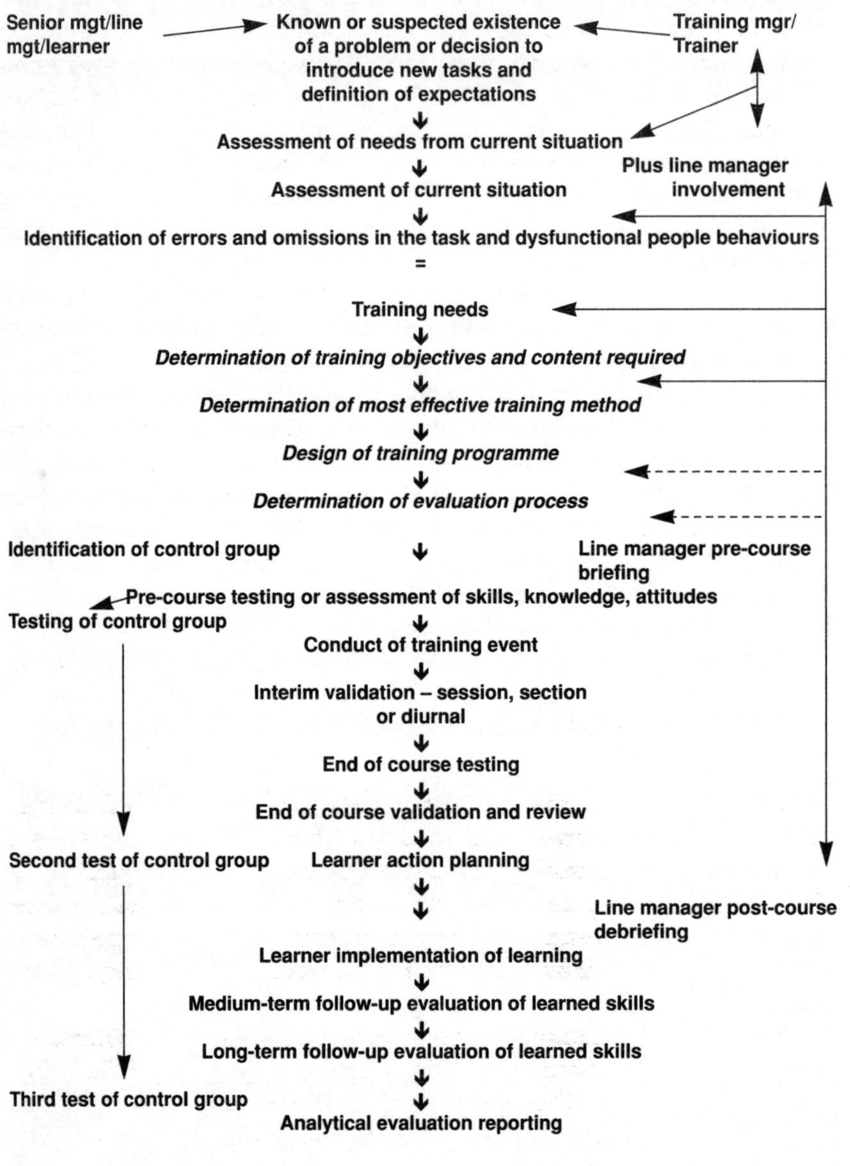

Figure 1.1 *The training cycle*

Areas of responsibility

A number of specific responsibilities are shown at the various stages of the training cycle. Some trainers, indeed some organizations, feel that because the whole is related to training the training department must be responsible for carrying out the full spectrum of activities. This is a traditional attitude, but experience has shown that in many cases only a very small part is carried out by the training department. This can usually be attributed to the fact that trainers have insufficient time to carry out the full cycle, the argument generally proposed being that if they had to do it all there would be no time left for training. This is not only not an acceptable reason, but indicates a basic fault in the thinking – the trainer is not always the best person to carry out certain stages of the training cycle, whether or not they have time to do so. Other people should/must be involved and be given their own responsibilities that they should be carrying out.

In previous writing I have introduced the concept of the training quintet, usually in connection with who does what in the evaluation process. But similar considerations apply when we are considering the planning of training and development. If you refer to Figure 1.1 the first area, that of making the initial decisions about general training needs, must fall squarely on the shoulders of senior management; the decisions about who participates in what training on those of the line manager, who is also responsible for certain activities prior to and after the training; and so on. There are specific areas where the knowledge, skill and expertise of the trainer decides that these are the areas in which they *must* be involved.

The training quintet is composed, as shown in Figure 1.2, also of the people who should be concerned with planning and design.

Senior management

Although not directly involved in the detailed planning and design of training programmes, senior management has the initial and the ultimate responsibility for the programme. It is frequently at their level that the decisions are made, with or without advice from a training manager, that new products, services or operations should be introduced and consequently 'some sort of training will be required'.

This is not sufficient involvement. Senior management is ultimately responsible for the effective training of their employees and the effective implementation of that training in order for it to have a positive effect on the business. This responsibility can only be fulfilled if the involvement is active:

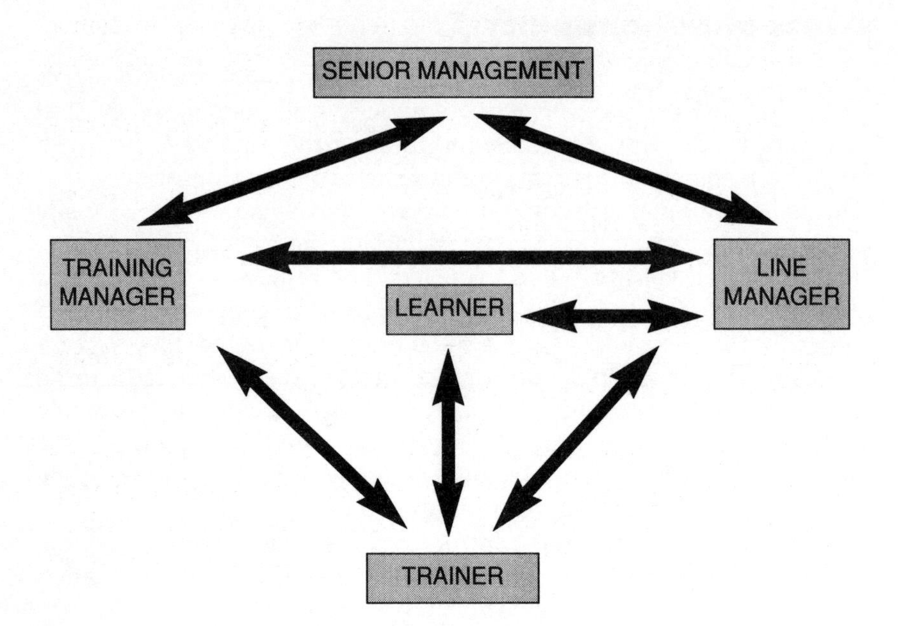

Figure 1.2 *The training quintet*

- giving more precise advice on training requirements as the senior management group sees them and authorizing necessary resources;
- taking advice from the training manager who should be involved at an early stage;
- requiring reports at an agreed point in the planning stage and (linked with the evaluation reports after the programme) following the programme;
- supporting planning from their knowledge and experience.

There is little value in clients and sponsors of training offering only a superficial and apparently uninterested attitude, frequently demonstrated by their stating their support without showing their support in a realistic and practical manner.

The training manager

These principal tasks of role holders are described in the second part of the title – manager. They must act as the moving and maintenance force in the progress of the development of the necessary training:

- frequent involvement and linking with the sponsoring senior management group from the earliest possible stage, encouraging positive decisions and active interest;
- agreeing with the training team the specific training programme needs;
- ensuring provision of sufficient resources to perform the planning task – staff, time, and so on;
- maintaining a continuing interest and support in the progress of the planning;
- liaising with line management ;
- reporting at agreed times on the progress of the training programme to the senior management sponsors.

The responsibility for the effective planning and design of the training and development programme falls directly on the training manager, and consequently it is in their interest to ensure that the responsibilities listed above are carried out with interest in and commitment to both the training and the training staff.

The line manager

'What have we got to do with all this? Training is the training department's job. We've got more than enough work to do.' This has frequently been the cry of line managers in the past (still commonly?), but there is a convenient forgetting of the responsibility of line managers that 'they are responsible for the training and development of their staff'. This does not mean that they have to train and develop their staff themselves, but that it is their *responsibility* to see that it happens.

The line manager is habitually underused in the training and development area – in the TNIA process, in evaluation, and even more so in the planning and design of the training of *their staff*. Much of this is because of the enforced divide between the line and training – 'training is the responsibility of training, and the line is responsible for operations'. The fact of the matter is that both are interlinked and dependent on each other. Trainers must be fully aware of what is happening and developing in the line, and line managers must be involved in training functions. There is considerable sympathy for the cry of line managers that they do not have sufficient time, but the trite, albeit true, response must be that they cannot afford not to be involved. After all they have the responsibility quoted earlier, and must also ensure, for their own satisfaction and task outcome, that they know what the training is about, that it is effective, satisfies their objectives and can be realistically implemented at work. Failure to take this interest, and related activity, will be reflected in the work of their staff and the efficiency of their budget operation.

As noted above, the training department has a responsibility for liaising with line management, but, as will be seen later, it also has an educative responsibility in this area of interlinking and positive activity.

Consequently the responsibilities of the line manager in the specific planning and designing processes are:

- being aware of what has been proposed and how the proposals are to be processed;
- having an input into the planning and design process;
- ensuring full awareness of the final product, and that this satisfies their operations' objectives;
- giving whatever support is requested, and is feasible, to the training department to enable or improve the planning and design.

The second responsibility in the list above is either ignored or not taken up in almost 100 per cent of training situations. Many trainers see an invitation to line managers actively to participate in the planning and design of a training programme in terms of 'What do they know about training programmes?' The line managers similarly react that they haven't the time, are not training experts, and that this is the job of the training department. These views from both parties could not be further from the truth. If the trainers do not take account of the views of line management there is every possibility that the learners will be trained, if not in the wrong skills, in skills that do not fully satisfy the line objectives.

Organizations that have good relationships between the training department and the line commonly involve line managers during the planning and design of training programmes. This co-operation helps to ensure that the manager feels some ownership of, and hence commitment to the training of *their* staff. It is for the training department to ensure that the managers are invited to participate, and for the managers to let the trainers know of their interest and willingness to help. Such joint actions are frequently practised at workshops set up specifically for the purpose. A big danger, that is not unknown , is for lip service to be paid to the support and assistance of the line managers, while in the event it is ignored.

This co-operation and active inter-involvement is not a simple and easy process, but its effective operation will be repaid many times over.

The trainer

The responsibilities of the trainer in this area are, in the main, obvious and clear, since they take the major role in the planning and design of training and development programmes that, most likely, they will be directly involved in offering. It is therefore to their advantage to ensure that the material they are planning and producing is required, fully relevant, completely up to date, and presented in the most effective (and enjoyable) way. In order to fulfil these basic responsibilities they will need to:

- ensure that they have been given a clear and as precise as possible a brief from the senior management, via the training manager;
- ensure, before the activities start, that they have sufficient resources to perform the task;
- working from the brief given, conduct all the necessary research to ensure that the training content will be relevant, up to date, and realistic;
- invite and involve line management representatives in the planning and design process, if necessary conducting educative programmes with these managers to ensure: a) their active interest and b) their capabilities;
- plan and design the training and development programme;
- ensure that the senior management is kept informed of progress, via the training manager;
- ensure that the line management is kept informed of the progress and content of the planned programme;
- construct either: a) as a written general brief, the detailed outline of the programme for the trainers who will be offering the programme to the learners; or b) if the planners will also be the practitioners themselves, detailed briefs for the programme.

The learner

It is fairly rare for the learner to be actively considered when a training programme is being developed, usually they are considered as the participant when the programme is being run. But the learner is important at all stages and in all aspects of the training cycle and should be so considered.

There are a number of ways in which the learners or potential learners can be involved in the process. Hopefully they will have been involved at the TNIA stages of the training cycle – planning and design involvement is a natural, more detailed extension of these contacts. It will probably be more difficult to bring the learners together to design workshops in the same way as that suggested for line managers. First, there are many more potential learners than there are line managers, and second, the likely learners may not be known at this stage.

Learner workshops

As far as learner workshops are concerned, line management can be asked to identify likely learners and release them for short workshops to assist with the design process. These workshops will have the objective of determining what the learners see as the most important or key factors they would be looking for in the training programme that has been proposed. Common views would be collected and promises made by the trainers that these views would be taken into account in the final planning and design of the programme. There must be absolute honesty on the part of the trainers in these promises, not only because it would be unfair otherwise, but also it is very likely that these same learners will attend the actual courses when they are mounted. Chickens will come home to roost!

Other learner approaches

In many cases there is not the resource time to hold live workshops, but approaches should still be made to potential learners to obtain their views and suggestions. This will most effectively be by mail, whether ordinary mail or e-mail. A questionnaire can be constructed, commencing with specific questions to which the planners need responses, followed by open questions. The specific questions will be directly related to the training subject, based on the information revealed in the TNIA, and the open questions will simply ask the respondents for their views on what they would like to see included in (and excluded from) a training programme of this nature. Naturally the questionnaire would be prefaced by a clear description of the proposed programme and a commitment to take full account of the responses (this commitment must be as real as the one shown at the live workshops).

It may seem a time-consuming exercise to practise this learner approach, but account taken of the responses of both these potential participants and those of the line managers will ensure (as far as this is ever possible) that the training content will be close to 100 per cent of the learning that is needed. Without this exercise there is always the possibility that the planners may omit an important (to the learners and their managers) aspect of the skills in question, perhaps so important that the training course fails on this account.

PRE-COURSE AND ON-COURSE CONFIRMATION OF CONTENT

If it is possible to contact the potential learners at the planning and design stage, it is also desirable that something is done at the stage when the programme is being introduced. Two principal methods are in general use for this:

1. a pre-course questionnaire;
2. an on-course activity.

Pre-course questionnaires

This is a very common approach, although it, and even more so the second method, is shutting the stable door after the horse has bolted. A fortnight to a month prior to the start of the programme, when a person's attendance has been confirmed, a questionnaire is sent to them, usually via the line manager, who may also be asked to comment. In the document the programme is detailed and the key or important learning points or subjects listed. The learner is asked to comment on the inclusion of these subjects and their personal need for these skills, whether any of the subjects are not relevant and should be excluded, and whether any omitted subjects should be included (if possible). If this questionnaire is sent there should be the time and opportunity to take account of any suggestions made by the learners. At least, if the responses are received in reasonable time before the start of the programme, obviously necessary modifications can be made, these taking less time at this stage than later on.

The principal caveat must again be:

IF NO NOTICE IS GOING TO BE TAKEN OF THE LEARNERS' RESPONSES, DO NOT SEND THE QUESTIONNAIRE.

On-course activities

A number of activities can be introduced at the start of a training programme or course:

- some when there is no intention to modify the training, but that are used to identify the key needs of the learners; and
- some where the intention is take instant action to modify the training content in the light of the learners' views.

Identifying the key needs of the learners

The general approach here is to ask the learners to take part in some activity in which they describe items such as what they are expecting from the programme, what they want from the programme etc.

The T-chart

In this activity the learners are given a sheet of paper, basically divided vertically into two sections – one section headed Hopes/Expectations, the other Concerns, as shown in Figure 1.3.

HOPES/EXPECTATIONS	CONCERNS

Figure 1.3 *A T-chart*

The learners are asked to record in the left section their views and feelings on what they are expecting out of the course, or alternatively what they are hoping will come out of it (there is a difference!). In the right section, they are asked to record their views or feelings of concern – nervousness about courses, fear that this course will not give them what they want, fear that they are on the wrong course, and so on. With the learners' agreement these sheets are displayed on the walls and the various aspects discussed and, if possible agreed for action by the trainer. The sheets can be left on the walls for the duration of the course, the learners being invited to cross out or add items as the course progresses, a final discussion being held at the end of the course.

This is a relatively 'safe' start-of-course invitation to the learners to comment. The activity described next is similarly 'safe' but, like the T-chart, it is revealing of the views and feelings of the learners.

The 'Who am I?' activity

This is an extension of a general activity used at the start of a course to settle the participants and start the process of their getting to know each other; but it can also be used to obtain information about participants' views and feelings about the coming training course. Flipchart sheets are distributed to the learners with a block diagram pre-drawn, as shown in Figure 1.4.

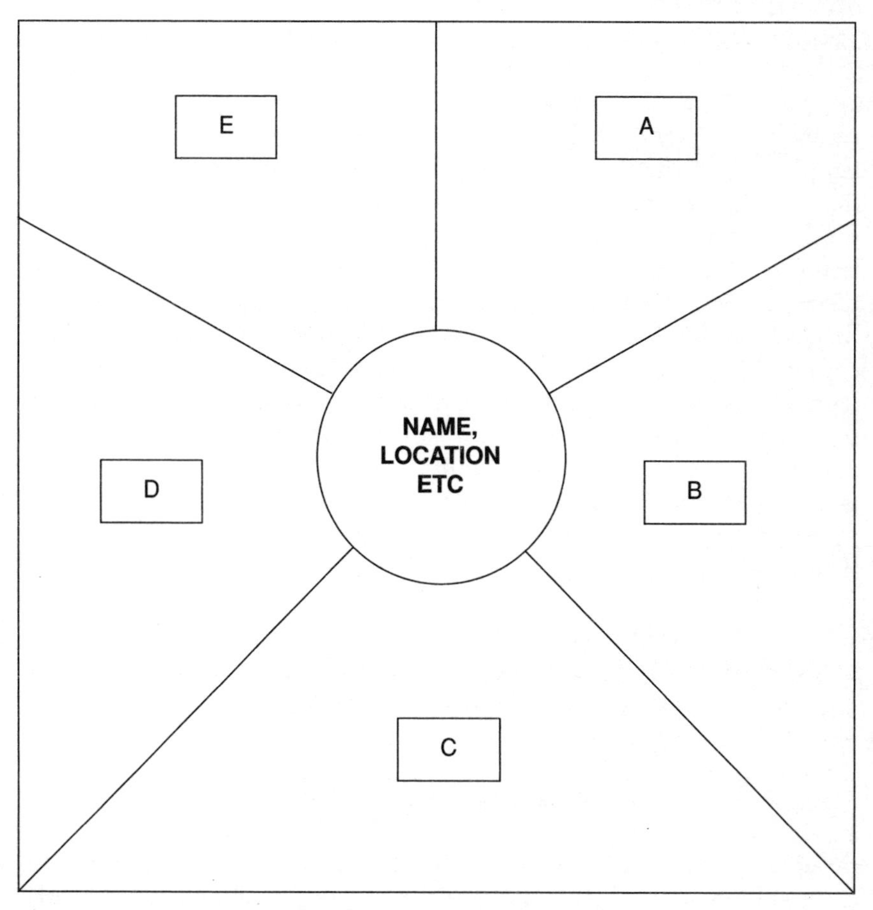

Figure 1.4 *A 'Who am I?' chart*

Within the centre circle the learner enters her/his name and other location/personal identification details. In the boxes around the centre 'A' might be concerned with the problems they have experienced in the learning area; 'B' – what they hope to get out of the programme; 'C' – how supportive their boss is of their learning and what he/she has done about this; 'D' – how they feel about taking part in the event. Alternatives for the boxes can be: 'A' – concerns about the course; 'B' – hopes for or expectations of the course; 'C' – personal strengths; 'D' – personal objectives; 'E' – their boss's expectations.

As with the T-chart, once the sheet is completed it is displayed on the training room walls, discussed and retained for during-course maintenance and end-of-course discussion.

The 'What do you want?' activity

This third activity is much more risky than the two just described, and should certainly not be introduced if: a) there is no intention of taking any notice of the responses; or b) there is no time in the course/programme to take action on the responses. The activity is simply to put the learning group into sub-groups with the brief to discuss the programme that is 'suggested' for the course, to agree which aspects they want and do not want, and to make recommendations about how the course should be modified. These agreements are discussed and collated and the trainers must then make a response as to what can be done about the learners' requirements. As suggested earlier this must be taken both seriously and practically and the learners' requests acceded to both as far as is possible and also within the context of the programme's overall objectives.

It will be seen that this is not only a risky activity, but also one that is very demanding on the trainers, who may accordingly have to modify the programme and their approaches significantly. Remember the caveat:

IF YOU DO NOT INTEND TO TAKE ACTION ON
THE RESPONSES, OR WILL BE UNABLE TO, DO NOT ASK
THE QUESTIONS.

SETTING THE SCENE

Before any planning can start, it is essential that as much information as possible is obtained. It is the planner's responsibility to seek this rather than expect it to be handed out completely, and without its being sought. One of the major signs of the poor planner is to keep returning to sources for further and further information. The ideal is to plan what you need to know in order to plan!

As suggested earlier, the initiative for new or revised training needs will come down from the sponsors/senior management. Unless the initial discussions have been supported by the training manager it is unlikely that a full description will be immediately forthcoming – after all the senior managers are not trainers and may not know the range of information required. If you feel that the information given to you or the demands made upon you to provide new or revised training programmes are not the full set of data, ASK. Depending on the organization culture, the person from whom you should seek the further information you as the planner have identified will be the training manager, or senior trainer if there is no specific training manager role. The information you require will include:

- Any TNIA report that initiated the demand for new or revised training. This report should pinpoint accurately the problem(s); identify the size of the problem; identify the scale of the need; indicate the type and nature of the solution; and (this is where the TNIA links and overlaps with the planning process) provide or suggest training objectives.
- The exact nature of the training required, its level and other factors related to the organizational requirements. It is not sufficient, for example, to be told to provide customer service training – you need to know whether this is for the shop floor staff, the supervisors or the management. Is it concerned with external or internal customers or both? Are there any specific types of customer approaches agreed in the organization? Does the complaints procedure have to be included?
- How many learners will be involved? At what level and from what locations?
- When does the training programme have to start and is there a completion deadline, or is this a continuing requirement?
- Has the training to be provided by the organization's internal training department, external consultants, a mixture of the two, by external consultants within their arrangements, etc?
- Where is the training to be held? Organization's premises, organization's residential training centre, external residential/day training centre, hotel?
- What resources are authorized? People – how many trainers will be available/needed; money – what budget has been allocated;

training resources – technological equipment, video purchase or rental, etc; research resources – content research, etc?

- What are the learner call-up arrangements and who will be responsible for performing these? What level of 'conscription' is approved or is recruitment completely in the hands of the line management?
- Is the training to be performed by the planner(s) or by a separate training team? If the latter, to what extent has the planning team to provide detailed training briefs?
- What evaluation guidelines have been given?
- Has a programme report (for whom) to be prepared (at what stage – after first course; at end of programme) and does it have to follow a particular format (organization's culture)? How has this report to be presented?
- Any other factors relevant to the particular type and nature of the training.

With this information you are now ready to consider in more detail the learners and their requirements, and the factors that will have an effect on these.

2

Considering the Potential Participants

This chapter suggests that the planner should take into account:

- the learning qualities, styles and preferences of the potential participants;
- communication, a learning model and an alternative learning model;
- the application of learning models to practical situations;
- the barriers to training and learning and how to resolve them.

From this point in the planning process we shall assume that the preceding TNIA has shown that a training and development programme needs to be produced, and that all the necessary information has been obtained from the various sources. While the TNIA produces the basic recommendations, the planning process is responsible for putting 'the flesh on the bones', including the translation of the identified aims into actionable plans.

Consideration of the various training and learning factors that affect people must be a strong priority in the planning process, since training involves people, changing their skills and frequently their attitudes. Where people are concerned there are so many contributory factors that the possible influences must be taken into account.

At this stage it is worth commenting on other 'technical' words in use in training and development. The principal one is concerned with the people attending the course or programme. Various terms are used, including:

- students;
- trainees;

- participants;
- learners.

Training and development programmes have progressed a long way in recent years from the severely academic approaches in which the learners were indeed 'students': from the didactic events that they attended to be *trained* – hence 'trainees'; and, although perhaps a pedantic differentiation, to me a 'participant' is one who attends and takes part, but does not necessarily learn from the participation. Consequently I prefer the term 'learner', although 'participant' is acceptable, particularly where the person is taking part in an experiential activity.

INDIVIDUAL LEARNER QUALITIES

At one time (not so very long ago, and in fact still quite a common approach) the almost universal reaction to the identification of a training need was 'Let's put on a course'. In this statement, 'course' was translated as a series of lectures, roughly approximating to the identified needs but also reflecting the performance preferences of the trainers or lecturers. Rarely were the learning preferences or attitudes of the learners considered – in fact rarely were they known – and the assumption was that, because they needed to, the people concerned would benefit from the course irrespective of its nature. Fortunately this attitude started to fade, to be replaced by trainer awareness that different forms of training events could produce more effective learning. The charted pattern of violent change from didactic, lecture-based courses, through free-for-all, almost totally experiential events to more balanced programmes containing mixtures of input sessions, discussions, activities, projects, video and computer interactions, is well known. Although well known, this does not necessarily mean that it is followed, nor is the balance achieved easily or always successfully.

KOLB'S LEARNING CYCLE

Alongside this revolution in the nature of the training programme developed an awareness of the differing nature of learners as individuals or groups of individuals. Following the personality type studies of psychological gurus such as Freud, David Kolb became the architect of modern concepts of the way people learn. In the 1960s and

1970s he developed what has become known as *Kolb's Learning Cycle,* from which grew a model of learning styles and preferences.

The Learning Cycle, shown in Figure 2.1, proposes that the process of learning in most cases starts with the learner experiencing an event, a feeling, an emotion, etc.

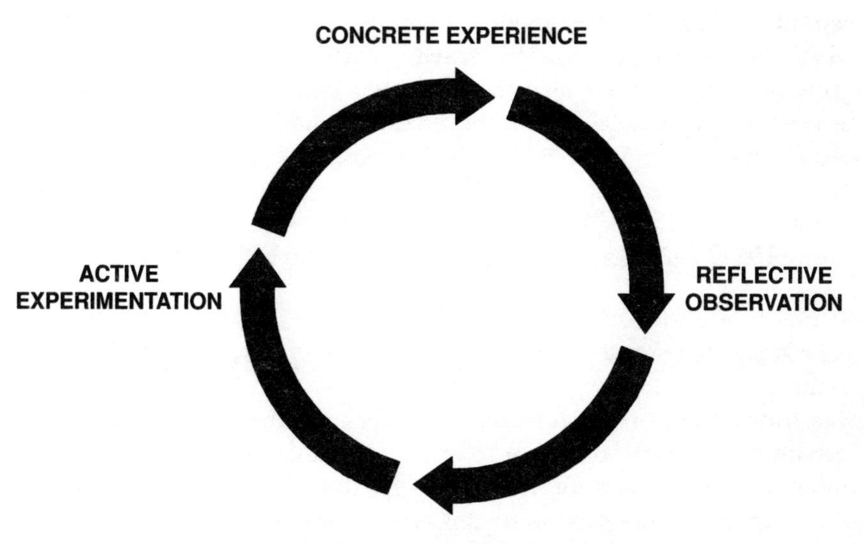

Figure 2.1 *Kolb's Learning Cycle*

In order to learn from this *experience* it is necessary simply to let it happen, then move on to the other aspects of the cycle. What tends to happen all too frequently is that people simply stop at this stage, accepting the experience. What should happen is that the experience should be reflected on in terms of what happened, when certain things happened, who made them happen, what resulted from these actions, etc. From this *reflection* the next stage is to draw conclusions about the experience – what was good and bad about it and why, what worked and what didn't (and why). As a result of *conceptualizing* in this way and identifying what you have learned, the final stage is *experimenting* with how you might behave in a future, similar situation, and certainly what you intend to do with the learning that you have achieved from the preceding stages of the cycle. It is an unfortunate fact that in most people situations the *reflecting, conceptualizing* and *experimenting* stages are most likely to be ignored. Well-balanced learning events should ensure that the content includes the opportunity to follow the full cycle, and that encouragement and time is given to the learners to take full account of all the stages.

In some ways this model can be considered too simplistic, as it gives the impression that *all* learning must commence with an experience, and that the model is a simple progressive cycle from experience round to planning. In practice learning does not always follow the cycle in a neat progression: learning frequently commences at a different point in the cycle; and, although the cycle describes effective learning, a large number of people do not take advantage of all the stages, because most people have different approaches or preferences towards learning and doing. My experience is that although learning can begin with an experience itself, and the learning stages can follow from that event, much commences at an earlier stage.

AN ALTERNATIVE LEARNING MODEL

Figure 2.2 suggests a model that describes an alternative approach, in which the learning does not follow a simple cycle but moves to and from different parts of the cycle. In this alternative experiential learning model the process begins with the realization that a potential learning situation exists.

This need or situation is then reflected on before considering what action can be taken. This consideration is then agreed either with yourself or a third party. In this model there are events, principally reflective, occurring before the experience.

The central sector of the alternative learning model then follows Kolb's model, which suggests experiencing, reflecting on the experience and concluding from this. It is often then necessary to reconsider the position and approach as a result of errors and omissions in the original path, before laying plans for a repetition of the experience, trying a new experience to extend the learning, or implementing the learning. The various stages can, therefore, be visited and revisited within a single learning experience before final learning is achieved.

LEARNING STYLES

The Learning Style Questionnaire

The research that produced Kolb's Learning Cycle and the associated Learning Style Inventory was carried out in the United States.

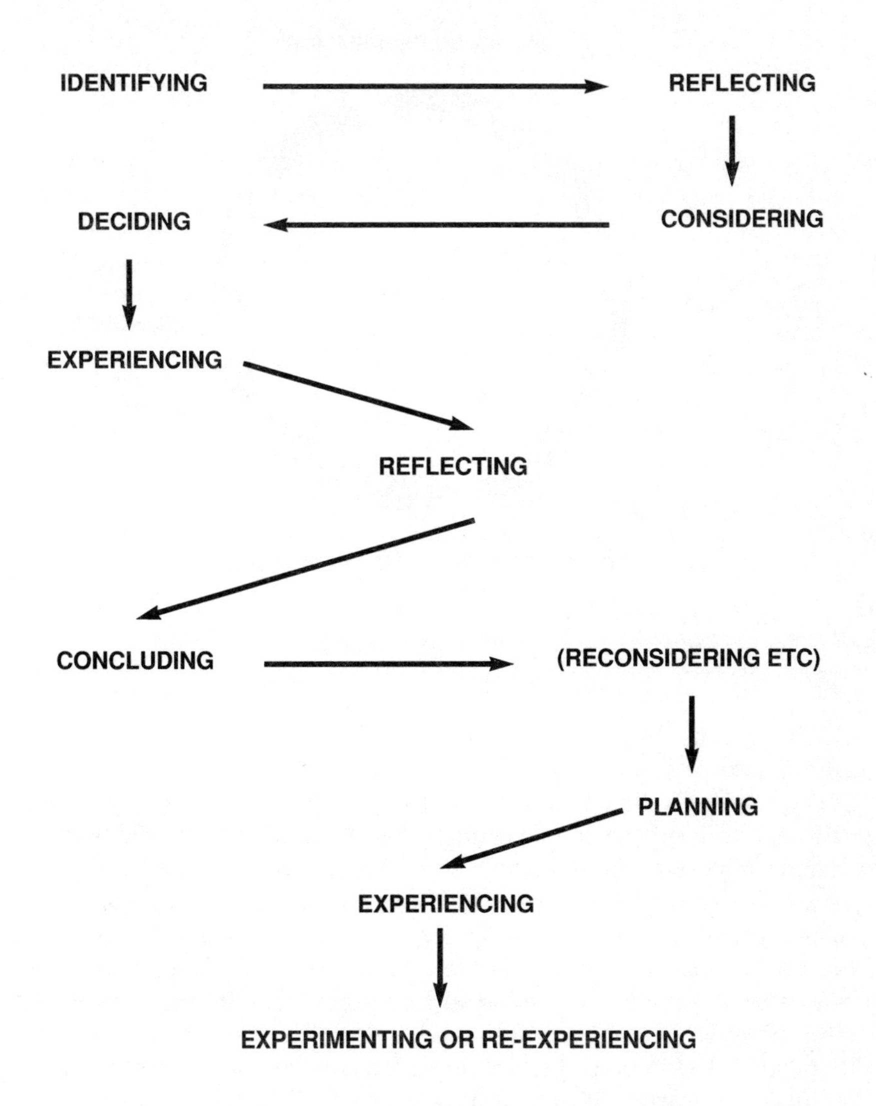

Figure 2.2 *An alternative learning model*

Somewhat similar studies were conducted in the United Kingdom by Peter Honey and Alan Mumford. However, these two management development consultants and psychologists followed a much more pragmatic path than that of Kolb and the result, the Learning Style Questionnaire, is a more practical instrument for general and training use.

The Honey/Mumford approach is also based on the classical

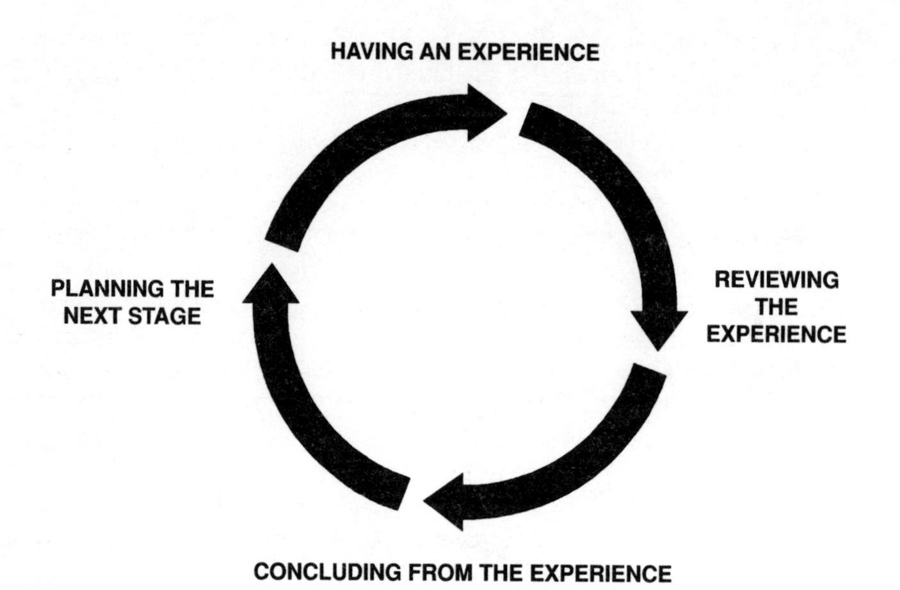

Figure 2.3 *The Honey/Mumford Learning Cycle*

Learning Cycle, but uses less academic labels than those of Kolb. This more practical model is shown in Figure 2.3.

The concept of this model is that, like Kolb's, it represents the ideal, fully effective approach to learning. This cycle 'starts' with the learner doing something, experiencing something, feeling something – an incident, whether factual, practical or emotional. Following the experience learning is reinforced by a period during which the learner reflects on what has been observed during the experience and what can be recalled about it – **what** in fact happened, **how** it happened, **who** did it, **what** the result was, and so – all the observable incidents that can be stored as factual, detailed information. This activity requires the learner to stop any other or further action in order to 'catalogue' the reflections.

In the third stage the data collected is analysed in terms of the reasons for what happened, alternative ways in which the experience might have taken place, an identification of the most effective option, and many other theoretical considerations based on what was done and what was seen to be done. This is the stage of the theorist or Kolb's conceptualizer.

But conceptualization has to be translated into action if it is to have any worth. This takes place in the fourth stage, when the pragmatist reigns supreme. The watchword of this person is 'if it isn't practical, then it isn't worth anything'. This is the area and the time when the historical considerations are translated into future action by people who care about practicalities.

The cycle then returns to the experience, which may be a repeat of the original experience, incorporating the lessons learnt in the previous stages. The cycle recommences, hopefully with a shorter lifetime, the lessons learnt on the first occasion producing a fully effective event.

The learner progressing through these stages has learnt something at all stages, to the extent that an effective function can be performed. This, of course, is the ideal. Most people however have a preference for one or more of these learning stages, and if these singular preferences are strong and overpowering, problems of complete learning exist.

For example, a learner who becomes 'locked in' on the active, doing stage is less likely to stop to reflect or analyse, and consequently will repeat the original mistakes or even make new ones. The reflector who is so enamoured with considering what has happened will let life pass by with others making decisions, taking action and so on. The locked-in theorist will become so interested in the convolutions of the internal intricacies that nothing will be done. The pragmatist at the end of the cycle might destroy or ignore all that has gone before because if it is not a practical event it must be of no value or interest.

Naturally, not everybody has only one preference. The ideal must be to have a balance of all stage preferences, but in practice most people have one or two strong preferences with the others either weak or just appearing.

LEARNING PREFERENCES

Using the Learning Cycle as their basis, Peter Honey and Alan Mumford considered the cycle on the basis of what managers and professional people do. Several thousand people have now been involved in their research, which has led them to a number of conclusions, namely the identification of four preferred common styles of learning. From this research they constructed an instrument, the Learning Style Questionnaire, to identify these preferred learning approaches within the Learning Cycle. Naturally, some individuals will have a preference and ability to learn in more than one mode, but Honey and Mumford found that most people, rather than follow the full learning cycle in a totally effective learning manner, tended to prefer one or two modes and 'lock in' on a preferred style, often to the detriment of their learning.

The four styles identified are the *activist*, the *reflector*, the *theorist* and the *pragmatist*, and these relate to the Learning Cycle as shown in Figure 2.4.

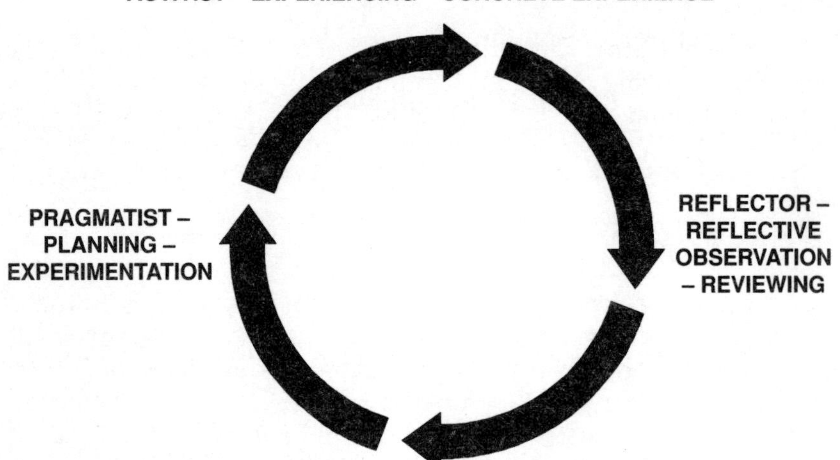

Figure 2.4 *The relationship between the Learning Cycle (Honey and Mumford; Kolb) and learning preferences*

Activists

These are people who enjoy doing something, sometimes just for the sake of doing it. They revel in innovation, but tend to get bored quickly and look for other interests. The activist learner prefers experiential learning events with lots of activities, games and exercises, and a minimum of input sessions. The activist preference trainer includes many activities, questionnaires and tasks in his/her events and while the learners are performing these can be at a loss as to what to do – thinking 'I wish they'd get on with it', 'Should I join in and help them?', 'Why are they taking so long?' and so on.

Reflectors

People with this preference are usually the quieter learners who, although interested in new concepts and ideas, would rather sit back and observe others taking part, extracting learning from their observations. They like to look at all angles and are cautious before making a move. If this is a very strong preference they can be locked into it and become very annoyed with the activist who wants to 'get on with it'. The reflector trainer can tend to build into the programmes too many periods to sit and think as opposed to doing something or seeking deeper reasons and learning.

Theorists

This type of learner must also reflect, but to a deeper extent, as they insist on knowing and understanding all the principles, models and theories behind any learning ideas. The various approaches are weighed against each other and the 'best' approach analysed. They tend to think in objective, rational, logical ways and are disturbed by subjective approaches and impressions. Their attitude is: 'If it can't be explained logically, I don't want to know.'

Pragmatists

The pragmatist is an activist who is keen to try out new ideas and methods, but only if these are practical and they can see a direct and specific application at work. They are essentially practical, down-to-earth people who will immerse themselves in problem-solving and decision-making events, so long as there is a real end product that can be put to good use.

THE PRACTICAL SIGNIFICANCE OF LEARNING MODELS

When one of these models is used in a training event the planners and trainers must be aware that the results have two significances – one for learners and the other for trainers. The significances for learners include:

1. how the preferences affect the learning events they are most likely to attend;
2. how the preferences affect the amount of learning they achieve in an event, whether this event links with their stronger preferences or weaker ones;
3. that fully effective learning only occurs if they do not allow themselves to become locked in on one or two preference roles.

As far as the significance of styles for trainers is concerned, in addition to the ones listed above, the list will also include:

1. a realization of their own preferences and how these might affect the design and implementation of training events;
2. their relationships with learners who have either the same or opposite preference characteristics;
3. their behaviour during a training event.

Figure 2.5 summarizes the significances and implications of learning styles and their preferences for training events.

LEARNING STYLE	PREFERRED ACTIVITIES	YOU MAY OVERLOOK POSSIBILITIES	MODIFY ACTION
ACTIVIST	Practical games, exercises and activities	Some learners prefer inputs in addition to practical events	Offer wide range of learning opportunities
	Encouraging group to be responsible for all the learning	Support by you when learning risk is high	Leading, but not directing
	Changing the programme several times	Learners may prefer a forecast progression to unforeseen change	Discuss changes with group before taking action
	Keeping the event moving all the time	Learners require opportunities to consider, reflect and consolidate	Build in reflection and discussion periods
REFLECTOR	Learning events with a large amount of reflection and discussion	The event has to be kept moving, with different activities	Plan varied programme with balance of activity and consideration
	Emphasis in feedback on what happened rather than why	Learners may want to examine the event in depth	Make reviews of events wide ranging and searching
	Events which are 'quiet' and contemplative	Many learners want a more lively type of event	Again, plan a varied type of programme
THEORIST	Complex learning programmes with detailed examinations of theories, models and 'academic' arguments and concepts	Some learners will be become bored with what they consider to be overlong arguments	Plan the reviews to the depth in line with the level and interests of the learners
	A preponderance of lectures and input sessions	The need for lighter, more active sessions, even though the material may still be essentially 'taught'	Vary the event to replace some of the inputs with activities that will still allow the learning to emerge

Figure 2.5 *Learning style preferences and the training event*

LEARNING STYLE	PREFERRED ACTIVITIES	YOU MAY OVERLOOK POSSIBILITIES	MODIFY ACTION
Ensure that the in-depth objectives that require a teaching approach are essential to the objectives of the event and that the lecture is the only relevant and effective technique.			
PRAGMATIST	Where the learning material is based firmly on 'real-world' material, case studies and activities	Wider aspects can be presented with constructed activities, planned to include all the learning points	Plan a balanced event which has real-life and constructed experiences
	The learners are used frequently in practical activities as they are accustomed to this at work	Although real-life events tend to repeat, the full circumstances may not always be the same	Use experience and experiences and describe the differences
	There is considerable emphasis on planning action on return to work to help the learning process	It is often necessary to include some 'fun' activities in a programme for mere mortals	Make the planning of future action, if not voluntary, then one in which the learner has considerable personal control

Figure 2.5 *Learning style preferences and the training event (continued)*

Learning, people's attitude and approaches to it, and the problems involved exist in the wide senses discussed in this chapter. The planner must be aware of them from the start, otherwise the questions 'I'm doing everything right. Why aren't they learning?' or 'They are all receiving the same training. Why are some of them not learning, even though they are as intelligent as the others?' will be raised. When the significance of styles is appreciated the answers to these questions become obvious.

OTHER LEARNING INFLUENCES

Sensory learning

Learning preferences are not only controlled by the types identified by Honey and Mumford, but the basic senses also come into the picture. The ability of people to learn can vary according to their senses, and their preferred use of senses, hearing, seeing, touching, smelling, visualizing, doing, and so on. Balanced learning programmes must take these into account.

Sensory learning includes five distinctive preferences that rely on the following.

The sense of sight

- *Learning by reading.* Sight can be used in reading information, either about skill techniques or procedural written material. Many find it a difficult learning approach and it is fraught with problems caused by the level of intellect, understanding capabilities and other considerations such as language, particularly where a number of races and cultures might be involved. Reflectors and theorists are usually more at home in this medium. Research and experience shows that when the words are accompanied by some form of pictures, people find it easier to accept the words. However, this is not an easy or cheap addition to the pages of most books, which are dominated by text.
- *Learning by seeing.* Many people have to see something before they can understand and, as a result, learn. This might be viewing the object itself, a model of the object, or even a graphic visual aid or computer graphic. Seeing the object of learning avoids the learners' having to attempt to visualize. Use of such objects should be easily introduced in most, if not all, learning events.
- *Learning by visualization.* This is a difficult approach that requires the learners, from verbal or written descriptions, to visualize an object, event or concept. Frequently this approach is used in conjunction with sight of the item after a visualizing description has been made to prepare the learners.
- *Learning by writing.* Whether it is the act of copying something from an existing text; interpreting, analysing and summarizing an extended text; or making notes from a verbal presentation, many people find the act of writing something down helps their learning, retention and recall.

The sense of hearing

This can have a significant effect on learning through:

- *Learning by listening.* Those who find it difficult to learn via the written word, whether through difficulties of understanding or an inherent problem with that medium, will frequently understand and learn from the spoken word (provided the verbal style is clear and related to the level of the listener). This approach to learning takes place most favourably in an environment where questioning and discussion can occur.

The sense of touch

This sense, if it is considered in terms of **doing**, can become the most important of all, although other learning aspects can be involved:

- *Learning by touching*. Touching has a more limited, but still significant application in the learning of certain skills, particularly those where a few minutes of hands-on experience can be worth hours of description. In the training environment the opportunity to 'have a go' can avoid many problems if the first practice is to be in the real world of work – try to describe the feel of a snake's skin if neither you nor the learner has previously held a snake. In other cases, an operation can succeed or fail where the event is very reliant on the sense of touch.
- *Learning by doing*. This approach is considered by many as the ultimate in learning processes, usually preceded by other forms such as verbal descriptions, graphical representations and so on (the classical Tell – Show – Do approach). The learners are given the opportunity, usually under supervision or observation, to perform an act, whether it is practically operational, procedural or one requiring the performance of task or people skills.

Smell and taste

These two senses are perhaps even more limited in application, but in specific forms of training must be considered as a major aid to learning. If the training of a gas meter reader ignores the opportunity to actually smell escaping gas, the training is not as effective as it should be, particularly if the learners have lived in an all-electric environment and have never smelled domestic gas. Similarly, learner-perfume practitioners need an effective sense of smell; and tea-blenders an effective sense of taste.

BARRIERS TO LEARNING

In spite of all our knowledge of learning styles and preferences and our attempts at applying them to the construction of an effective programme, success can still be thwarted because of the almost infinite ability of people to resist learning, sometimes unconsciously. When input sessions are being planned it must not be assumed that the learners will hang on every word uttered by the trainer, even if they want to learn; nor will all the participants take part to the full extent in experiential activities, even if their preferences are for being active. An appreciation of some of the barriers to learning that exist can help to avoid some of the pitfalls that can be encountered. The barriers can be classified under:

- language and speech barriers;

- psychological barriers;
- barriers attributable to the trainers themselves;
- environmental barriers;
- the learning attention span.

Language and speech barriers

Vocabulary

It is essential that programme designers and trainers use a vocabulary that can be understood by the listener/reader, otherwise a foreign language might as well be used. Jargon particularly has to be used carefully. It quickly becomes the 'shorthand' talk within an organization, and can even vary from one part of the organization to another. Jargon can be useful if everyone is fully acquainted with it, otherwise it will not only be misunderstood but will annoy and inhibit the learning process. Many people are finding the developing jargon of the computer world and the Internet difficult and annoying; this is demonstrated by the extent to which computer magazines have to publish regularly and use continuously updated glossaries.

The growing e-mail activity is developing a language (or jargon) of its own, the use of acronyms and quasi-graphics being used extensively by some e-mailers, in some cases almost to the extent of 'acronymania'. Such acronyms include BTW – 'by the way'; IMO – 'in my opinion' (IMHO – a patronizing form saying 'in my humble opinion'); TTFN – 'ta ta for now', an acronym dating back many years from wartime radio programmes; FAQ – 'frequently asked questions'; etc. These acronyms can be very useful shorthand forms, provided the recipient knows what they mean.

Quasi-graphics or 'emoticons' fulfil a similar shorthand purpose. For example, **:-)** or **:)** = a smile; **:(** = a frown; **:/** = a grimace, and so on. These acronyms and emoticons have become so extensive that books have had to be written to list and explain them.

Ambiguity

Whatever is written, whether as a general planning guide, a brief, a handout or a slide for projection, must say exactly what is meant, not simply what was intended. This can be a particular problem when multi-cultural learners are to be involved, in view of the different meanings that can be afforded to some words and sayings. This problem is not restricted to multi-racial situations – ask both a Geordie and a Scot what they mean when they use the word 'canny'! There will even be variations in the use of that word by inhabitants of the same region. The meaning is usually clear in the spoken word and in the context in which it is used, but the written word presents more problems.

Woolly or rambling speech or writing

Remember the classical acronym 'KISS' – 'Keep It Short and Simple', or alternatively 'Keep It Simple Stupid'! Readers and listeners very quickly turn off if the writer/speaker continues interminably, this syndrome usually taking the form of using 20 words where one might suffice. Such ramblers enjoy the sound of their own voice or the sight of their writing, but they have to remember that this may not be reflected in the audience.

Unusual words and phrases

The words and phrases to be used in a plan, presentation or handout must be straightforward. Is the word/phrase the best/only/correct/most appropriate/relevant one, or is it simply being used for effect or because it is a favourite of the originator? Is the receiver likely to understand it easily?

Psychological barriers

These barriers to listening, understanding and learning are the most problematical for both programme planners to forecast and include solutions for in the planning, and for the trainers presenting the training programme. They can be apparently overt, becoming evident by attitudes and behaviours, or covert (or at least the reasons for them are). The range of ways in which psychological barriers are demonstrated is almost endless – remember we are dealing with people!

Mood

People have moods – both negative and positive ones – and these can affect their approach to learning. In a negative mood learning will not be a priority for the participants, and it will be principally up to the trainer on the spot to note the occurrence and take action to resolve the problems. The planner can try to resolve such problems in advance by producing a programme that will be sufficiently interesting and enjoyable to modify the mood, and let the participant see that the learning will be significant for them.

Pressures

Many types of pressures have a bearing on the learning capabilities and desires to learn of the participants. Pressures can detract from learning and distract people from taking a full part in the learning – thoughts of work outstanding on their return; problems that occurred at work before they left for the training; health worries (both their own and that of others); domestic situations that were unresolved before attendance on the event; money problems; learning difficulties; social problems; and so on. Many of these will be included in a participant's hidden agenda, and can result from the person being forced unwillingly to attend the programme.

Some of the problems, if solvable, can only be solved by the trainer on the spot when a barrier is identified, although the planner can support the trainer to some extent by producing a programme with such interest, importance and relevance that the trainer will be helped in his/her attempts.

Attitudes and behaviours

These very quickly make themselves evident on a training programme, and can be the result of many base causes. Barriers in this area can result from:

- *Shyness.* The learner has overcome the first shyness barrier by attending the programme. The planner can support the trainer's efforts to overcome the shyness by including items that encourage participation without undue pressure.
- *Aggression.* This usually emanates from an enforced cause. For example, the learner who has been forced to attend the programme against their will, interest or need will almost certainly exhibit an aggressive attitude – 'Go on then. Train me!' Unless controls can be built into the lead-up to the training to avoid such attendance, the planner can support the trainer by producing a programme that is interesting and enjoyable, relevant to the learners' work and needs, and including sessions in which the person can be included specifically, perhaps by utilizing their knowledge, experience and skill.
- *Impending retirement.* 'Why have I been sent on this course? After all I retire in a month's time.' Hopefully the material and the trainer's skill can show this person that the skills they will learn can be applied in a variety of situations, including those when they are in retirement.
- *Failure to see the reason for the training.* The reason behind this failure can be attributed to the learner's line manager, who did not discuss the training fully with the learner beforehand; the inadequacy of the pre-course material in explaining the training;

or the inadequacy of the initial course material to ensure understanding.

- *Resistance to change.* Why is the learner resistant to change, ie training? It may be an integral part of their personality, although it is more likely to be the result of the person saying 'Why change? Things are going well as they are' or 'If change happens, how is it going to affect me?' Again the planner and the trainer should ensure that sufficient information is given to the learner to get rid of feelings of this nature. This, may be easier said than done, however, particularly when the person is demanding guarantees that may not be available.
- *Know-it-all.* Again by producing a programme that is full of real learning opportunities this barrier might be reduced, perhaps supported by acknowledging the person's knowledge, skill and experience. People with this barrier are difficult to plan for and reliance must be placed on the skills of the trainer on the spot to overcome the attitude without taking negative actions.
- *Too old to learn.* This is a common attitudinal barrier among older learners, who follow the principle that 'You can't teach an old dog new tricks'. This, of course, is completely false as it has been shown that the older learner can in many cases be more effective than the younger learner because of their prior knowledge and experience, and experience of learning, solving problems and so on. Depending on the 'age' (actual or virtual) of the learner, there may have to be some simplification of the programme material, but the necessity of this must not be assumed.
- *Status differences.* Learning programmes can often be severely disrupted because the learners are at different status levels in the organization and allow this to have an effect on their learning capability. Higher status participants may not wish to comment or act in front of junior colleagues, and vice versa, for a variety of status-based reasons. If this is identified as a potential problem part of the programme design must be an identification of the most suitable learning population on each occasion, thus avoiding any conflict.
- *Previous experience.* Most people, whether in education establishments, at work or during adult training events, have experienced episodes that they recall either consciously or subconsciously and that act as a learning barrier. You may have been embarrassed in front of others by the trainer on a course (whether or not the trainer realized what was happening). All these factors can contribute towards an attitude of 'I don't want to learn' and must be broken down by the trainer as soon as there is realization that a

problem exists. It is of course sometimes very difficult for the reasons for the barrier to emerge, perhaps this may only happen after the training day, in a more social situation.

- *Lack of confidence.* If learners attending a training event or taking on an open learning package have experienced severe learning difficulties previously, it is possible that they will approach the current event with the feeling that 'This is going to be too difficult for me'. The planner and the trainer must ensure that at the start of the learning event the process and content are described fully and its level explained. Doubts should then be sought and clarified, and above all the trainer should ensure that every assistance is given to the learners if difficulties are experienced. A start-of-course knowledge test can often help in this respect, particularly if two tests are given – the first will contain questions that the learners should be able to answer (the confidence builder) and the second related more to new material that forms the content of the event. There is, of course, the danger that the second test will reduce the confidence resulting from the first test, but this risk should be minimized by an appropriate introduction.
- *Lack of motivation.* Motivation is an internally generated attitude, and every learner comes to a training event with a range of motivational attitudes and levels. Again some may have been forced to attend against their wishes; others may not see the reason for the training; yet others may feel that they already know what the training is all about.

  One fact is certain – you cannot motivate people to learn. What you *can* do is provide all the factors to encourage them to motivate themselves. If motivational needs are satisfied, although not motivating a person, they will encourage them to self-motivate. A logical and acceptable explanation should be given about how the learner will benefit from the new skill, how they will 'grow' as a result of the experience, how their chances of progressing will be enhanced with the learning, and so on.
- *Old dog syndrome.* This is based on the common expression that 'you can't teach old dogs new tricks'. This is not entirely true. If an older person has kept their mind active and in a learning mode, they are often in a better position to learn, with their background of experience, than the younger person who has only youth on which to rely. Obviously, if an older person has allowed their mind to atrophy learning is almost impossible. Quite often this syndrome emerges when older workers attend training events during the last few years of their careers and the 'old dog' excuse is used for a variety of other barriers, including 'Why bother at

this stage in my life'. As in the case of the approaching retirement participant, the learner can be shown that they can learn, and it will be worth it; or if there is very difficult material, with which the older mind might encounter problems, the planner should construct sessions that take these problems into account.

- *Unlearning.* Resistance to learning can exist if the potential learners have experience of the type of material, but of an outdated nature. The training will be intended to introduce new systems, procedures or methods, but the earlier knowledge, skills and attitudes have to be cleared before the learners' minds are receptive to the new. Some may resist this unlearning, perhaps because of some of the barriers already discussed; others may find it difficult to clear their minds sufficiently. But if the training is to be effective the trainer must be sufficiently skilled to ensure that the message is offered and accepted.

Barriers attributable to the trainer

The allocation of trainers to particular programmes is another factor that is frequently out of the hands of the programme designer and planner, allocation depending commonly on availability. This allocation frequently results in unsuitable trainers being selected – unsuitable because they are either unskilled in the particular nature of the programme or are simply unskilled trainers in a situation requiring training experience.

So not all the barriers to learning are attributable to the learners themselves; the trainer and the planner must be aware that they can inhibit learning in a number of ways. These can include:

- *Inappropriate content.* This obviously should not occur if the TNIA has been carried out effectively and the planning continued in line with the TNIA findings. However, some aspects can get in the way of fulfilling this need, for example training content being included not because it has been shown that this material was needed, but because it was a favourite topic of the trainer or planner! If the TNIA final briefing requires specific elements to be included then this is what should be done, even in the face of other demands.
- *Wrong techniques of approach.* These barriers can be laid at the feet of either the planner or the trainer. The planner should, having identified the subject, considered the most effective and appropriate method of including it in the training and development programme. The trainer should follow this briefing on the basis

that it has been carefully researched as the most effective approach for the various parts of the programme. If the trainer has any query about the effectiveness of a proposed technique this should be cleared prior to the launch of the programme.

- *The unskilled trainer.* An unskilled trainer, in spite of advice about how to progress, might use methods and techniques that are not the most effective for making an impact on the learners and thus encouraging learning. This, of course, may not be the fault of the trainer who has not yet gained sufficient experience to have an extensive training toolkit. If there is sufficient time these failings can be corrected by trainer training in the additional skills required.
- *The unskilled speaker.* Perhaps more difficult to remedy, particularly in a short interval, is the trainer or guest speaker who has deficiencies in the actual presentation of material. This might even be evident in the more restricted input required in the introduction of activities, rather than the more demanding input sessions. Too many hesitations, verbal noises ('ers'), distracting mannerisms, etc will be noted by the learners, and can so easily distract from learning as the learners take more notice of these than what is being said. Most people can be trained to become *more effective* speakers, albeit not completely expert, but this can take time, and practice in safe conditions is essential.
- *Accents.* Where is the training programme to be held? Who will the learners be? How strong a regional accent has the trainer who might be selected to run the programme? At one time regional accents were not acceptable in many areas of public speaking, but this has to a large extent been discounted and their use in fact encouraged, particularly if the particular accent is one of the more attractive ones. However, if the accent is too strong it may not be understandable and thus negate the learning situation. I recall the television series *When the Boat Comes In* in which the Geordie accent was frequently very strong – my wife turned away from this excellent programme because there was so much she could not understand.

  Dialect words, however, must not be used as these might not be widely understood; this barrier should be avoidable with advice to the trainer on the use of language.
- *Manner.* This is a much more difficult trainer trait for the designer to take into account or take action to resolve, as a person's manner is often integral to their personality. However, overt manner and behaviours once identified can usually be modified, even if only for the period required. Aggressive, patronizing, abrasive, self-

centred, exaggerating, obviously lying, over-casual, negatively critical manners can be modified with interpersonal training following identification of the behaviours.

- *Prejudices include the following:*
  - those concerning a trainer's views on race, sex, age, disability, which can emerge without the trainer realizing;
  - judgemental views that try to enforce the trainer's attitudes on the learners;
  - ignoring or rejecting out of hand the views of the learners because they do not fit in with those of the trainer;
  - over-direction to the trainer's viewpoint, however well intentioned;
  - non-acceptance by the trainer of the learners' rights to have a say in their learning.
- *Lack of knowledge.* All the efforts of the programme designer can be aborted if the trainer involved in presenting the programme has a substantial lack of knowledge of the subject. This is not as rare as might be thought: say an organization has a training department that is told to mount a particular type of programme, but none of the available trainers have knowledge of the subject demanded. Learners will have sympathy or empathy with a trainer who has reduced training or presentation skills, but lack of knowledge of the subject will rarely be countenanced. Again, the designer must ensure trainer familiarity with the subject or take the necessary steps to develop this.

Environmental barriers

- *Noise. Heat. Cold. Ventilation. Space available. Interruptions/Work intrusion.* These are all potential barriers for a training programme and should certainly form a significant part of the planning and preparation of the event. Although there will be occasions when a negative aspect cannot be avoided most potential problems can be forecast and resolved before the event.
- *Restricted time.* This is an important factor that must be taken into account when the programme is being designed. It is not uncommon for the designer to be told that three days are available and a programme should be designed to *fit this time.* This is the wrong way to approach the design of a programme. The TNIA will have identified what is required of a training programme and the calculation then should be 'How long a period is necessary to include the TNIA requirements?' Unfortunately this is not always possible, and the result must be a compromise between what is

needed and what is available. Other factors are the level of the learners and their capacity to learn a particular competence in a certain period of time; and the complexity of the material when compared with the normal material for which learning times have been established. The designer, supported by the trainer, must be prepared to argue with the time allocators about what is realistically necessary and should be allowed.

Many of these barriers, on both the learners' and trainers' sides, may not be present when the designer is planning the programme, but their existence must be considered if success is to be achieved. Many of them may appear trivial, but trivia can often have the maximum effect on a situation. It may be that in the long run the designer may not have the means or the opportunity to resolve any of the problems identified; this must be recognized as a potential hazard to the level of success of the programme.

The learning attention span

A further important aspect that the programme planner must bear in mind when designing a training and development programme is the length of time for the session, particularly input sessions that will need to be delivered in the more traditional manner.

In almost every learning situation there is the problem that, however interesting the material and however well motivated and skilled the trainer, learners have a limited attention span. This of course can vary, depending on such factors as the motivation of the learners, the enthusiasm of the trainer, the skills of the trainer, and the presence of the other barriers described above. But research has suggested that, for input sessions or lectures given by a trainer in the traditional presentational manner, attention starts to fade after about 20 minutes and continues reducing until there is little remaining, particularly if the presentation continues beyond 30–40 minutes. In the shorter sessions there is frequently a re-emergence of some attention towards the end of the session – this can unfortunately be attributed to the learners' realization that the session is drawing to a close and perhaps lunch is the next item on the programme.

This factor will have a strong influence on the designer's construction of the learning programme. There will almost certainly be a number of inputs during the programme and obviously not all of these can be contained within the 20-minute period. However, the 20-minute period relates to the single stretch over which attention will be reasonable. At or before this point a change in the session can be introduced – a break might be suggested, even though this adds to the total time for the session; a discussion might be held rather than just the trainer's input; an activity conducted related to the material covered so far; an appropriate video or computer program inserted; and so on. In fact any other type of activity can take place rather than continuance of the input approach, although the change must be relevant to the session and not appear to be simply an add-on.

POSITIVE FEATURES OF LEARNING

Not all is doom and gloom as far as learning is concerned, since learners can come to training programmes with motivation and the ability to learn. Also, dealing with the negative barriers described above will give the planner and trainer insight into why it is that people do want to learn. These factors will include:

- *If they need to.* Probably the strongest motivational factor for learning is when the learner has a specific need – to learn a new skill and thus ensure that their jobs are retained; or to learn the new skills of a different role.
- *If they want to.* Wanting is frequently strongly linked with needing, but there are occasions when people want to learn, whether this is for a particular purpose – as described in the 'need' above – or simply for the pleasure of learning something new. But neither will necessarily make the learner want to learn – somebody may have to make this desire emerge.
- *They have some control.* Young or younger learners are dominated in the majority of cases by the need to learn and are more willing to accept direction and trainer-controlled situations. As people mature, become more experienced and more selective in their learning, they become less willing to be trainer led all the time and demand that they are given some control over the event and their learning. This factor of course reflects high motivation and is something a trainer should capitalize on – self-learning is a more powerful medium than having to learn from someone else or being taught. The successful trainer will balance an event so that the control, and hence the maximum learning, lies between the trainer and the learners. In learning events of this nature the trainer question 'How would you like to tackle this?' becomes a common one.
- *Balance of input and practical training.* At one time training was of a singular nature; the 'trainees' attended a training course and were

told in a lecture-type presentation what they had to learn. After the 1939–45 war there was a strong swing to experiential training, in which there were few input sessions but many practical activities. It was eventually realized that neither approach on its own was completely successful and a balanced mixture within a training event began to evolve. Such approaches as input sessions, discussions, practical activities, role plays, games, simulations, videos, computer programs and so on all have a place in effective training/learning. This is not to say that they should all be used at once, but the value of each with regard to a particular learning activity should be assessed and the appropriate method(s) implemented.

- *Their experience can be used and is valued.* Many adult learners have experience to a greater or lesser degree in a variety of areas and consequently there is little that will be completely new to them. This must be recognized and, where relevant, made full use of. When subjects are introduced it is always valuable to seek from the learners the extent of their existing knowledge. Those with knowledge and experience can be used to confirm the techniques proposed and to add realism to the training with accounts of their experiences. Using them in this way not only helps the trainer and the learners, but shows the experienced learner that this experience is valued.
- *Realism.* The greater the experience, skill and knowledge of the adult learner, the less likely they are to accept learning approaches that are not related in some way to their world of work. Even apparently non-work-related activities must be shown to have a relationship, otherwise they will be treated as 'games' in the worst sense of the word. Although the activity may not have any obvious work relationship, this can emerge in the review and feedback session following the activity.
- *Expression and mistakes without fear of ridicule or censure.* Much more so than with young learners, adult learners have a hatred of being ridiculed or censured in public, in front of their peers, subordinates or senior managers. The atmosphere of the learning event must be developed in such a way that the participants will not hesitate to respond to a question, make a statement or do something in an activity. This can be developed only by showing in the early stages that there are no sanctions, and it is often useful for the trainers to put themselves in the learners' position. Encourage laughter *with* people rather than *at* them.

3

Setting Training Objectives

This chapter will:

- discuss the nature of the training objectives that will develop from the TNIA;
- consider the methods of writing effective objectives;
- describe a process for setting objectives;
- suggest the practical applications of objectives.

'If you don't know where you are going, how will you know when/if you get there?' This oft-quoted truism is for me the ultimate message in support of setting objectives. Any journey, real or virtual, on which the voyager sets out without any idea of the ultimate destination in mind will fail. The person or group who has completed the TNIA will have set out in general terms the aims and objectives of the proposed training; it is for the planner and designer to translate these into a specific training programme. The final training and development objectives must state in clear and unambiguous terms what the training is setting out to achieve and what the learners will have gained by the end of it.

An objective, for training or whatever, can be defined as an unambiguous formal statement of desired end results, normally to be achieved through a series of activities that will be detailed in the programme. It should specify:

- what the learners will be able to know or do at the end of the programme differently to that at the start of the programme – that is to say, the change intended or other outcomes;
- how they will demonstrate the extent of this learning – conditions for evaluation;

- the standards they will need to achieve to confirm their new competence levels – standards;
- any time constraints that will be imposed to achieve the objectives – conditions.

THE ELEMENTS OF OBJECTIVES

A frequently used acronym to remember the elements of objectives is SMART. This translates as:

- **S**pecific;
- **M**easurable;
- **A**chievable;
- **R**elevant;
- **T**ime-bound.

BENEFITS OF USING 'SMART'

As opposed to the determination of objectives in a more general and unguided way, SMART objectives are challenging and allow progress and success to be measured against predetermined benchmarks and criteria.

Specific

If the objective is specific it:

- provides clarity and direction;
- lets everyone know exactly what is expected of them without vagueness or ambiguity;
- allows you to test for measurability (a link with another aspect of SMART);
- allows you to test that the objective is achievable (another link with another aspect of SMART);
- allows you to define timescales based on specific information;
- helps in the effective allocation of resources;
- clarifies the plan so that weaker points might be identified and other problem areas highlighted.

When setting objectives, in spite of some of the apparent criteria suggested by SMART, it must be remembered that at no stage in the planning process are the objectives carved in stone – they are guidelines by which speedier and more efficient progress might be made. Even if flexibility is not written into the objectives directly the users must be aware of the guideline status, although deviation must be for credible reasons. This, of course, is because objectives are based on knowledge at a particular stage; circumstances can change and the objectives may need to change too.

Measurable

Objectives:

- ensure that standards are set that are as far as possible measurable and are identified at the start of the planning;
- enable you to monitor progress of the planning and evaluate final results, determining whether the desired content has been included;
- allow you to make amendments if the measurement system exposes problems.

It must be recognized that not every aspect of training and development is measurable in fully objective terms. Knowledge and skills learning and achievements are more easily 'measurable'; 'people' skills, behavioural, attitude, value and judgement aspects are less easily measured and, because they are the 'soft' forms of training or are subjective in nature, may require some form of subjective measurement.

Achievable

- There is little sense in setting a target that cannot be achieved. This results in frustration. Similarly, objectives that are too easily achieved do not provide sufficient learning (other than perhaps a historical confirmation) and suggest to the learners that they are not going to learn anything. Objectives that appear to be too big and frightening can always be broken down into smaller, more digestible elements (after all, who eats an elephant in one swallow?!).
- The practical effect of setting unrealistic targets will result in frustration and low morale among the eventual learners, and will, if they have any conscience, make the planners feel uneasy at what they have done.
- Having to ensure that targets are realistic (not easy) encourages the planners to think through the stages of the training and identify possible problems at a realistic stage in the process.

- Setting realistic objectives will help the learners to progress in a logical and realistic manner, rather than to try to cut corners on safety, quality and process issues to meet objectives that are not achievable.

Relevant

- Planners must ensure that the objectives and the content of the training material being designed is fully relevant: a) to the learning group; and b) to the training programme. Some sessions and activities, etc are favourites of both the planners and the trainers, but the question is whether they are relevant to the programme. This does not rule out the 'irrelevant' icebreakers and learning span extenders that might need to be included in certain types of programme – they are relevant in their irrelevancy!

Time-bound

- Time-bound objectives (and content) are essential at the planning stage, although in some cases it may be very difficult to do. This is particularly so with new training material, as the time needed will in many cases be an educated guess. However, time-bounding must be attempted, particularly if a specific number of items have to be included in a particular length of programme.
- Having to set deadlines can provide an impetus to get things done and ensure that everything essential is contained.
- Having definite deadlines imposed helps the planners to achieve their task on time, to prioritize workloads, and helps the learners to correlate the training activities with work-based ones where they have to keep to a timetable of work.

Agreement

- Where more than one person is involved in setting objectives – eg several planners, planners and trainers, and so on – it is essential that, before finalization, the objectives are agreed. It is not unknown when this has not been the case that during the training programme the trainers have manipulated material, etc simply because agreement had not been reached.
- With full agreement all parties are working towards common targets.
- People always feel more committed when they feel more involved, and agreement provides this involvement and commitment.

- The agreed objectives must be *written* to avoid mental or actual manipulation, which is always possible if they are constructed and retained in the mind only. It is only too easy, without a black and white record, to excuse a failing by saying 'Well, I didn't think that was really a firm objective that had been agreed'. Recording enables the evaluation of success or failure to be made unequivocally.

The objectives described and the manner in which they are constructed are usually used as the end result of the complete planning and/or training, and are referred to as *terminal objectives*. There are also *enabling* and *lesson* objectives, both important for the detailed construction of individual learning sessions within the full programme. Enabling objectives describe what the learner will need to *do* to achieve the terminal objective, and the lesson objectives further define what has to be included so that the learners can achieve the terminal objectives once the programme has been completed successfully.

Figure 3.1 is a simplified comparison of how these objectives relate to each other within the overall aim, which is the general statement of intent. At the planning and design stage the planners will be more concerned with the terminal objectives, but will also need to keep in mind the other sub-objectives, particularly if they are also involved in the smaller detail of the programme they are planning.

LEVEL	OBJECTIVE
Aims	Improve training programme effectiveness.
Terminal objectives	The learner will be able to present a 20-minute session using a minimum of three training aids, having a written brief in a style preferred by the learner, and allowing five minutes at the end for questions.
Enabling objective	Give a 20-minute training input session.
Lesson objective	Develop a good knowledge of, and be able to adjust, the session brief to take account of the barriers to learning.

Figure 3.1 *Relationship of aims and objectives*

THE ADVANTAGES OF OBJECTIVES

The following list summarizes the benefits and advantages of formulating and using objectives when planning training and development programmes and, for trainers, when formulating their own specific training sessions.

Objectives:

- help to ensure that the appropriate amount of training is given, defining the type and level of content appropriate to the programme and the learning population;
- avoid irrelevant and unnecessary programme content, thus ensuring that the time required by the programme is not excessive;
- avoid irrelevant and unnecessary programme content, so that the learning messages are clear to the learners;
- provide guidelines for the design and planning of the programme as a whole and its more detailed constituent parts;
- give comprehensive advice to the trainers about what is expected of them and the programme;
- provide a base from which the programme can be evaluated for success or otherwise – without identified objectives at the start of the programme validation at its end is worthless as it is not measuring any change, and longer-term evaluation becomes baseless;
- when written, provide quantitative material on which any review for possible revision can be based.

THE DISADVANTAGES OF OBJECTIVES

The use of objectives is not universally accepted, although in my view the arguments against them are not sufficient to negate their use. It is only fair to demonstrate both sides of the argument, so some of the anti-arguments include:

- Some trainers find the rigorous approach too severe to accept within their more open practitioner style.
- Objectives make training programmes inflexible by limiting the trainers to the objective-defined material.
- Designers and trainers find that writing down objectives restricts flexibility as the written form suggests that the objectives cannot be modified.

- Objectives require the categoric demonstration of outcomes. Practitioners claim that some forms of learning are not capable of quantitative demonstration and evaluation and that, as a result, the more subjective forms of 'soft' training must be excluded.
- Too much time can be expended in formulating objectives and writing them down in the form required.
- Training objectives are seen as behaviourally anchored outcome measures and exclude the programme's theory and knowledge content.

WRITING TRAINING OBJECTIVES

It was suggested earlier that objectives should always be written down to avoid possible manipulation; however, the written word gives the impression of being final and is not completely free from ambiguity. Consequently the use of correct words and phrases is important and the constant use of active verbs will help to avoid many problems and make the action clear to the objectives' recipient. Figure 3.2 lists many of the relevant active verbs used in writing objectives. It is not necessarily complete, but additions should always be challenged in terms of what the result of the action would be.

Many of the verbs in the list can be and are usually combined to demonstrate the action flow. For example, 'Having *recognized* the various factors, *list* and *analyse* the most important, *combine* them with the list provided and *determine* a total action plan'.

BROAD AREA	POSSIBLE WORDING		
KNOWLEDGE	Define State Recognize	Write Recall Be aware of	Underline Select
COMPREHENSION	Identify Justify Select Indicate Perceive	Illustrate Represent Name Formulate	Explain Judge Label Classify
APPLICATION	Predict List Find Show Perform	Choose Reproduce Compute Use Demonstrate	Construct Select Assess Explain

ANALYSIS	Analyse Identify Conclude Criticize	Select Separate Compare Contrast	Justify Resolve Break down Differentiate
SYNTHESIS	Combine Restate Summarize Précis	Argue Discuss Organize Derive	Select Relate Generalize Conclude
EVALUATION	Judge Evaluate Avoid Recognize	Support Validate Determine Criticize	Identify Defend Attack Choose
ATTITUDE	Prefer Relate to Be aware of	Recognize Accept Identify with	Be motivated to Be committed to

Figure 3.2 *Action verbs for writing training objectives*

THE PRACTICAL APPLICATION OF THE TRAINING OBJECTIVES

1. Identify the aims and objectives from the TNIA.
2. Clarify and agree the actionable training objectives.
3. Establish priorities.
4. Check for feasibility.
5. Check for errors and omissions.

Figure 3.3 *Objectives process checklist*

CLARIFY AND AGREE THE ACTIONABLE TRAINING OBJECTIVES

The TNIA will have identified all the training needs in the area of investigation and it is common for the TNIA to show needs that can be met by a variety of means. It is essential that there is early identification of the needs that can be met by more formal training, those that can be met by informal measures at work and those that can be met by more formal work processes, including coaching, mentoring, open learning, CBT and Web-based programs. Obviously the final decisions will depend on a number of circumstances, including the organization's culture and 'politics', availability of resources and finance, etc, but a rule of thumb can indicate:

- *Large group needs in the organization.* Construction of an internal training programme to cover the identified needs; if appropriate, an open learning package for use by all learners; if appropriate, CBT or Web-based training programs.
- *Small group needs in the organization.* Depending on the size of the total group requiring training, a similar approach to the larger group methods, including an internal Net training contact, or attendance at a relevant externally provided training programme.
- *Individual needs.* These will normally be met most effectively by some form of one-to-one interaction – mentoring and coaching, and the use of open learning packages, CBT, and Web-based training. Practical training needs can be met by work station training conducted by an experienced worker who has been trained in the on-the-job training methods.
- *Group needs for individuals located in a widespread organization.* These learners can have their needs satisfied by either bringing them together for a central internal training programme or using any of the approaches suggested above. If it is available, a Net-based collective learning programme can be used, or an open learning package for each learner, the trainer acting as a central co-ordinator over the Net, by telephone and fax, and with the extensive use of e-mail on a pre-arranged programme.

  A different approach that planners might find useful is included in Diane Bailey's chapter, 'Designing Effective Training', in *Handbook of Training and Development* (1999, 3rd edn, ed A Landale, Gower). Diane considers possible training approaches for groups, on-the-job development, and self-study. This is shown in Figure 3.4.

There will be occasions when the types of approaches recommended for the groups mentioned above, although the most effective, are not suitable or available. One important identification must be the division between at-work based training and that provided by more formal training approaches. Both are important and serve different needs in appropriate ways, but the first question should always be 'Can training for this person (these persons) be provided at work rather than on a training course?'. Provided that the facilities and skills are available without the learner leaving their place of work, and with work providing the vehicle for training, this is usually the most effective way of satisfying the learning needs.

MECHANISM/STRATEGY	POSSIBLE APPROACHES
GROUP TRAINING	■ Lectures/presentations ■ Courses/workshops/seminars ■ Peer study groups ■ Action learning sets ■ Focus groups ■ Discussion groups ■ Guided practical activities and exercises ■ Project planning and management
ON-THE-JOB DEVELOPMENT	■ Coaching interventions ■ 'Sitting next to Nellie' ■ Mentor support ■ Supervised practice ■ Properly briefed delegation ■ One-to-one instruction ■ Workplace practice and experimentation ■ Tasks and projects ■ Personal development plans and management feedback
SELF-STUDY	■ Distance learning/open learning courses ■ Self-study material, eg CD-ROMs ■ Planned reading/research ■ Individual written activities and exercises ■ Video and interactive video ■ Intranet or Internet ■ Practical experience linked to learning logs

Figure 3.4 *Possible training approaches*

ESTABLISH PRIORITIES

It will be evident from the TNIA that, with a large number of training needs or for a large number of people, all the training cannot be provided at once and at the same time. Consequently the planners must agree a prioritization programme, taking into account the availability and suitability of all the resources.

These priorities can be determined in the majority of cases by posing a number of questions to both senior and line management and, if possible, the learners. These questions would include:

- What is the minimum amount of knowledge, skills and attitudes needed by the learners to enable them to carry out the task to a satisfactory level?
- Which other items would be desirable in addition to the basic needs?
- Which items would it be helpful, but not essential for the learners to know and be able to do?

Experienced training practitioners will recognize these levels of need as the three priority decisions that are made in connection with a range of training questions and decisions, including full programmes and sessions:

MUST KNOW **SHOULD KNOW** **COULD KNOW**

FEASIBILITY

Linked with the identification of the priorities of the different approaches to satisfying the identified training needs are questions relating to the feasibility of the approach and hence construction of the objectives:

- Is the learner target population sufficiently small to be covered in the time allocated or should additional time/resources be sought?
- If additional time cannot be authorized, can authority be sought for consultant provision either in-house or externally?
- Is the learner target population capable of learning what is required within the time allocated?
- Are all the objectives identified as essential included within the time constraints linked with the prioritization of objectives?
- Must all the objectives be covered in detail, or might some be left for follow-up training or for coverage by other learning methods?
- Must the skills be learned to the highest level, or is a satisfactory 'can-do' level all that is required?

AN OBJECTIVES ACTION PLAN

We have now considered the various elements of starting to plan and design a training programme in terms of the numerous factors concerned with people, their learning problems and aids, and the construction of objectives once the overall planning and, to a limited extent, the construction of specific session objectives. I have also recommended the writing down of the objectives once they have been framed. An action plan for completing the planning process can now be considered, and again it is recommended that, when considered, this plan is written down, principally as a continuing *aide-mémoire* during the planning process.

Figure 3.5 summarizes this plan, which can be used not only with the planning objectives, but also as a practical check by the planner or training practitioner of the objectives of individual sessions.

1. Read the objective.	Go to paragraph 2
2. Can you say in concrete and active terms what the learner is expected to know or do?	If yes, go to paragraph 4 If no, go to paragraph 3
3. The objective is defective and must be rewritten. It must state clearly what is expected of the learner in terms of behaviour that can be observed and measured. Rewrite.	Go to paragraph 1
4. From reading the objective, do you know precisely what standard of performance you expect from the learner?	If yes, go to paragraph 6 If no, go to paragraph 5
5. The objective does not enable you to decide how much or how well the learner will have learned. If a level of acceptable performance is stated it enables you to make accurate judgements. Rewrite.	Go to paragraph 1
6. Does the objective say under what conditions the learner will carry out the required activity? Is there a time constraint? Where will the activity be performed, etc?	If yes, go to paragraph 8 If no, go to paragraph 7
7. Verify that these aspects do not have any bearing on the learner's level of acceptable performance. If you think they do, the objective must be rewritten to include them.	If rewriting, go to paragraph 1
8. The objective would appear to be satisfactory.	

Figure 3.5 *Checking a training objective*

THE PRACTICAL USES OF OBJECTIVES

The obvious use of objectives as the basis for planning and designing training programmes has been described, but they have further uses within the programme itself, whether used by the planner or the training practitioner.

Prior to the programme

The objectives can be introduced into the pre-event activity of a programme in a number of ways. In most cases the objectives for a training programme have been finalized by the TNIA practitioner – this is frequently the trainer, who might then go on to design the programme from the objectives. Although the potential learners should have been involved to lesser or greater degrees in the TNIA, their input has been as a contribution to the final objectives. It is an infrequent occurrence for any further reference to be made to them, but this would reflect good practice. At least two practical approaches can be suggested:

1. Before the final objectives are applied to the construction of a training programme copies of the objectives should be sent to, at least, the people who took part in and contributed to the TNIA. This serves a number of purposes, not least of which is that it paves the way for a return to these contributors or their further use on another occasion. In so many cases of training activities the learners complain that something happens in which they are involved but they never hear anything further – this does not lay a good foundation for their future co-operation. The objectives can also be sent to the wider population who might be affected by a training programme based on the objectives. In both cases the recipients should be asked for their reactions to the objectives in the context of the proposed training programme. This serves two purposes – it gives people an opportunity to comment (favourably or otherwise) on the objectives as they affect them, and also to correct any misinterpretations or misstatements.
2. When learners are being invited to take part in a training programme the invitation should also include a clear statement of the objectives for the event, whether it is a training course or some form of open learning. This will give them the opportunity to confirm or otherwise the suitability of the programme, possibly at the time of the pre-programme discussion with their line manager. The action also ensures that the learner has as much

information as possible prior to the programme, a move that certainly helps to encourage motivation and co-operation.

At the start of the programme

The objectives can also be used once the programme has started – let us assume that the programme starts with a training course. At this stage, the objectives can be used in at least five ways:

1. It is very common for pre-programme training material not to be read, or read very superficially by the learners. Whether you suspect this or not, it is always a useful training move to start your programme with a restatement of the objectives, clarifying them as necessary.
2. Present, or re-present, the objectives, and seek the views of the learners: a) about the objectives, their relevance, the learners' understanding of them, and so on; and b) whether they wish to suggest any further objectives at this stage.
3. As part of an introductory session, while displaying the programme objectives, the learners can be asked to introduce themselves, including comments about: a) the programme objectives; and b) their personal objectives, preferably linking these to those of the programme. In this way 'objectives' start to become much more person-related features than ethereal ones.
4. The objectives, programme and personal, can be used as or linked with programme evaluation measures by seeking the learners' views on how everybody will know at the end of the programme whether the objectives have been achieved or not.
5. Using the objectives directly with the training programme brings home the fact that all the stages of the training/learning cycle are linked substantially, particularly the early stages of TNIA and objectives and the evaluation of the programme. Objectives state in effect the overall deficiencies in the skills of the learning group, but within that group individual skills, etc can vary considerably. As we shall see in Chapter 11, start of programme tests or other assessments can take place in order to identify the individual level of skills at that stage. The process will be repeated at the end of the programme to validate any change resulting from the training.

The actual process for this assessment will depend on the nature of the programme – knowledge, skills or attitudes.

Knowledge will normally be assessed by the setting of written tests; skill assessment will depend on the type of skill – practical, technical or operational skills are the simplest, with direct observation of the learner trying to perform the skill task. People skills are more difficult to assess and require a rather more subjective assessment, frequently based on a concept or model, of the learners performing, usually, training exercises. Behaviours as part of attitude assessment can be approached by an observational method such as behaviour analysis. Other self-assessment instruments are also in use – these will be considered in Chapter 11.

During and at the end of the programme

Objectives used on these occasions are virtually indistinguishable from validation and evaluation measures, as these are intended to check the satisfaction of the objectives against the learning by the participants. Consequently descriptions of approaches and methods will be included in Chapter 11. But this important association must be kept in mind in view of the integrated and comprehensive nature of the training process.

PART TWO

Planning and Designing On-the-job Training and Development

The chapters in this part will consider in detail the various aspects that need to be taken into account when planning and designing an on-the-job training programme or approach.

4

On-the-job Training and Development – I

This chapter will:

- describe the initial considerations necessary for the planning and design of on-the-job training and development programmes;
- suggest the steps to be followed in planning and designing the content of an on-the-job programme;
- describe two of the training approaches available – GAFO and coaching.

ON-THE-JOB TRAINING PROGRAMME PLANNING STAGES

The initial stages in the planning and design of an on-the job programme are:

1. Refer to the agreed objectives for the training programme as produced in the TNIA or the initial planning stages.
2. Consider the identified target learning population and how they might affect the training design.
3. List the ways in which each objective might best be met.
4. Decide whether the learning might be best achieved by an on-the-job or off-the-job programme.

REFERENCE TO THE AGREED OBJECTIVES

Although considerable work will have been done in the overall planning stage on the objectives, they may not have been specifically considered in terms of on-the-job training and certainly are not set in stone, being capable of modification in the light of local and specific knowledge. The overall objectives should be considered as a guideline blueprint from which the final, working objectives are derived. An example of this might be the order in which the objectives and plans are detailed – in the light of the facilities available this order may have to be modified to ensure that it is practicable.

CONSIDER THE TARGET LEARNING POPULATION

- How many people are to be covered by the learning programme? This is very relevant when on-the-job training is being considered – the individual coaches, mentors, packages, etc will be restricted and this in turn will restrict the number of learners who can be dealt with in a timescale. Do these investigations determine that the number is too large for this approach and off-the-job training will have to be considered instead?
- What will the age range, experience, sex, physical capabilities, status, etc of the learning population be, and who might be involved in the training process? Significant differences and factors will require a different approach – eg new entrants, young, inexperienced workers will require a different approach from existing, older and experienced employees and the advice given to the planners and eventually the people involved as coaches, etc will need to be imparted accordingly.
- What are the learning preferences likely to be? Planners are in a favourable position if this can determined beforehand, as the programmes can be planned with these preferences in mind. Decisions will need to be made whether to plan the training accepting the learning preferences, or to try to ensure that the learners take into account all the stages of the Learning Cycle. Pre-knowledge is a rare occurrence and the planners will probably have to take into account the distribution of learning preferences in the population as a whole. Peter Honey and Alan Mumford demonstrated that most people have a strong preference for one or two of the learning styles, some are locked in on one style, and few have preferences over the full range. Locking in is a particularly difficult learning style to cope with as people with strong, singular preferences tend to reject the other approaches. For example, a very strong preference activist will find it very difficult to sit down after an interesting activity and reflect and conclude

on what happened – they will most likely be looking for the next activity! Similar problems arise with learners locked in on the other preferences of pragmatist ('I'm only interested in something that can be done at work'); reflector ('I want to sit and think about this. Don't disturb me with something else to do'); or theorist ('Look. Before we do anything else, are we quite sure that what we have seen means what it appears to be? What other aspects are there that can suggest other causes? Has there been any research or models to explain what happened and what we can do about it?). And so on. Multiple preferences are not unusual – eg reflector and theorist; activist and pragmatist – and, approaching the fully rounded person, the reflector, theorist, pragmatist. A typical example of the latter multi-preference type is the engineer who, presented with a mechanical problem, thinks beforehand of all the errors that are occurring and investigates whether any others are present; he/she then considers possible reasons why these should occur, coming to a solution from the reasons considered and rejected; then the faults are put right by practical action.

If the preferences are known, or can be determined to some extent, three approaches can be considered:

1. If the learning preferences of the people who are to be involved are known, the training can be planned to concentrate on these preferences. For example, if there is to be a group of theorists they will probably react more favourably to a programme that includes a number of inputs or lectures, perhaps introducing controversial themes, but presenting models or concepts for them to consider and discuss in depth. Activists will react more favourably to programmes in which they take part in a large number of activities, with not too much emphasis on 'talking about it' and with relatively passive input time at a minimum. Similar considerations apply to reflector or pragmatist strong preferences.
2. Similarly, where the learning preferences of the group or learner are known it might be decided to widen these preferences and undo the locks that have been preventing them from fully utilizing the other approaches. Reflectors must be given time to reflect, but would have to take part in activist or pragmatist types of activities to enable them to do this. In the same way theorists would also have to take part in activities, giving them food from which they could develop their theoretical and concluding skills,

perhaps being provided with a subject expert with whom to discuss their views. Pragmatists could usefully be exposed to non-work activities to show them that lessons that could be related to their work could be identified in these types of situations.

3. It is more usual for planners to have no prior knowledge of the learners and their preferences or to be presented with learners who have mixed preferences, particularly in a group. This is much more akin to a general population group, as suggested earlier. The safest and most effective approach in such circumstances is to produce a balanced learning plan in which all the preferences are taken care of in the learning cycle model, experiences being followed by periods given over to reflection on what happened, then a deeper consideration of the meaning of what was observed to happen, followed by planning to try the activity again or translate the learning to the work situation. In programmes of this nature, probably the most common in on and off-the-job training, an additional learning objective might be 'to widen the learning preferences and skills of the learners by exposing them to and helping them learn from the full range of learning situations and activities'.

Whatever the pre-knowledge of the learners' preferences (or lack of it) there is considerable value in identifying these preferences before or at the start of the learning experiences, modifications being introduced to take them into account. The information may not be known by the planner at the general planning stage, so either a composite programme can be designed or several appropriate programmes suggested.

Level of starting knowledge

It is important to know, as completely as possible, the level of the starting knowledge of the learners. Again the ideal will be to have pre-knowledge of this, and to a substantial extent there should be data about this level as a result of the TNIA – this will probably show, except in the case of completely new work of which no one could have previous experience, that there is a range of level. This will obviously produce problems for the planner and trainer in terms of at what level to pitch the training – too low, to suit the ones with little skill level and the more skilled participants will be lost. Pitch the level too high and the lower skill level learners will not learn and may cease trying to do so. However, although most training programmes have to cope with a mixed range, every attempt should be made in your liaison with the line manager in the training quintet to select learners for particular training events on the basis of their level of experience and existing skill.

Location

In the case of on-the-job training there should be few problems about where the training should be held, the location and type of location usually being dictated by the form of the training. If a group is being supported at work the training might be in the organization's training suite or, if the group is sufficiently small, in an unoccupied office. Other approaches will be, for example in a one-to-one coaching session, at the manager's or another's desk, or, in a practical approach, on the operational work line or a separate area set aside for this purpose, with CBT, interactive video, other open learning programmes, or with the use of the organization's computer network or intranet.

Timing

Although there can still be problems with the timing of training on the job – non-availability of the company trainer, coach or training room; non-availability or delayed availability of computer hardware or software, open learning packages, etc – most of these can be solved more easily than in off-the-job training. There will still be, however, complaints by the trainers that the learners are not made available at the relevant times, and by the line managers that the training department does not make the training opportunities available when they are needed! Effective planning following the TNIA should help to avoid problems of this nature.

ON-THE-JOB TRAINING AND DEVELOPMENT PLANNING AND DESIGN

In addition to the normal aspects of planning and design of training programmes, on-the-job programmes require some specific activities. These will include:

- Specific decisions on the type of training approaches that are relevant to on-the-job training – one-to-one instruction, coaching, mentoring, etc.

- The likelihood of planning a number of different programmes and approaches for a significant number of individuals, each with their own requirements.
- Preparation of outline programmes based on the variety and number required.
- Discussion of the proposed programmes with the people who are to be involved, including the potential learners and their line managers. This aspect should be an easier task than with off-the-job training planning, particularly where the potential learners are spread widely throughout the organization and possibly many locations.

A COMPETENCES APPROACH TO PROGRAMME MATERIAL

Although competences and National Vocation Qualifications (NVQs) are relevant to all forms of training and development, because of their work-related nature, they are significantly appropriate to on-the-job training. Consistent standards of competence at work have formed the bases of NVQs and these standards have been produced for a large number of occupations and industry sectors. These standards are detailed and describe the activities in an occupation that determine the outcome of the job in a more realistic way than many other approaches to job descriptions. The individual is assessed by an experienced and qualified assessor against their ability to perform the skills laid out in the standards, principally for the award of a relevant NVQ, but the standards and the approach can be used in a variety of other ways, including the planning and construction of training programmes.

Each NVQ is defined in overall terms by a Key Purpose, Key Areas and Key Roles. The more practical aspects of the NVQ are described in the Units of Competence, Elements of Competence and Performance Criteria included in the Key factors.

UNITS OF COMPETENCE

Each Key Role contains a number of Units of Competence, the basic building brick of an NVQ and the areas in which NVQs are assessed for award. One NVQ is that of Training and Development (T&D), which has various levels, such as those for practitioners, training managers and training directors. Key Role E2 in the T & D NVQ Level 3 (the NVQ principally for training practitioners/training officers) – *'Evaluate the effectiveness of training and development programmes'* – contains three Units:

Unit E21 Evaluate training and development programmes.
Unit E22 Improve training and development programmes.
Unit E23 Evaluate training and development sessions.

ELEMENTS OF COMPETENCE

The Units are not sufficiently detailed to obtain a realistic assessment of competence in the function to be performed. Thus each Unit is further described in terms of Elements – statements of the detailed aspects of the function. The Units vary in having (in the T & D NVQ) from two to five Elements each. For example, the Elements contained in Unit E21 quoted above are:

Element E211 Select methods for evaluating training and development programmes.
Element E212 Collect information to evaluate training and development programmes.
Element E213 Analyse information to improve training and development programmes.

You will see that the Elements describe the progressive involvement of the practitioner in that particular competence, from selecting methods to analysing the result.

PERFORMANCE CRITERIA

The Units and Elements define what is included as functions in the competence standards. The Performance Criteria, what a practitioner must be able to do and what an assessor must look for to determine whether the functions are being carried out satisfactorily – the test of competence – and it is this area that the programme planner will find the most value.

Each Element has a number of associated Performance Criteria, ranging from 5–10 or more. Following our T & D NVQ example, in Element 211 the nine Performance Criteria are:

Unit E21 Evaluate training and development programmes
Element E211 Select methods for evaluating training and development programmes
Performance criteria:

a) *The training and development programmes being evaluated are clearly identified and used as the focus for the evaluation process.*
b) *The specific objectives and desired outcomes of the training and development programmes are clearly identified.*

c) *The purpose, scope and level of evaluation is clearly identified.*
d) *Methods that are capable of evaluating training and development programmes are clearly identified.*
e) *The advantages and disadvantages of each evaluation method are suitably assessed and an appropriate method selected.*
f) *Evaluation criteria are appropriate to the training and development programme and clearly specified.*
g) *Evaluation methods are capable of being implemented within the resources available.*
h) *All aspects of the evaluation method are clearly identified and agreed with the appropriate people.*
i) *A plan for implementing the evaluation is clearly specified.*

PERFORMANCE EVIDENCE

In addition to the Performance Criteria listed, notes are included in the Element giving guidance on the type of evidence – performance and knowledge – required to satisfy the criteria. For the Performance Criteria described above:

The performance evidence required is:

Identification of training and development programmes being evaluated
Specification of evaluation methods and rationale for their selection
Specification of evaluation criteria and rationale for their selection
Explanation of scope and purpose of evaluation
Plan for the implementation of the evaluation
Notes of agreement made.

The knowledge evidence required is:

Methods of evaluating training and development programmes
Range of evaluation criteria available
How to identify criteria for evaluation
Employment and equal opportunities legislation and good practice
Relevant national and organizational debates concerning learning
Relevant national and organizational debates relating to evaluation and quality improvement.

As the Units, Elements and Performance Criteria describe the occupation in sufficient detail that the skill of the performer can be assessed, the standards are ready-made listings of the skills necessary to identify areas that figure in the training identified in the TNIA. Consequently they represent a valuable source of information on which the planning for a particular programme can be made. Again the NVQ competence standards are valuable tools not only in on-the-job training (where competence is readily observable and available), but also in other forms of training, the standards identifying the details of what should be included in the training.

TYPES OF ON-THE-JOB TRAINING APPROACHES

The criteria described earlier in the chapter will help the planner to decide on the type or types of training approach that will be most appropriate in the circumstances – large group, small group, experienced individual, inexperienced individual, and so on. The range of approaches available includes:

- GAFO;
- coaching;
- one-to-one instruction – the 'sitting with Nellie' or desk training approach;
- project management;
- mentoring;
- team development;
- open learning – audio material, video material, interactive video, comprehensive packages;
- computer-based training.

GAFO

This is an acronym for 'Go Away and Find Out' and can be the simplest form of training at work, although only if done for the right reasons and handled properly. At its crudest, a learner approaches someone who would be expected to have the appropriate knowledge or information, and is constructively told to GAFO. How this is done can give the learner the impression that the person is not interested in helping them, but applied in an effective manner can help the learner to become non-trainer-dependent. The learning is achieved forcibly, with the learner having to seek the answer for himself or herself. If used in the most deliberate and constructive way, by helping the learner to identify general areas where the finding out will be possible, and the learner returning with the information for a discussion on the material and the method of obtaining it, the approach becomes one of guided self-learning.

COACHING

Coaching is a training and development technique that is used when a manager has only one or two staff who need training and development and a personal involvement and approach can be utilized. The learner follows a training programme while at work, using real-work tasks as the vehicles for learning. In this it differs from most traditional forms of training by using actual work rather than the more artificial training course activities.

The uses of coaching

Coaching is a multi-purpose training and development approach, ideally suited for on-the-job training. The initial planner can only go so far in planning for coaching – identifying it as the most suitable training vehicle; identifying the objectives to be achieved; suggesting approaches, eg coaching by the line manager, subject experts, experienced colleagues, and so on. This initial planning will need to be followed up with specific arrangements – these can be made direct with the learners' line managers or the training practitioners can perform this function, depending on the discrete nature of the planner.

The uses of coaching include:

- *Remedial training.* In many cases where training appears to be required a TNIA may demonstrate that, although the learners may at some time have received training in the skills, etc required to perform their work, this training may have been forgotten, misinterpreted or implemented erroneously, so that the required level of work performance is not being achieved.
- *New or extended duties of work.* In such cases the individual is required to extend or increase their skills beyond the existing situation as a result of having to undertake new work or increase the range of their current work. These increased skills can be achieved by the learners attending training courses, but at the expense of resource time and the possible failings of a training course as opposed to learning from 'real' work.
- *Career development.* A skilled and efficient worker may be on the point of promotion to higher duties or may need job enhancement to stretch their abilities and ensure career development or continued job satisfaction. Coaching can offer a very effective method of introducing the learners to these more demanding tasks by taking on projects that would normally be carried out by their supervisor or manager. This higher-grade work would be

delegated to the learner, giving them the authority to carry out the work, but the boss would retain final responsibility for the results of the task.

- *Training consolidation.* Attendance on a training course is not often an end in itself and requires substantial follow up when the learner returns to work. Training course material is often very general, deliberately so to give a base for a range of situations in which the skills have to be implemented. Back at work the more general training skill may need to be translated or interpreted to the particular work situation; real-life practice in the skills will certainly be necessary; at-work training in additional parts of the skill might be needed; and so on. If the training is to be made worthwhile as work practice the supervisor or manager must accept this continuing need and their responsibility to support it, and start coaching projects and assignments to achieve this. Frequently good training is condemned as having failed when the real cause of the failure is the lack of opportunity, encouragement or support to put the training into practice.
- *Complete training events.* A coaching approach might be the alternative to sending learners on expensive training courses, provided sufficient skill exists in the work area to cover the material effectively, particularly when this is linked with real-job tasks. The costs and effectiveness of both approaches will have to be considered so that a cost and value-effective choice can be made. This approach, of course, can be considered a form of one-to-one, on-the-job instruction when the 'instructor' is either a member of the work staff or a trainer brought to the workplace to support the coaching/training.

There is no guarantee that coaching, of whatever nature, is less costly than a training course, particularly where there are several people requiring the learning, and in some aspects coaching is more expensive in resource time than a course. However, the benefit of the learning taking place at work and the value of real-work tasks being undertaken must be significant factors in the cost/value balance. Many learners find that effective coaching has more impact on them than a training course, which they may see as divorced from the working situation.

The basis for coaching

Coaching by the learners' line managers has its foundation in the accepted (but not always practised) basis of management that:

ONE OF THE PRIME RESPONSIBILITIES OF MANAGERS IS THE TRAINING AND DEVELOPMENT OF THEIR STAFF.

This does not mean that the line managers carry out the training themselves; some of this responsibility will be taken by the training department where applicable, but the line manager, supported by others, can help individuals in many ways in their development.

Apart from this responsibility the line manager is ideally situated to focus their power, influence, expertise and skills on the development of their staff:

- They have the inescapable management responsibility for the training and development of their staff as described above.
- In spite of improved formalized training programmes, most of an individual's real development still takes place while performing the job – often as a result of trial and error.
- They are in an ideal position to help the learners translate more formal training into the practicalities of the job, supporting their action plans and continued development and evaluating this progress.
- The most powerful training and development relationship should be that between manager and subordinate.

BENEFITS AND DISADVANTAGES OF COACHING

Benefits

The benefits of coaching to the individual, the line manager and the organization include:

- improved individual staff performance;
- improved team performance;
- cumulative improved performance of the organization;
- staff are better informed and more aware;
- staff are better equipped for any changes that occur;
- staff are encouraged to be more innovative;
- increased job satisfaction usually results;
- manager has eventually more time for management level tasks;
- more systematic management progression is possible;
- learning is performed at the workplace;
- there is no need for learners to be away from work and home to attend training courses;

- real work is used, and consequently there is increased credibility in the eyes of the learners;
- the translation from learning to work is eased;
- the coaches themselves develop skills.

Disadvantages

Wherever there are advantages for actions there are almost certainly some disadvantages, real or assumed; coaching is no exception:

- time is required for both the learner and coach for the coaching process;
- the organization may not really want the closer relationships that almost invariably develop between managers and staff;
- the coached skills are not always followed up by opportunities to practise them on a permanent basis;
- expectations can be falsely raised, the failures often out of the hands of the line managers;
- some learners see going away on a training course as a bonus (not necessarily a learning bonus!);
- the line manager has to take personal action and be involved in the development of a better relationship with his/her staff – this may be alien to the manager's preferred style of management;
- decisions to exclude some staff from coaching might damage existing staff relationships.

COACHING PRACTICE

The coaching process has techniques and processes similar to those of many other forms of training and development. Many of the practical steps after the initial planning has been done will fall on the training practitioner and the line manager, the trainer taking on a more advisory role once the initial organization steps have been taken. Eight stages can be recognized in the planning of the specific coaching process:

1. Recognizing the need.
2. Identifying the opportunity.
3. Setting the coaching climate.
4. Meeting the learner.
5. Agreeing the assignment.
6. Agreeing the assignment reviews and final review.

7. Implementation.
8. Review.

Stage 1 Recognizing the need

The training and development need when coaching is involved will have been identified in a number of ways – the TNIA, problems thrown up in the appraisal process, problems identified by the manager in the course of work, problems identified by the trainer when the person is attending another training course, requests for development by the people themselves, and so on. It is the line managers' responsibility to take action if the need is recognized by them or reported to them by others.

Whom to coach?

Identify the individuals requiring training and development

Although it may be desirable, a manager cannot coach all his staff at once, even if in theory they are all potential candidates. The process should not be seen solely for the high flyer or the favoured worker, nor should there be a concentration on remedial coaching for the poor performer. All staff should be considered on their merits, with the possible long-term aim of providing coaching for everybody. The principal groups of people for whom coaching will be appropriate are:

- the potential promotee – the high flyers;
- succession candidates and those who are interested in their career development;
- the poor performer who requires remedial training;
- staff required to perform new or extended duties or tasks;
- those needing consolidation of learning following participation in some other training form;
- frustrated workers who need to have their commitment and energy rekindled.

A useful guide for line managers in the control of staff development is the maintenance of a skills matrix, as shown in Figure 4.1. The vertical columns are headed by the skills to be recorded; the horizontal rows for in the individuals involved. Existing skills are plotted for each individual. In the example, against individual 1 a * signifies 'can do' and X 'can't do yet'. Thus this individual has all the skills required except E and F.

NAME	SKILLS								
	A	B	C	D	E	F	G	H	I
1	*	*	*	*	X	X	*	*	*
2	***	**	**	***	X	X	***	**	*
3									
4									
5									

Figure 4.1 *A skills matrix*

The detail of the matrix can be increased by showing the level of 'can do' as entered against individual 2:

X = can't do yet;
* = has knowledge of the skill, but is not yet a practitioner;
** = can perform the skills, but only with difficulty;
*** = can perform the skill well.

The training needs stand out clearly in the matrix, particularly if the Xs are entered in a different colour to the *s. The matrix will also help the coach to identify which individuals are coaching priorities. Consequently the matrix demonstrates not only the development needs of each individual but also records their progress.

Training needs

The training needs of the working group will have been established in an earlier TNIA and these will need to be further refined into specific objectives for the individuals or small groups of individuals, relating them to the nature of the coaching process required. Whoever has been responsible for the original needs identification, the line manager/coach will need to:

- *Confirm that coaching will be the most effective and or most cost value-effective form of satisfying the training needs.* Provided that coaches are available, in addition to resource time, this should be a relatively easy process based on earlier comments of whether the people to be developed are individuals, small homogeneous groups, small heterogeneous groups, large groups and so on, the first three sets being the ones immediately suitable for coaching.

- *Identify the specific training and development objectives of the individuals or groups.* The coaching objectives will need similar treatment to the identification and setting of training objectives described in Chapter 3. These objectives will relate to both the learner and the task to be achieved in the coaching process. They should:
  - Describe exactly what the learner will be able to do as a result of the coaching process, in terms of knowledge, skills, behaviour, task achievement and performance.
  - Define the standards the learner is expected to achieve, in as objective and measurable terms as possible. Where quantitative measures are not possible, clear guidance should be given for subjective assessment within these restraints.
  - Define the conditions under which the learner will be expected to achieve the standards – including time, resources, equipment and so on.

Stage 2 Identifying the opportunity

Selecting coaching projects

Most of the opportunities for coaching, and this is the principal advantage of the method, will be found in the day-to-day operation of the job. These will include:

- *Day-to-day work of the department.* The line manager or supervisor will come into contact with their staff every day in the course of their, and the managers' duties. In these circumstances virtually every contact will be an opportunity for coaching, whether it is asking for a job to be done, discussing or asking for progress reports, etc.
- *Following mistakes, failures or setbacks.* When negative events occur they can be turned into positive coaching opportunities. This not only helps the person responsible to understand what has happened and how to avoid it in the future, but can also help to restore the individual's confidence.
- *Following successes and achievements.* Coaching is not all concerned with using negative events at work, although there is no doubt that much learning occurs from our recognizing and analysing our mistakes. In the same way we should be able to benefit from our successes, recognizing and analysing them in the same way as failures – why they have succeeded, what can be learned from this, and how can this learning be applied.
- *Planned delegation.* In delegation, some of the manager's work is passed to another person to perform. This can become an integral

part of the coaching process and be used as a learning event rather than a time management or resources event.

- *Relief coverage.* Managers and supervisors sometimes need to be away from their work. A good manager will always ensure that the work carries on in his absence just as if he/she were there. This requires the development of a 'deputy' who can be developed to undertake some of these tasks or make other 'absent manager' decisions.
- *Promotion or career development.* Any change of job, particularly promotion or a move to assist career development, can be an ideal opportunity for coaching.
- *Secondments or departmental moves.* Staff can be seconded to another area of work, either to help out in a crisis or as part of a career development plan. These are opportunities for planned coaching by linking the actual work with development. The worker can be briefed prior to the secondment on how to take advantage of this move as an opportunity for development, preferably also introducing the secondment manager into the plan. Following the secondment, a full debriefing will take place to consolidate the learning.
- *Projects, assignments, working parties, research or pilot studies.* These opportunities can all help to widen skills and knowledge, either as one-off events or ongoing tasks, if the learner is guided into seeing them as coaching events.
- *Following training events.* The return from, say, formal training courses can be used as an opportunity to consolidate the individual's learning, and also to widen the skills and knowledge of other staff. The returnee can give presentations to other staff or hold mini-workshops and facilitate learning events for them. This can have the additional effect of developing the individual into an on-the-job trainer or coach.
- *Deputizing at meetings for the manager.* Meetings that the manager cannot attend are ideal opportunities to send a representative, not simply to determine the content of the meeting, but also to act for the manager, the representative having been coached in the extent of authority allowed. Or the learner can deputize for the manager in departmental meetings when the manager is not available but the meeting should go ahead.
- *Introduction of new work.* In addition to the learning that ensues from the introduction of the new work, individuals can be assigned to roles in its introduction and follow-through as a learning process.

Stage 3 Setting the coaching climate

Following the basic vein of this book, as in all aspects of training and development attempts to introduce coaching without preparation are certain to lead to failure. Setting the climate is essential, and although there is no magic recipe for this, it must be sought. Nor is it an instant fix: the coach must demonstrate an open, honest and sincere interest in the learners as a permanent attitude, a sincere intention of involvement and support, and of developing the members of staff. A devious or manipulative approach will soon be recognized or (even worse) suspected. A good coaching climate should include:

- high performance and clear, quantified standards set, with agreement to review them regularly;
- an environment in which learners are encouraged to develop their motivation;
- expectations for personal development created and job descriptions regularly reviewed;
- a visible acceptance that seeking help or admitting weaknesses is not wrong;
- encouragement for creative risk taking;
- concentration, particularly at appraisal times, on the future rather than dwelling on the past;
- learning encouraged from mistakes and successes;
- demonstration that coaching is not a once and for all process but an ongoing one;
- fully open, frank and participative group or team meetings, some of which are held to discuss people development rather than always concentrating on the task;
- all group or team members encouraged to seek and offer help;
- a working environment of openness and trust is developed.

Stage 4 Meeting the learner

A meeting with the proposed learners, encompassing many of the aspects expressed in stage 3, is essential, and equally essential is the planning and preparation for this meeting. The meeting and the reason for it should not come as a surprise and it is very helpful, a few days before the meeting, to ask the learner to think about the proposed process and be ready to progress from the start.

The meeting itself will start with an iteration of the reason for the meeting and the proposed outcomes. The coach should aim to lead the learner to express the need to change or develop rather than this having to come completely from the coach.

The coaching plan and its objectives

When these essential opening gambits have been successfully covered, the coaching plan can be proposed, discussed and agreed, prescription by the coach being kept to a minimum. Objectives should be discussed and agreed, in the case of coaching these being stated in more detail than in general objectives. For example, the coaching objective might be for the learner to be able to produce a written report on ..., the report being grammatically correct and in a style and to a standard acceptable to the coach (defined as quantifiably as possible by the coach) by ..., making use of the resources available from ...

For practical coaching the learning points within the objectives must also be detailed. For example:

- the learner to report on his/her research methods;
- the learner to explain the structuring plans;
- emphasis to be placed on effective spelling and use of words;
- the report must be as correct as possible within the rules of grammar and syntax without making the construction a slave to these;
- the learner will develop an effective and acceptable writing style, appropriate to the situation;
- the report, before final printing, to be edited by the learner and their support for clarity and conciseness;
- the learner to show effective use of all the resources available.

Stage 5 Agreeing the assignment

Once the coaching task and its objectives have been described, discussed and agreed, the method of achieving the task should be discussed. Again, the coach should plan not to prescribe how this should be done, rather encouraging the learner, with supportive advice, to propose how they intend to proceed. Too much advice, guidance and prescription by the coach can lead to a lack of commitment by the learner as they do not develop any ownership of the process. Of course if the action proposed is so wide of the required mark the coach will have to help the learner to the realization of this problem – again by questioning rather than prescribing.

Stage 6 Assignment reviews

A final agreement at the meeting will be the number, extent and timing of reviews during the performance of the coaching task, and also the date of the final review. Although the interim, ongoing reviews will be more informal and reliant on the progress of the assignment, the format of the final review will usefully be determined at the initial meeting. This review will be based on the coaching assignment objectives and will be concerned not only with the completion of the task but also the learning achieved during the process. A review plan can be determined for the learner's continuing reference and use at the final review by the coach and the learner.

Stage 7 Implementation

Once the coach and the learner are satisfied with all the plans for the assignment, the task should start as soon as possible to avoid loss of momentum. This stage is in the hands of the learner, but the coach must make definite personal decisions *not* to interfere while the assignment is being undertaken. The learner must be given the opportunities to seek the guidance of the coach, but otherwise meetings between the coach and learner will be at the agreed reviews. The caveat to this must be that if the learner is seen to be going badly wrong, with no chance of redemption, then an intervention is essential. Also, an assignment must never be taken back from the learner because they are not progressing as the coach would wish – there must be a much stronger reason for doing this.

Stage 8 Review

The importance of interim and final reviews has been stressed as these are almost as important as the task itself, since they give both the coach and the learner the opportunity to reflect on, conclude about and plan the continuance of the assignment. Of similar significant importance is the final review, which will concentrate on *achievement of the task* and *the learning achieved*.

For the review to be useful to the learner the comments must be honest. If praise is due this must be given, not just implied and, equally, if performance has been wanting this too must be said. However, if a system of interim reviews has been effectively implemented there should be little of the latter involved.

What next?

Not everything in the assignment may have been done well, so part of the final review is a discussion and planning for an extension of the learner's development, perhaps with a further, similar task. Few coaching plans can stand alone with one assignment, and the review meeting can include agreement on what should then be done for this continuance and further development, in effect repeating the initial investigatory interview.

5

On-the-job Training and Development – 2

This chapter will:

- describe the further on-the-job training approaches available – 'sitting with Nellie' or training by exposure; one-to-one instruction; project management; mentoring; team development; delegation; and action learning.

ONE-TO-ONE INSTRUCTION

The one-to-one approach used to be referred to derogatively as 'sitting with Nellie' or more formally 'training by exposure'. A new worker or one changing jobs, was immediately placed alongside an experienced worker, told to watch what was done, then given their own machine and told to 'get on with it'. The amount of waste that must have occurred over the years that this 'approach' was practised must be astronomical, but it was a very common method, particularly in the clothing trade where sewing machines were used and it really was possible for the learner to sit beside 'Nellie'.

The realization that more effective training methods could: a) produce a more skilled worker in a shorter time; with b) less waste of materials, enabled the 'Nellie' method to be retained, but in a much improved form. This modern approach, generically known as 'one-to-one instruction' can in many cases be more effective than the 'artificiality' of training courses. To ensure that the method is effective, a number of criteria for the instructor must be satisfied:

- must be efficient and effective at the task/job in question;
- must have been taught how to instruct;

- must be given the necessary resources to enable the instruction to be performed;
- must be allowed sufficient time to prepare for and perform the training;
- must not be expected to maintain personal job output (eg no effect on bonus pay systems).

The extent to which individuals are dealt with in an organization will vary from one company to another. In larger companies a full-time instructor or instructors are found where there is a steady flow of people requiring training/instruction. (The borderline between 'instructor' and 'trainer' in these situations is very vague.)

In other situations the instructor is part time, and will concentrate on the instruction of individuals only on an occasional basis. The role of the part-time instructor can be more difficult than that of the full timer because of problems of continuity.

Criteria for effectiveness

The criteria necessary for effectiveness in one-to-one instruction include:

- a clear commitment to the philosophy of training and a real interest in creating the conditions for effective training;
- an insistence that the conditions are made available for the needs of the individual and the organization and the task or job has been fully investigated so that real and comprehensive objectives can be set (ie a preceding full TNIA);
- the instructor, if a part timer taken from production work, is willing to pass on their skills and knowledge to a learner;
- a clear, logical and comprehensive programme has been developed and established, to include content quantity and quality; appropriate locations of training and practice; relevant aids and resources; necessary time allowance; objective and (if possible) quantifiable standards are described;
- instruction will continue until the learner is capable of performing the task or job to the required standard;
- the learner's progress is monitored and evaluated;
- realistic support is guaranteed by more senior management.

The cycle of instruction

Following the normal TNIA processes, the cycle of one-to-one instruction can be summarized as:

1. Be fully aware of the apparent training need.
2. Obtain authority to proceed.
3. Identify a person or persons already skilled in the processes to be learned. Confirm that the person is also skilled in training and one-to-one instruction techniques – if they are not, it will be necessary to make arrangements for them to receive training in these techniques.
4. Unless it has already been done, analyse the job and/or task and produce a job/task specification.
5. Produce a person specification (again unless already produced in a TNIA).
6. Identify training gap.
7. Set specific, comprehensive training objectives.
8. Decide on the most appropriate training/instructional strategy.
9. Design an instructional event or obtain a relevant training package.
10. Produce instruction brief, instructional aids and handouts (or obtain manual).
11. Arrange instruction environment and other administration details.
12. Perform instructional event or issue training package.
13. The learner within the training area, or under the continuous supervision of 'Nellie', is allocated production tasks (preferably in small bites) to perform until they are ready to progress to full production work.
14. Review training and learning.
15. Reassess any instruction or learning needs.

Planning the instruction approach

It is essential that a one-to-one instructor is fully aware and capable of effective methods of instruction, and in this type of training it is essential that the learning steps are clear and in sufficiently small progression for easy understanding. This can be achieved by a detailed task step analysis produced prior to the instruction by the instructor.

Let us consider the task of making a cup of tea. Simple! Boil a kettle of water, place tea in a teapot, pour the water into the teapot, allow to brew, pour out the tea, add sugar and milk. But a moment's consideration will suggest that the task is not as simple as this and there are a number of questions to be answered. A fuller procedure could be as follows, the steps being sufficiently detailed for a learner who has never previously made a cup of tea:

1. Unplug the electric kettle from the socket.
2. Take the kettle to the cold tap and remove the lid.
3. Place the kettle under the tap, turn on the tap and fill the kettle.
4. Turn off tap and replace lid.
5. Return kettle to socket and reinsert the plug.
6. Switch on socket (if applicable) and switch on kettle, and while the kettle is coming to the boil.
7. Lay tray with cup, saucer, teaspoon, milk jug (filled with milk), sugar bowl (filled with white or brown sugar), sugar spoon.
8. Open receptacle that holds tea and check availability of measuring scoop.
9. When the kettle boils, take the teapot to the kettle and, having taken off teapot lid, pour in a little hot water.
10. Swirl hot water around in teapot until it is warm. Pour out water.
11. Replace kettle at socket and replace teapot lid.
12. Bring kettle to boil again.
13. While kettle is boiling a second time, place necessary tea in the teapot (having removed the lid) using tea scoop – one scoop per person and 'one for the pot'.
14. When kettle boils, take teapot to the kettle and fill the teapot to the appropriate level.
15. Replace teapot lid and return kettle to its own location.
16. Allow tea to stand in teapot for required time.
17. Place teapot on tray and take tray to person requiring the tea.
18. Either first add milk to cup and pour tea into cup, or pour tea into cup, allowing space for the milk, and add the milk to taste
19. Add sugar to taste from sugar bowl using sugar spoon. Stir tea with teaspoon until sugar has dissolved.

Planning instructional methods

The actual methods of instruction will, of course, depend what the instruction is to be given – mechanical operation, desk systems, computer operation etc – but in the majority of cases a traditional approach should be followed. This is known as the Tell – Show – Do system.

Example of mechanical operation instruction

With the learner seated beside the instructor at a special training machine, the instructor explains the operation, with relevant aids (most effectively the materials themselves) to the learner – the *tell* section. The instructor then *shows* the learner how the process works, describing again the operations as they are followed through and ensuring that there is full understanding (this stage may need to be repeated until understanding is achieved). Finally the learner practises the process themselves under the supervision of 'Nellie' – the *do* section of the instruction.

Following the initial practice of the operation by the learner, the instructor gives the learner feedback on their performance and, if necessary, the Do stage is repeated until the learner has achieved a satisfactory or agreed level.

Example of a more complex task, eg clerical or computer operation

The process for non-mechanical operation follows the one just described, the principal difference being, because of the more complex nature, the introduction of more stages or steps:

1. The instructor gives the learner a short talk describing the (new) procedure, its overall detail and the reason for its introduction. This can be followed by a general discussion between the instructor and the learner.
2. The manual and/or instruction sheets and any supporting documents can then be given to the learner, who should be given sufficient time, not to learn the instructions, but to become familiar with the procedures.
3. The instructor will have identified the main steps in the procedure and treat these as the staged, divisible learning points. Each stage can then be dealt with in a Tell – Show – Do manner, movement to the next stage only occurring when the instructor is satisfied with the understanding and skill of the learner.
4. After each stage the process and the learning should be discussed to ensure that any problems are resolved before moving on to the next stage.
5. After the final stage the full process and learning is discussed and any remaining problems resolved.
6. The learner can then be given a task (preferably a real one taken from work) to perform, using the new learning. An example of this, when, for example, computer programs are being taught, might be the production on Microsoft Word of a letter or report, in which the grammar and spelling have errors and inconsistencies and the format is not shown.
7. The final action is to discuss the practical session and the learning with the learner, giving feedback on their newly acquired skills and confirming any further action necessary.

If managed in this way the approach can be used with a wide range of occupational training – clerical procedures, reception duties, using office machinery, computer operation and programming, ancillary medical and dental duties and so on, in addition to the more practical tasks such as machine operating. It works most effectively with operations of a relatively routine and/or repetitive nature, although the same principles can be applied to the higher level complexities of training.

Designing training/instruction events

Instructional events have a duration of from three or four minutes to much longer periods, depending on the complexity of the task. However, all events need to be designed in exactly the same way, with individual differences of scale, and can follow a pattern:

1. introduction;
2. development;
3. consolidation.

The introductory period is self-evident and is essential as a settling-down period, the worst strategy being to launch immediately into the instruction. The learner may be feeling nervous with the environment, the situation, what is to ensue, and the instructor. Similarly, particularly if the instructor is only an infrequent, part-time instructor, there could be nervousness on the instructor's part, with the settling-in period also helping that person.

The development period is when the actual instruction takes place, following the guidelines suggested earlier. The Tell – Show – Do guideline is a basic rule to be followed, the other being KISS (Keep It Short and Simple). Few people can take in complex instructions in one bite – a five-course meal is more enjoyable and more easily eaten if each course is served separately rather than all the courses being served at the same time! So the preferred approach is to use small units of instruction in a natural, sequential order – the key teaching or learning points.

The consolidation stage: on too many occasions instruction finishes with a set of assumptions by the instructor:

- the instruction method used has been the most effective;
- the instructor has performed in the most effective way;
- the learner has learned as required;
- the objectives have been satisfied;
- the learning is implemented at work.

These assumptions need to hold true, and can be tested by simple observation of the learning implementation against the objectives.

PROJECT MANAGEMENT

Project management is a task and management tool in itself, but it also has a place in on-the-job training alternatives. It follows on naturally from coaching, either as a coaching tool or as real-works tasks to be practised following a coaching approach. With its closeness to coaching as a training and development approach it has similar procedures, and the planning will include:

- the identification of the learners and their particular needs;
- the satisfaction that the learner has sufficient skill and/or experience to enable them to carry out the project and learn from the experience;
- the identification of suitable projects ;
- discussion and agreement of the project and its management activities and objectives with the learner;
- discussion of methods and approaches with the delegated project managers, giving supportive advice as necessary;
- agreeing levels of authority and responsibility where a project team is involved, the manager retaining the final responsibility for the success of the project;
- agreeing starting and finishing dates; interim review dates; and a final review and reporting date at the end of the project;
- discussion of the learning achieved by the event and consideration of future action.

Using projects and project management is most usefully performed with the more skilled and experienced workers, as a significant amount of responsibility is held by the person completing the project or acting as project leader. Other similar reasons include:

- giving the person the new experience of following a project through;
- giving the person the opportunity to manage a group of people in order to perform the project;
- using the project approach for special learning situations.

As an example of the last-named, as a training manager I was asked by my director to pair with a psychologist and complete a project relating to the relationships between the trainers and the support psychologists, a matter that had been causing some concern. This was the particular specific objective, but there was also a secondary one that related to the psychologist, whose work experience had always been as an individual worker but who needed to obtain experience of cross-discipline working, something in which she had shown herself as not too effective. As the project proceeded she realized that her individualistic approaches were not helping the support role in which she now found herself, that she had to take positive behavioural steps to modify this and to develop cross-cultural/discipline relationships. I too learned that I had developed ingrained attitudes about psychologists that were obviously completely unfounded. We both found this a particularly effective approach and learning event.

MENTORING

Planning for mentoring involves similar approaches to those for coaching, but on a wider organizational scale. Whereas coaching is usually applied to operative and similar tasks, mentoring is an approach that has application to the higher levels and/or more complex situations. Mentoring can be managed in a number of different ways, and part of the planning process is to decide which method will be the most effective. However, the more normal approach is for one experienced person to act, usually over an extended period, as the mentor, supporter, adviser, event arranger, etc for the learner.

One example of mentoring might be with a newly appointed management trainee. Following more formal induction training and following or running alongside management training, a departmental line manager or series of managers might be appointed in a progressive plan as mentors to the trainee. During the period of mentoring the mentor and learner would have a close association, during which arrangements might be made for the learner to:

- shadow the mentor for a period of time;
- undertake some of the mentor's tasks (under supervision and with coaching);
- complete projects – artificial and real – set up by the mentor;
- attend training events suggested by the mentor;
- discuss a range of relevant topics with the mentor;
- follow a planned programme of visits to various departments, either simply as visits or for periods of secondment (under the supervision of the mentor linking with the department head);
- have review and forward planning meetings with the mentor.

An important aspect of the mentoring process is the identification and selection of suitable mentors, because they must be highly committed themselves, not only to the organization but also to the active support of the learners. Mentoring will at times make substantial inroads into their time and resourcefulness, but one pay-off, as described regularly by mentors, is the satisfaction of seeing their learners progressing upwards in the organization, knowing they had a significant role in helping this progression.

TEAM DEVELOPMENT

The essence of teamwork is that all the members of the team work together towards a common goal, each member relating to the others and their roles, respecting each other's abilities and disabilities in their progression towards completion of the task. The team members of an effective team are also interested and active in the team development process. This involves not only the team's progress towards completion of the task but also the development of each member and, where relevant, good interrelationships with other teams in the organization.

The team process was well expressed in a simple model by John Adair (1986), as shown in Figures 5.1 and 5.2. The basis of the model is that the team process consists of three factors.

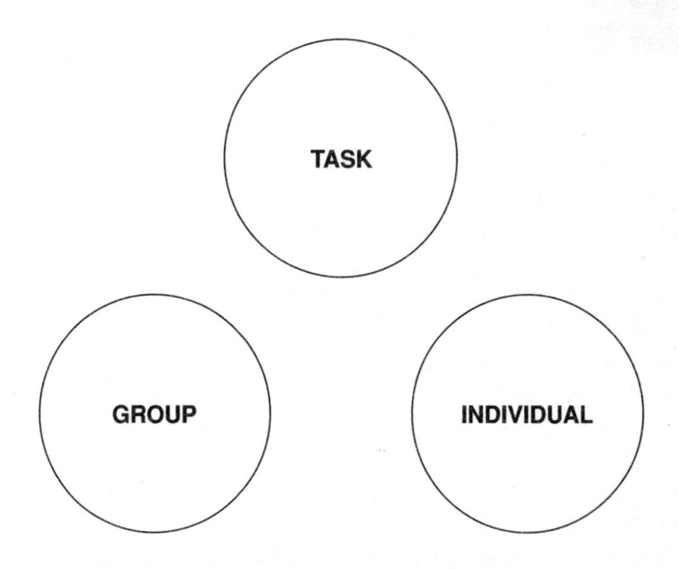

Figure 5.1 *The three factors of the team process*

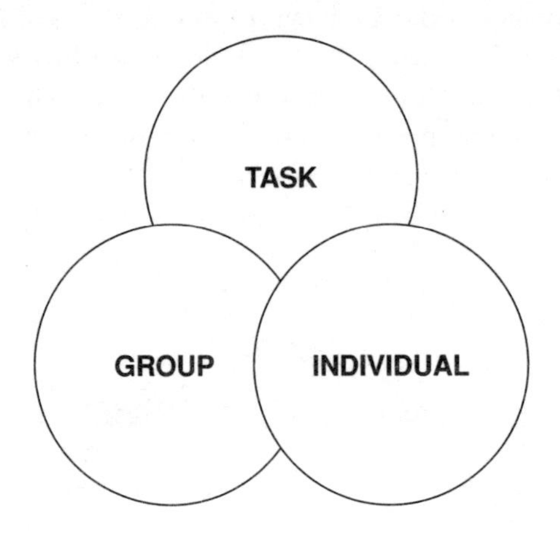

Figure 5.2 *The three factors of the team process*

Although any team contains these three factors, the team is not effective if they are isolated factors, rather they should be considered as mutually dependent, overlapping areas. This is demonstrated in Figure 5.2.

If the team members concentrate only on the task, the feelings, needs and development of the individuals are ignored and there will be reactions by the team members, usually to the detriment of achieving of the task. If only the needs of the *group* receive attention the task completion will suffer and the individuals might not all be in tune and not support the group needs and what is being done for them. If the concentration is on the individuals the time spent can jeopardize the achievement of the task and the group may not develop as a complete team. However, if the needs of the task, the group and the individuals are treated in a balanced manner task achievement and human resource progress are much more likely.

Teams do not just happen. A new 'team' starts as a group of people performing jobs towards the completion of a task, but basically seeing themselves as individuals in this process, probably because it had been expedient to form them into this group. A group such as this, where it has common goals and objectives and requires the interrelationship and co-support of each member, is ripe for team development, a process that will result in an efficient, effective and cohesive team. But, as said above, 'teams do not just happen', they need a planned, logical programme of development.

A number of concepts and models of team development have been produced over the years, the earliest being with the research of Mayo in the 1920s in the 'Hawthorne Experiment' and, later, a classification of the categories of team members – a rather arbitrary classification. These and other research programmes show that teams, to develop, move from a *forming* stage, through *storming* and *norming* to the end stage of *performing*. This is illustrated in Figure 5.3.

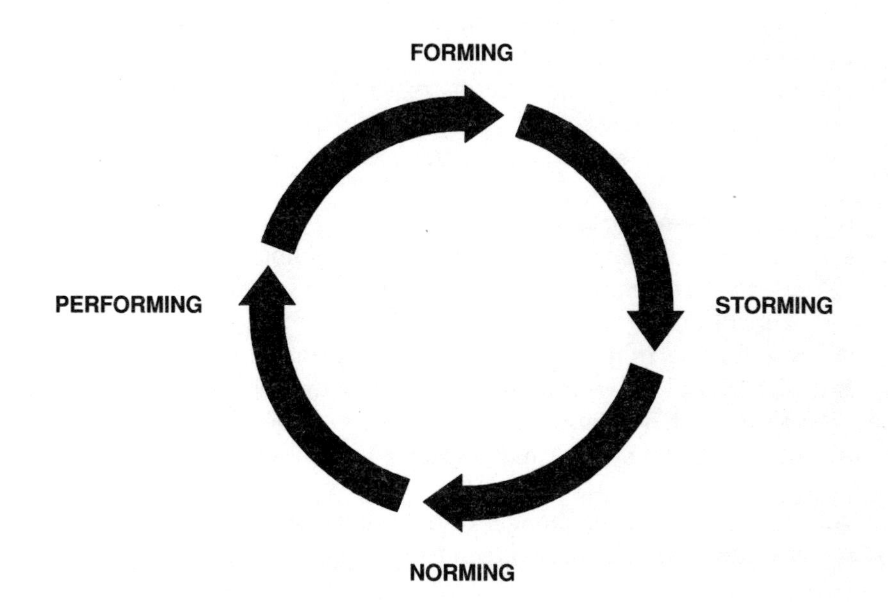

Figure 5.3 *The four stages of group/team development*

Each stage is unique and separate, and team members exhibit particular behaviours which, if identified and discussed, can help the team to progress through the various stages.

In the *forming* stage, the behaviours exhibited include:

- being formal and polite with each other, with internal feelings of whether they will be accepted by the rest of the group;
- contributions are rarely contentious or controversial – 'Let's not rock the boat';
- keeping contributions to a minimum – 'If I let people get to know me too much, they might not like me';
- avoiding serious contributions – 'They may think I'm an egghead';
- avoiding disclosure;
- not commenting on others' views or giving feedback.

The types of behaviour described might suggest another title for this stage – that of *avoiding*, although as the stage continues these behaviours start to be minimized and modified.

When the group/team has been together for a little time the barriers start to come down and the behaviours start to represent the true attitudes of the members – attitudes that can be affected by a wide range of factors not connected with the event, but having an interactive effect. This *storming* stage is when the members are starting to say to themselves, 'I'm not going to sit here like this for the whole event. So here goes...' and in many cases the forming behaviours reverse themselves and the stage is characterized by:

- the expression of strong views;
- challenges made to the views of other members;
- restricted listening to the views of others, with increased own contribution;
- resolute reactivity, attacking and defending;
- withdrawal by some members, particularly if they become victims or have their views disagreed with;
- challenges by several members for leadership and control of the group;
- overt and active challenges to the trainer or team leader;
- emotions taking over from considered behaviour.

This stage can become so stormy that a large number of the members just give up and the team never matures beyond this point. But if the members are helped to consider their attitudes, behaviours and objectives, progress can start to be made. If this is successful the cliques and sub-groups start to dissolve and a sense of team identity starts to emerge. The typical behaviours in the *norming* stage include:

- sharing of leadership according to individual abilities;
- listening and receptiveness to the ideas of others;
- active participation and contribution by all, even the quieter members;
- non-participators being brought into discussions and activities;
- an open exchange of ideas;
- dealing with any conflict of ideas or proposals as win-win rather than win-lose
- easy self-disclosure;
- looking towards a more methodical way of working, with methods agreed by the group.

The positive approach in the *norming* stage, when the team is maturing and realizing the benefits of working together, leads naturally into the final stage, *performing*. This is the mature stage of the team in which there is intense loyalty to the group (this is a danger that has to be watched carefully as the team can become too closed and fail to improve inter-team relationships). Some of the indicative behaviours for this stage include:

- less dependency on structure and rules;
- accepting individual actions more readily as talents that will help the team;
- high creativity and flexibility;
- openness and trust between the members and the team leader;
- strong relationships and supportive behaviour;
- feelings of 'belonging' to a family;
- recognizing and accepting individual failing, and offering support;
- willingness to discuss failings and learn from these as well as successes.

Team roles

An essential element in the development of teams that must be included in the planning is concerned with who forms part of the team. The team members can be identified as performing various roles – not necessarily only one role per member – and an effective team must contain members who are capable of fulfilling these roles. A number of researchers have produced models of team roles, but the one I have found most pragmatic and practically useful is that by Margerison and McCann (1984). They suggest a model of team behaviour based on eight main roles within an effective team and show these as directly related to the key work functions in a team:

1. *Advising* – the role function in which information is obtained and disseminated;
2. *Innovating* – proposing experimentation with new ideas;
3. *Promoting* – the search for and persuasion of others to engage in new opportunities;
4. *Developing* – the testing of the applicability of new ideas and their development;
5. *Organizing* – the functional establishment and implementation of the ways and means of getting things done;
6. *Producing* – establishing systems and operating them on a regular basis;

7. *Inspecting* – the essential checking and auditing of progress functions to ensure that installed systems are working effectively;
8. *Maintaining* – ensuring that standards and processes within and without the system are maintained.

These terms can be applied equally to tasks and people roles. When a new task has to be performed by the team, the logical and effective path would be an initial search by the *adviser* for precedents, research, other practices and so on. If they have not already been set down, the *innovator* offers or produces options for methods, procedures, systems and practices. The creative ideas will be picked up by the *promoter*, who will try to sell them within the team; the options being assessed by the *developer*, who will also suggest ways of achieving them. The next stage is the pragmatic one and it will be the *organizer* who will press for action to be taken on the agreed items, this action being taken over by the *producer* to ensure that there is an outcome and that the schedules and plans are implemented. Once the system is up and running the *inspector* ensures that the agreed systems, etc are being followed accurately, with the *maintainer* the one who ensures that the wheels continue to run smoothly.

These are not necessarily discrete roles and people are not given the titles. Rather they act naturally within the roles, more than one person usually fulfilling more than one role. But it is the essence of team development that the role functions are all present and fulfilled in some way – team training is planned to ensure this overall coverage. It may be that some role figures are missing from the team, so steps need to be taken to develop in members the missing skills, even though they may be alien behaviours.

Team development and learning activities can be held both on and off-the-job, the planning requirements being very similar in both cases. On-the-job team development utilizes the involvement of the whole team in tasks that not only require real solutions in the course of the team work but can also be used as learning situations. This is usually processed by the team leader allocating work time for the team to meet and discuss the project/task they have taken part in, its successes or problems, the participation and roles of the team members, any learning that evolved from the task, and an action plan for the future. Similar learning discussion events can also be planned to be held at the end of the regular team meetings. After the meeting proper a more informal discussion meeting is held so that the various aspects of team process and development raised by the meeting can be considered. These might be the level of participation in the meeting by the team members; an analysis of the behaviour pattern of the meeting; interpersonal agreements made between the members to 'do more of, do less of, continue doing' various aspects of their behaviour, etc. A planned pattern of meetings such as this can be considered so that the team has the opportunity to meet regularly for purposes other than direct task fulfilment and to give an opportunity for them to speak openly about the team and support each other.

More specific training events for the team can be held away from work; team development training along with other group training methods are considered later in Chapters 7 and 8.

DELEGATION

Delegation is normally seen as a mechanism used by supervisors and managers either to control their time management or simply to get rid of some of their work. But it can be a powerful training tool at work, especially when combined with the coaching process.

It is not an easy process to introduce, however, as there are strong barriers raised against it, and hence it requires considerable planning before it is instituted. But these barriers can be overcome and if it is introduced with care it can be a strong aid to the development of individuals at work.

Delegation can be defined as the structured and controlled allocation of the supervisor's/manager's tasks or parts of tasks to subordinates for the purpose of enabling learning to take place. The learning is usually either for remedial or pure developmental learning purposes.

Barriers to delegation

The common barriers to delegation include the following.

It's my job to do the work: after all I'm the supervisor/manager

It is not job of the supervisor or manager to *do* the work, rather to ensure that it is done. There are certainly tasks that *must* be done by the boss, but if they try to do everything they will succeed at very little. The role of a manager is to ensure that the work for which they are responsible is performed – this means utilizing the time, skills and experience of others whenever it is possible and/or appropriate. If others are given work of a higher nature than that to which they are accustomed, and they are supported, guided and advised in this, not only will the task be performed, but learning will result.

How do I know what to delegate?

The simple answer to this is that almost any of the manager's tasks can be delegated, whether as a full task or broken down into appropriate and manageable chunks. The manager is personally responsible for some tasks – eg appraisal of subordinates, people reports to senior management – but there are many that do not require personal attention. These are tasks that are ripe for delegation.

By the time I've explained it, I could have done it myself!

Of course you could have done it yourself, but think of the training/learning opportunities that would be lost if it were a delegatable task. The first time a job is delegated a significant amount of time is involved in planning and setting it up, but on each successive occasion the time required becomes less until there is no expenditure of management time. Then you will have more time to do the jobs that you have to do.

How do I know it will be done right?

The responsibility for the effectiveness of the task remains the manager's, but if authority and agreed responsibilities are given for the project and a series of reviews is installed there will be no loss of control and straying from the path will not be allowed to carry on for too long. But do not keep on looking over their shoulder, otherwise you might be told 'You might as well do it yourself if you don't trust me!'

If I show them what to do, they'll be after my job

And why not? If your staff are sufficiently skilled and experienced to feel they could do your job they will be performing their own efficiently and effectively. When you are promoted you will leave your old post knowing that it will stay in good hands and it will reflect well on you at any stage if others say 'So-and-so (a member of your staff) must be good; they come from (your) unit'. And remember it may even be possible that they will pass you going up the ladder, and you will have another friend at court.

It's too risky

If you give some of your work to a subordinate, who by the nature of the exercise is less skilled than you are, there will always be some element of risk. But the wise delegator takes care in planning – selection of the right person for the right task; ensuring that any necessary training is given; holding a full discussion with the delegatee about the task and how they might go about it; and, above all, agreement on interim and final review meetings. The decision must be made as to whether any remaining risk is worth taking. The delegatee must know where the final responsibility lies – with you – and if there are problems you will get the blame; but success will also rebound on you. So in both cases 'The buck stops here'.

But I enjoy doing it myself

Of course you do, and if you examine the work you do you will almost certainly find that the tasks you enjoy most are the ones you do first; the least enjoyable ones are the ones you put off – the former are also probably the least urgent and important – one of the first lessons learned in time management! There is every likelihood that if you find certain tasks enjoyable so will a delegatee, and this will be part of the recipe for their success, certainly at least for the first few delegated tasks.

I daren't just sit and think – I've got to be seen to be doing something

Delegation will give the manager more time to sit and think and plan, but many people feel uncomfortable when they can be seen doing apparently nothing (and this is often part of the organization's culture). If this worries you once you have given yourself more time, always sit with a pencil in your hand and a piece of paper in front of you (if you're not actually writing anything, have something already written on the paper!). Also, if as a result of your delegation and other training actions the work of your department improves, let others know how you did it.

They might do it better than me!

Great! You can't be master of everything, and current advances in technology certainly increase the likelihood of this being true. By delegation and other means build up around you a group of 'experts' in a range of disciplines and skills to whom more and more difficult tasks can be delegated. Most of your staff will respect the trust you put in them and the opportunities for them to develop.

They might not like me giving them my work

Much will depend on how you introduce delegation and how well you operate it, with the maximum advantages to your staff seen by them. In most cases your staff will welcome these opportunities and will respect your management skills in arranging them.

The process of delegation

One of the commonest reasons why delegation fails is because it has been introduced with insufficient thought and planning. The delegation process benefits from a logical format, the principal elements of introducing it including:

1. *Tasks to delegate*
   - What do you want to delegate?
   - What can you delegate?
2. *Who should do it and why? You:*
   - To improve your staff's performance and motivation.
   - To develop your staff's knowledge and skills.
   - To reduce your personal workload at the same time as developing your staff.
   - Are there any strong resistors?
3. *Meet the delegatee*
   - Agree willingness.
   - Describe the task.
   - Test understanding.
   - Discuss how the task might be performed.
   - Agree training.
   - Agree progress reviews.
   - Agree deadline and final review.
4. *Task implementation*
   - Establish interim review.
   - Don't interfere.
   - Don't take back a delegated task unless unavoidably forced to do so.
5. *Final review and evaluation*
   - How did it go?
   - What learning was achieved?
   - What else is now needed?
6. *Self-evaluation as delegator*
   - How well did you delegate?
   - Would you repeat the process?

Many of these actions and methods of achieving them are very similar to those of the coaching process, and the task and the delegatee should be approached in the same way as the coaching task and the person being coached; after all delegation can form a significant part of a coaching assignment.

ALTERNATIVE ON-THE-JOB TRAINING APPROACHES

The approaches described so far for on-the-job training have involved the instructor or some form of leader or manager in direct contact during the learning period with the learner. This is the traditional method, but more recent, more remote training innovations can be as effective, if not more so, and in some cases can be more cost and value effective. However the case for these possibilities is not proven, and all situations must be considered for the most relevant and/or appropriate approach.

The alternative training approaches include:

- books;
- text-based, open learning packages;
- interactive video programmes;
- multi-media packages;
- computer-based training programs (CBT).

These approaches will be described in the next chapter.

6

Alternative On-the-job Training Approaches

This chapter will describe on-the-job training approaches that are alternatives to the direct contact methods described in the two preceding chapters, and will include comments on:

- secondments and job rotation;
- action learning;
- books;
- open learning packages;
- video programmes;
- computer-assisted (CAT) and computer-based (CBT) training programs.

SECONDMENTS AND JOB ROTATION

These two approaches involve no training as such, but rely on the performance of work in different ways to enable the learner to develop. These are development approaches for people with some experience rather than a training programme in the recognized sense.

Secondments

Where development is being planned for an individual who has reached at least satisfactory level in their present role secondment to another section or department can be considered. Apart from the occasions when secondment takes place for organizational contingency reasons, this temporary transfer of a learner to another role in another area of work extends their knowledge and skills and, consequently, gives them a broader base for advancement.

When secondment is being considered, the planner (trainer or line manager) considers two principal factors: 1) the development needs of the individual; and 2) the development opportunities offered by a suitable secondment.

For the first of these two considerations it will be necessary for the full range of skills of the individual to be assessed and the decision made that development will be best approached by secondment, or is desirable for some other reason. Where these considerations are positive it is usually because the person is sufficiently skilled in all the roles that they need in their present location and show every ability to assimilate the work of other roles in different departments of work.

The potential place of secondment must also be considered. The first step must be agreement with the manager of that area that secondment is possible for development reasons and the seconded person will be treated in this way, rather than as a dogsbody putting in time there. A planned, progressive programme of learning and experience with time bounds should be agreed, and regular reviews arranged for the learner with both the original line manager and the line manager of the 'new' department.

The new department manager should ensure that his or her staff are made fully aware of what is happening, and why, and every attempt made to overcome any suspicions by the existing staff (sometimes difficult) – 'Oh, somebody's coming in to learn our jobs so they can get rid of us', 'It's going to make extra work for us seeing that this person doesn't foul up the system', and so on. Openness and honesty are the order of the day for this purpose and a useful move is to have the 'secondee' meet the new staff before the secondment actually starts.

When the provisional arrangements have been agreed, final agreement should be made with the individual, who of course will have been involved in the preliminary discussions.

Job rotation

Job rotation within a department or section commonly takes place for reasons of contingency or expediency, for example when a job holder leaves or is promoted. But it can also be used as a deliberate approach in the development of members of staff. In the ideal situation every person would rotate to every other job so that in time every member of staff becomes multi-skilled and able to take over as necessary any of the jobs in the work area. In practice, this ideal is rarely attained – people leave and upset the plan; work emergencies halt the process; and, unfortunately more commonly, there is resistance by some of the staff to leave their 'safe' jobs for the uncertainties of learning another and/or the suspicion that this is a management ploy to increase their workload without recompense.

Planning and introduction of a developmental, work rotation scheme has to be approached with circumspection and, in a similar atmosphere to that of secondment, all the staff must be informed in an open and honest manner, giving them every opportunity to have their say and have their fears and suspicions allayed. Several of these initial motivation and commitment meetings need to be planned before interviews are held to obtain individual views and, hopefully, agreement. A rotation plan with timings should be produced, displayed and agreed, and (what may take a substantial period of time in many cases) job descriptions produced or brought up to date.

Contingency plans need to be made for such events as people leaving, being promoted, being absent on sick leave and so on, although these cannot be firm in their details until these events actually happen. However, a general contingency policy can be formulated, ready for detailed operation whenever necessary.

The ideal behind a completely multi-disciplined workforce also ensures that every worker is aware of the work and problems of others, thus helping the development of a team attitude. Finally, it ensures that each individual is developed within the range of the department to their maximum abilities and is given the opportunity to use and develop these abilities. They become people with broader attitudes and more skills, which makes them much more promotable. Job rotation helps them to develop as individuals and, with a wider range of job skills and experience, they are much more likely to become satisfied workers.

Managers who wish to introduce this system must not assume that it will be easy – without a history of manager/worker trust and openness there will be a mountain of suspicion to overcome. So in many cases it might be looked on as a long-term process, developing the necessary atmosphere before considering the introduction of the method.

ACTION LEARNING

Action learning can be considered a half-way house approach between training and instruction and absolute self-development. It is a group approach to learning developed by Reg Revans in the 1950s, originally with a group of colliery managers. It uses real-life problems, solving these through action research with consequent learning as a result. A number of variations exist, ranging from the group identifying and solving a common problem, through the group electing to solve a problem owned by one of their members, to individual members working on their own problems but using the set as a sounding board and support.

The action learning set meets regularly, the two full group approaches more frequently than when the concentration is on the individuals' method. The value of the meetings, in whatever format, is the opportunity for different interpretations and ideas to be made available and help with research by more than one person. If the use of instrumentation is intended, the set members can be used as guinea pigs for questionnaires or tests.

The principal danger can be that the task solution becomes the only objective; how the set members interact, how research is performed and reported, how solutions are proposed and considered and how the final solution is reached are all potential learning areas and must be kept in mind. It is essential that meetings are planned during the life of the set for these aspects to be reviewed along with the task progress, and a final meeting will review the overall learning and its implementation.

The 'half-way house' aspect is because the set has a responsible 'set adviser', whose purpose is to arrange the set and help the members in the early stages, but to gradually withdraw from an active role, being available whenever the set might request help or advice. Part of the learning intention of a set is to develop the means of operating independently, and the set adviser will encourage this. The set adviser will even withdraw whenever possible from being involved in specific learning needs, encouraging the set members to take these on themselves. In one set in which I was involved as set adviser the set needed to write an important report, but were unsure about their ability to produce a sufficiently impactive document. One of the set members was superb at written work and so, when the set started their report they arranged themselves some informal written skills teach-ins facilitated by the skilled member, and the report was eventually produced through the workshops.

SUPPORT GROUPS

Action learning need not be as formal as described above, and learning can be planned to take place through what are usually referred to as support groups. These are semi-formal groups with participating volunteers with similar interests who want to share their knowledge, skills and experience. Frequently these sessions are held during the lunch period away from the canteen or restaurant, with the members coming from a single part of the organization or as a heterogeneous group from various parts of the company. The meetings, once initiated, can be as regular or irregular, frequent or infrequent, formal or informal as the members themselves decide. If the members wish, the content of the discussions can extend beyond their own or other work areas to general life situations from which the members can learn. Some groups, realizing the benefits of some measure of control, elect chairpersons, often on a rotating basis – this is yet another learning opportunity.

QUALITY CIRCLES

Quality circles are very similar in composition and implementation to action learning sets, and are set up in organizations with groups, usually from the same section, department or discipline, under the leadership of a supervisor or manager. The circles meet in work time and commonly start by looking at existing problems identified within the work or discipline area, perhaps selected by the manager or senior managers. As the circle progresses and these initial problems are dealt with, the circle itself identifies further problems that they can consider.

Many of the circle members may have had little experience or training in the skills of identifying, analysing, solving problems and decision making and resultant presentations of findings. By working through these problems, the circle leader will ensure that learning results as well as achievement of the task, the pragmatic solution of the problem being the fundamental reason for the circle.

Although similar in many ways to an action learning set, the end result emphasis of the quality circle is different – task solution with peripheral learning compared with using a task as the learning vehicle. Both however share two factors – application to real-life problems and events at work with learning taking place in the process.

BOOKS

Learning can be achieved without the involvement, or only minimal involvement of other people, and the basic method by which this can be achieved is learning from a book or manual. However, this can be a difficult and/or lonely process, either because of the lack of clarity in the material or because the concept is too difficult to accept from the written word. In spite of this a significant amount of learning takes place from the reading of books and they are still an important and effective form of learning. They require motivation to start the process and to continue in spite of all the difficulties, but as a result this intention to learn aids the process. Their true effectiveness depends entirely on the learner's skills in understanding and the author's clarity and teaching skill.

Four aids that are recommended to the lone book learner are:

1. Don't try to learn the material in one chunk. Separate the book material into learnable chunks and do not pass on to the next until you are certain you have assessed a section properly.
2. Make your own learning notes as you read.
3. Practise the learning and translate the knowledge into practical skills as soon as possible.
4. Discuss the material and the learning to ensure that your interpretations have been correct.

Patterned notetaking

The suggestion above about making learning notes can unfortunately, with some people, produce almost as many notes as the original text. Most students will have encountered this, particularly at revision time when they are faced by a mountain of facts. One way of avoiding this is to use the patterned notetaking method developed by the master of creativity, Tony Buzan. Alternative words for the technique include spidergrams or mind maps, the latter because the format of the notes is intended to replicate the non-linear action of the brain. This action is much more chaotic than a 'logical' vertical format starting at the top and working down to the bottom, but within the apparent chaos a definite pattern can be identified.

The patterned note takes us away from the regular, logical format and produces a record in a pattern that replicates the working of the mind. Because the pattern produced is directly related to the individual producing it the patterns can be highly individualistic and perhaps unintelligible to others. This is perfectly acceptable, as in most cases the notes are intended for the use of the notetaker only.

A variety of formats can be used, the criterion being that they are meaningful to the notetaker, even after a long period of time. The problem, however, is that because they are written very much in a shorthand form, they can only be triggers to the memory of the full material. Colours can be effective, as can symbols enclosing parts of the note, eg a key part of the note can be contained within the shape of a key. Arrows from one part of the note to another can link similar or related subjects. The most important part of the construction of the note is the identification and summarizing of the key elements of the material being read – these are the triggers for the memory when the note is being used later.

A patterned note of key words or short phrases can be contained in a small space, say one sheet of A4 paper. This itself introduces a potential problem as notemakers can tend to try to put too much material on one sheet, the resulting complexity causing as much problem as the original material. One approach is to use one sheet for each chapter of the book or, if the chapter is complex, a sheet for each of the major components. Figure 6.1 demonstrates a 'typical' patterned note of the type I produce for my own use.

OPEN LEARNING PACKAGES

Open learning packages are in some ways the modern equivalent of the correspondence courses that have been with us for many years (and still exist for those who find this their best learning medium). In these a particular subject was studied – initially knowledge based, but eventually practical learning was included – and the student was supplied with text material that they had to read and learn. Then the course supplier sent them question papers or other instructions – 'Write a 1,000-word essay on *x*'; 'Answer the following set of questions'; 'Construct a 3-D wooden model from the 2-D drawing on page 7 of the notes'; etc. The tasks were performed, returned to the supplier who marked and commented on them, and moved them on to the next stage. This process, in the earlier days of correspondence courses, could last a substantial period of time as a result of the passing of lessons, the answers and the marking by post. This process can be speeded up today using e-mail.

Open learning or, as it is otherwise called, distance learning, has the same basis as the correspondence course, which is recognizable in these new forms. In open learning a self-learning package is purchased containing some or all of the following:

- a set of text-based learning material;
- a pre-recorded audio tape (perhaps with a set of 35mm slides for simultaneous projection);
- an interactive video;
- a CD, CD-ROM or interactive CD-ROM.

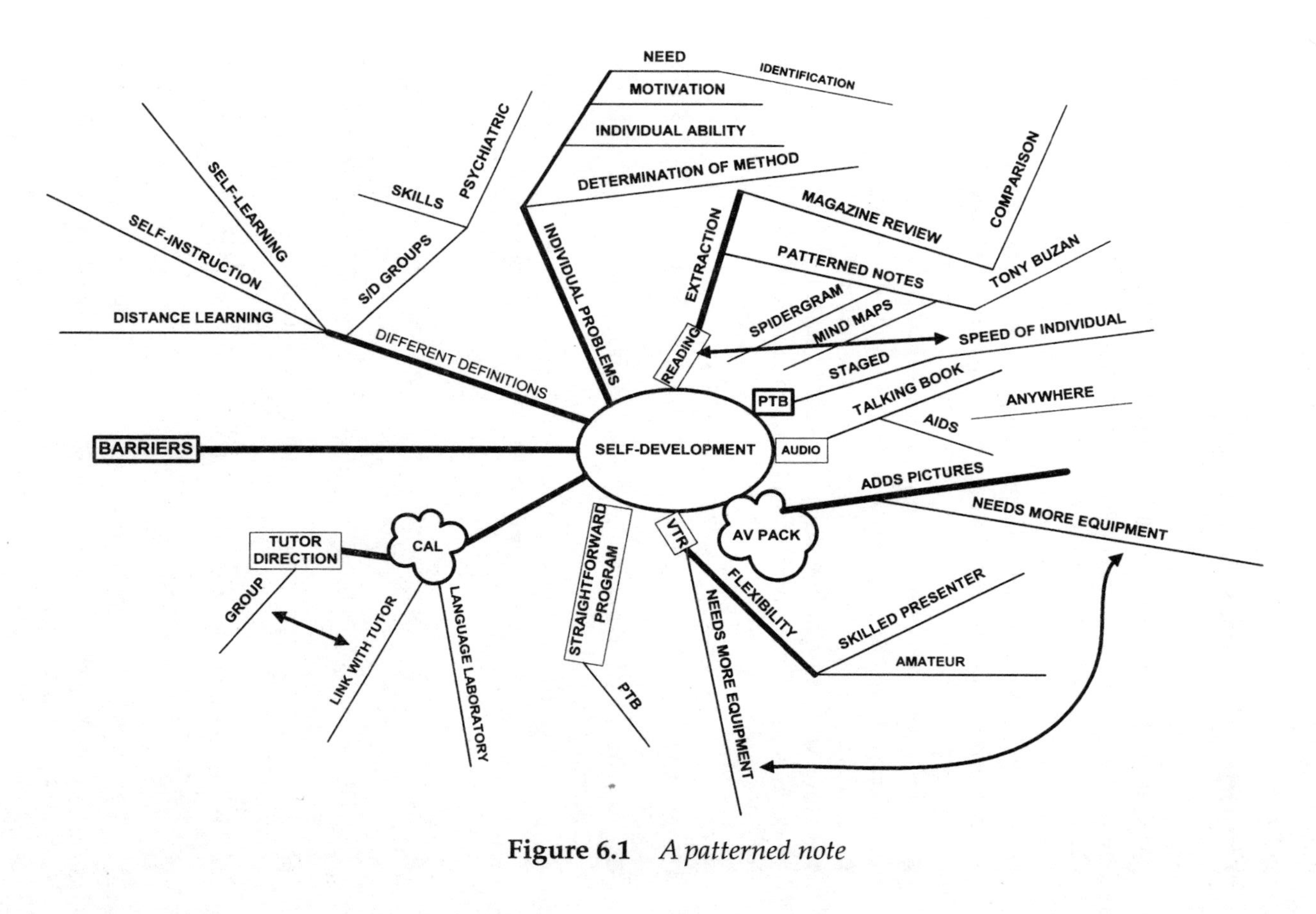

Figure 6.1 *A patterned note*

These programmes are basically intended for use by the solo, self-developing learner or by a group of learners, thus enabling a strong measure of mutual support.

Planning for open learning

The planner who is considering introducing an open learning package into a programme or organization will need to ensure that the package being considered is the best one for the situation. Questions that should be asked include:

- To what extent has the concept of open learning the support of the organization – senior management, line management, training department?
- Which type of open learning package will be the most suitable? (Descriptions of some of the different types follow this checklist.)
- Is this the best method of learning for this learner?
- How well are the package objectives stated? These should be sufficiently clear for the learners to understand them without difficulty.
- What is the balance between knowledge learning and practical activities? Skill will not be attained from a knowledge-only package.
- Are the activities and tasks pitched at the appropriate level for the learning population?
- What inclusion is there for feedback to the learner on the success or otherwise of their practical work? Will it be possible for the learner to determine *why* they have gone wrong if this is the case?
- Does the material provided in the package need to be supplemented in any way? (This may be the addition of more advanced material or material appropriate to the organization and its special needs.)
- Does the material provided need to be amended in any other way – eg some parts removed or deleted?
- Is the material structured effectively and should it cause minimal problems?
- What are the licensing arrangements? Is the use of the package restricted to one learner only or is multiple learner use approved – with or without the purchase of a relevant licence? What are the arrangements for material copying – a site licence?
- Are the materials up to date and complete for the purpose intended?

- How long does the package take to meet learning needs? Is the supplier's statement of this reliable? (This can be tested by a dummy run with a non-learner or the trainer him/herself.) Will the required time be (made) available?

Consequently planning the introduction of open learning to a learner or group of learners must be performed carefully, considering specific questions relating to the suitability of the learning package itself:

- Do I know about the availability of packages of the nature required? How do I know which package is the most suitable one for this purpose?
- Do I know anybody who has used this package and who can evaluate it?
- Has there been a published evaluation of the package and is this valid?
- What arrangements are there for learner/supplier contact?
- Can the organization produce its own package? Has the organization people who have the necessary open learning authoring skills? Has the organization a supply of experts to respond to learners with problems?

Text-based open learning

As suggested above, an open learning package can contain text-based materials designed to help personal learners work through them, learn and follow activities to consolidate the learning. These texts are usually in the form of programmed learning, written in impactive phrases and checklist blocks, rather than the flowing (sometimes long-winded) text found in normal books. Self-tests are included so that the learners can check their progress and the programme is completed by a self-evaluation instrument.

The principal criticisms levelled against these programmes are that:

- Not every learner can learn best from this text-based approach.
- Considerable motivation and determination is needed to complete the programme.
- Solo learning can be a very lonely process, the loneliness acting against easier learning.
- The training material is prescriptive and there is no opportunity to discuss the material of clarify misunderstanding and disagreement – fortunately some packages offer the opportunity for

learners to telephone or e-mail the supplier for these purposes, particularly where the 'supplier' might be the organization's central training department. A trainer in this location may be designated as the open learning contact to help learners in non-understanding or disagreements.

- Even if the learning is concerned with work subjects, time at work to follow the programme is not always given, or is not given freely.

MULTI-MEDIA OPEN LEARNING PACKAGES

Audio cassettes

Few open learning packages nowadays consist solely of text material, the earlier inclusions being audio cassettes. The learner listens to the audio cassette about the subject or part of the subject, perhaps reading the text at the same time and answering the questions posed on the cassette (answers are then usually found in the text material). This is a simple extension to the text and, in fact, the audio cassette can be used alone for open learning purposes. The cassette can be played anywhere that there is a suitable audio player. Few people however have the patience to sit and simply listen to a spoken cassette unless the material is particularly riveting or the presenter is very charismatic. One alternative is to play the cassette in the car while the learner is travelling to and from home or to work appointments (even in the all-too frequent traffic jams!).

Audio tapes are simple and cheap and a wide range of subjects is available commercially, including tapes of speakers at conferences and seminars. They are easily produced within an organization by an expert on the subject – the planning of such a tape must include ensuring the material is presented effectively by a presenter with an acceptable presentation manner.

Audio-visual packages

Audio cassettes alone have the disadvantage described above of being completely passive and without a real centre of attention – it is difficult to sit and look at a cassette when it is in the player! With universal TV we are used to having something to look at while we listen. An effective centre of attention is provided by the audio-visual package. In addition to the audio cassette and any supporting workbooks, the package also includes a number of 35 mm transparencies. These slides are intended for projection while the cassette is being played. Obviously there must be some indication when the slides have to be changed: this can be annotation in an accompanying script or the addition to the tape of an audible signal – usually a bleep or musical note. With a simple addition to the slide projector, an inaudible 1 kHz pulse is transmitted to the projector when the slide needs changing. This pulse is added to the tape when it is being produced, and obviates the need to have an audible signal that might annoy the listener(s). The most effective piece of equipment for marrying the slide and the tape is a combined tape-slide presenter that includes a cassette player, slide projection system and a screen on which the slide picture is displayed. The pulse coded tape signals the changes automatically and the resulting picture can be viewed on the integral screen (or projected onto a traditional screen) while the audio material is being listened to over the built-in speaker system.

Like the text-based package or the audio cassette approach alone, a considerable amount of planning and preparation is necessary for a production such as this, for once the pre-arranged programme starts it can only be varied by stopping, and also, of course, as with the text-based material it is firmly prescriptive.

Video and interactive video

The natural extension from audio material is to video presentations, and a wide range of this material exists for both self-learning practices and also for use in off-the-job training programmes.

The simplest form is a video directed at a particular subject consisting of either a 'talking head' presenting the material or a case study, or series of small case studies, describing the various aspects of the material. For example, there are many commercially produced videos that demonstrate, say, an appraisal, discipline, counselling or other type of interview; a negotiation in practice; a demonstration presentation using all the effective skills; and so on. Learners can view these videos in isolation or in a work group and learning becomes much greater if, following the video, there is at least a discussion on the learning points, led by either the in-company trainer or the workers' line manager. Both approaches require considerable planning and preparation concerning the questions that will need to be asked to initiate the discussion. The trainer/manager will also have to ensure that they have intimate knowledge of the video content and the problems it raises. These video/discussion sessions can be held at the end of the lunch period, during actual work time or, linking with team development, on team development events at or away from work.

Trigger videos

As a result of watching television most people, including many of the learners on an event, are used to watching a programme right the way through (apart, perhaps, from when they have recorded it and pause during it to make a cup of tea!). Training videos are not all meant to be viewed in this way. Any video can be stopped at any stage to have a discussion, to ask questions of the audience, or to make a supplementary comment. Trigger videos are ones that have been especially produced with the intention that they *should* be stopped. They usually consist of a number of cameos or mini-case studies. When a cameo has been played the video should be stopped and the learners are asked – either by the trainer or the video at the end of the cameo – questions such as 'What would you do now?'; 'What would you say in answer to this?'; 'What experience have you had of situations like this?'; and so on.

The trainer/manager must ensure that they have fully prepared for these videos by getting to know the material, the questions that will be asked and gathering additional information on the subject to help the discussion along.

Interactive videos

Interactive videos are usually intended for a person's self-learning rather than their having the direct help of a trainer/manager, although it is essential that the learner is not left completely on his/her own, the trainer/manager or subject expert always being available to respond to the learner's problems with the material. The interactive video is meant to negate the criticism of the video as a learning medium because the learner cannot interact with the video as with a trainer. It succeeds to some extent in this aim, but until technology advances considerably the interactivity will be very restricted and one-sided. A typical interactive video asks the viewer, at stages throughout the programme, to answer a question or suggest what should happen next. Usually a choice of alternative answers is given and the viewer keys in what they think is the correct response. If the *programme* thinks they are wrong, they are asked to think again and key in another response.

However, the arguments raised against 'straight' video or similar programmes are repeated with interactive video, namely that the video material is prescriptive and there is no opportunity for the viewer to discuss this situation if they disagree with the video concept. The learner is consequently expected to accept the correctness of the video material (or reject it and stop watching the video).

COMPUTER-ASSISTED AND COMPUTER-BASED TRAINING PROGRAMS

The involvement of computers in training and development has increased over the past decade and will obviously continue to do so in the future.

Computer-assisted training programs (CAT)

Computers started to be used in support of more traditional training approaches. This support was initially the inclusion of computer requirements and mini-programs in multi-media open learning packages, extending the audio and video elements described above to the much more flexible computer. Other CATs were used in training programmes at work, again being inserted into the more traditional approaches, taking the place of audio and video inserts. These inserts permitted instant practice of skills discussed, particularly those related to the use of the computer; for example, the learning subject might be the use of spreadsheets on the computer. Following 'Tell' and 'Show', using the computer to demonstrate an electronic spreadsheet, the learner can then 'Do' by working on sample spreadsheets or constructing their own from provided data.

Where the more logical procedures and methods are involved, the planner should consider whether the learning will be more effective with the computer being used to assist the learning.

Computer-based training programs (CBT)

CBT extends significantly the involvement of the computer in training, particularly self-learning and self-development approaches, and all indications are that this could be a significant learning force in the future. The programs nowadays customarily consist of a computer package, usually on CD-ROM or interactive CD-ROM, perhaps supported by text and/or video material, questionnaires, projects and activities.

The advantages of CBT packages include:

- the learners take part in an active form of learning;
- study can be at the learner's own pace;
- an ease of building in checks of understanding;
- learning can take place anywhere there is a computer, and, if an Internet program, a telephone line link to the Internet;
- time and resources are generally used more effectively.

The disadvantages are few, although they can be serious, and include:

- the learning requires a high motivation and commitment by the learner;
- managerial, trainer or other expert support should be readily available, although this is not always possible;
- some feelings of isolation may be felt with the learner sitting alone in front of a computer screen;
- some people have an aversion to, even a fear of working with a computer, although this is becoming less of problem with the increasing availability of PCs and today's generation growing up with these as normal tools.

Learning packages, usually on CD-ROM or interactive CD-ROM, are widely available commercially and many are of good quality. The interactive versions are a vast improvement on the fairly passive form of the straight CD-ROM and, like interactive video, give the learner the chance to input their responses to significant questions posed at various stages. However, CD-ROMs suffer from the same problem found with videos – they are fixed in their approach and are prescriptive with their messages, permitting no argument or disagreement – if the computer has been programmed that the answer to question *x* is *y*, then no other answer is acceptable. A reason for an 'incorrect' response may be given, but even this may be unacceptable to the learner.

Web- and Internet-based training

Probably the biggest 'revolution' in the world of training and development in recent years has been the increased and increasing use of the Internet to transport training programs to learners, whether they are individuals or groups within an organization, although not necessarily a group that has come together for training. This approach started quite simply with real-time, e-mail contact between a self-learning, open learning programme learner and the central expert or supporting trainer/manager. The logical development of this was a learning programme controlled over a Net of learners from a central source from which the learning material had been sent. This learning material could be in the form of traditional text, e-mail material or electronic Web pages. The learners respond to progress questions from the source, taking part in subsequent electronic (by e-mail or in an instantaneous 'chat room' format) discussions where necessary, before moving on to other parts of the programme.

The more revolutionary techniques (and these are seen by many people as the way in which electronic methods of learning will proceed) involve the Internet equivalent of traditional methods of training and development. The significant basis of these methods is that the presence of any social contact is unnecessary – contact is the interaction of the learner seated in front of the computer VDU with a program that originates with a Web site at any location in the world.

The take-up of these 'new' techniques was not as extensive as had been anticipated, perhaps because in their early days, the 1980s, the equipment available to view the programs was not too widely available and costs, of both the programs and the essential telephone links, were high – at least in the UK. This would particularly be the case where self-development was intended and the learner might be taking a personal initiative – this learner would have even less opportunity of access to expensive equipment. But in spite of costs, and recognizing the need to keep up with developments, organizations have been encouraged to consider alternatives to the traditional forms of training.

The caveat must be given, as in the case of all 'discrete' forms of training, that any one approach to learning will not suit every learner, and even less cost-effective learning may result if one method is introduced to the exclusion of any alternatives.

This certainly applies to CBT if it is considered on its own as the complete answer to the economics and effectiveness of training and learning. Although CBT is not the panacea for all training ills, it is a technique that has been delayed in introduction, for a number of reasons. Computers are often introduced or offered by enthusiasts, or establishment organizers from 'on high', and this over-enthusiasm or direction has often frightened trainers or organizations with limited experience of computers. The widespread use of and familiarity with computers has not been with us very long and there are still many people (including training practitioners) who are computer restricted, if not computer illiterate! Trainers were also suspicious of the introduction of computer training because they saw it as yet another management ploy that would reduce their control of the training situation, or even threaten their jobs.

Time has shown that these fears are, to a large extent, unfounded. An explosion of computer ownership and awareness, in homes as well as in commerce and industry, has educated many more people in the use and operation of computers and their programs, and the relative ease of working with them. More people continue to become more aware and at ease with the many computer applications and programs in use, and these developments have increased substantially the advantages *and* disadvantages of computer systems.

The benefits of CBT

The main benefits offered by CBT in training include:

- *Immediacy.* The learners do not have to wait for a viable number of participants before a training event can be offered. Training is therefore available almost on demand. When a new training demand arises there is often a considerable delay between this realization, the time taken for the training department to construct an effective programme, the administration to set up and complement the training event(s), and all the other necessary adjuncts of a live training programme. If the training is available on a computer program, is suitable for learning by this medium and the learners have computers available, the training can be provided almost immediately, which simplifies matters.
- *Reduction of training time.* In most cases training time is reduced. In group training activities the trainer has to pitch the training at a lower level than required by a number (often the greater number) of participants, with obvious consequences. If the learner is studying as an individual, using a flexible CBT program, he can pace his progress to suit his own knowledge and skills. This is a common feature of open or self-learning systems and can certainly occur in CBT.

  A further advantage linked to the learner's choice of pace is that the program need not necessarily be followed in one session or consecutive sessions. The program structure may allow it to be taken in sections, at intervals or on a part-time basis. This in itself could help both the learning and the availability of the learner.
- *Location of training.* CBT can be taken to the learner rather than the learners having to come to the training. The traditional approach can cause difficulties of release, cost of travelling and accommo-

dation, replacement while the job holder is absent from work, and so on. The CBT program can even be followed at home on a home computer, although this requires substantial commitment to learning on the part of the learner.

- *Consistency.* There is a higher degree of consistency than with exposure to live trainers. There are good and bad trainers and many in between: each trainer will present roughly the same material in a different way – some ways will be effective, others less so. Each trainer will have a different level of knowledge that will affect the way they put over the material. If the level is sufficient for the learner, all is well, but if not, problems can arise. Many trainers have different attitudes and values about the topics for which they are responsible – some may be biased, others have twisted views on the subject, and so on – ideally these are not reflected openly, but this will not always be the case. The CBT program is at least consistent every time it is run – hopefully to 'consistency' we can add 'correct'.

The disadvantages of CBT

- *Computer availability.* Problems of the availability of a suitable computer or even a computer at all have been discussed. This is a decreasing problem as more and more organizations are installing a wide and sufficient range of computers, and home PCs are similarly increasing in number. There may still however be problems of this nature for some potential learners.
- *Flexibility.* If there is a computer program available for the learning topic it will have only a limited degree of flexibility. This may mean that the learners may have to make considerable jumps in relating the material to their own circumstances, especially if other support is not available.
- *Learning limitations.* Not every subject can be learnt from a CBT program. However many, where the basis is the acquisition of knowledge, or knowledge from which skill can develop, are very suitable for CBT application. In general, however, learning areas with a high degree of human resource interaction are not usually very suitable. In cases such as this the learning often demands actual interaction under controlled circumstances with a group of other learners – something not normally associated with CBT. Again, however, and this supports the argument that few training techniques can stand alone, if the CBT program is linked with a short (short because of the prior learning) training event where the skills learnt in theory can be put into practice, there can be a

successful marriage of techniques. The use of CBT in prior learning for a direct training event not only reduces the length of the event but also helps to ensure that the learners are all at the same learning level. However, a training sponsor attitude can exist that says that the learner should/can use only one technique – *either* direct training courses or CBT/self-learning.

- *Inflexibility.* You cannot argue with a computer even though modern programs allow you to interact with it. Most CBT programs are set according to a fixed plan and produce what is, from the program author's point of view, the 'right' answer. In many cases this is no problem, but problems can arise for learners if they disagree with the point made in the program and/or do not understand the points made. The disadvantages here are the absence of a live peer group, trainer or expert with whom to discuss the problems, or gain explanations in understandable terms. This disadvantage can, of course, be overcome to some extent if the learner has access, perhaps by phone if not in person, to a trainer, expert or author of the program.

Trainer attitudes

The training practitioners and planners of the 21st century have to accept that there is a CBT application, that this facility is increasing and, whatever the eventual result, they must develop an awareness of what CBT is, what it can and cannot do, and develop skills in applying it to the learners for whom they have a responsibility. In this way the range and success of their clients' learning can be greatly extended and enhanced. The conclusion must be that in the training world, for certain purposes and approaches, CBT has a developing part to play in training and in particular the IT area of training. But trainers still have widely differing views, believing that the use of CBT is still at the crossroads. Planners of training programmes who might be considering the use of CBT must consider these views:

- First, trainers are at the stage of exploring with enthusiasm the opportunities available with the new technology. These enthusiasms are principally in seeking the most effective ways in which technology can make learning more enjoyable and enlightening. This committed group is already familiar with the hardware and software available and use the technology at every opportunity, not only to help the learning opportunities of the trainee, but also to demonstrate to management and other trainers the advantages of the developments. They have to be careful, however, that their enthusiasm does not take over completely and give the wrong image that CBT and other forms of training technology are *the* training answers.

- Even more trainers are still in the early courtship stage, wanting to develop new personal skills and learning methods for their trainees, but very apprehensive about the technological advances and the knowledge and skills necessary to use them. The more they learn, the more applications appear; and the addition of this technology to the trainer's toolkit still seems to have a high risk factor for them, apart from any expense. This group can, with benefit, meet members of the first group and interface with their enthusiasm, at the same time retaining controlled scepticism, and also take every opportunity to see and have hands-on experience of the materials available.
- A large body of trainers falls between the first two groups, having a strong personal commitment to the use of the technology, although perhaps not to the extent of the first group. However, they are not being allowed to progress by their employing organization, perhaps because of:
  - ignorance by the organization's senior managers of what is available;
  - doubt by the organization of the value of the methods;
  - restrictions in the availability of the organization's existing hardware;
  - the organization's refusal to invest in technology for training and/or company work.

  All that this group can do, if its members are really motivated to introduce the technology, is obtain as much experience as possible with the range of material available so that they can submit a strong case to the organization. They can, of course, move to an organization that is more in tune with the way they wish to work!
- A fourth major group in the training world is equivalent to the dinosaurs, the Luddites or simple reactionaries, who tend to claim, without any real knowledge or understanding, that the approach is valueless, want to have no knowledge of it, and are obviously hoping that it will simply go away. Go away it will not, and any trainer who takes this ostrich-like attitude is courting disaster for their training, their own careers, their organization and their learners.

Planning the use of CBT

Decisions! Decisions! The first one that the planner must make if CBT is raised as a training consideration is: 'Is CBT the most effective format of training for these particular needs?' This question, if answered positively, leads to further questions, additional to those detailed earlier when considering the use of open learning:

- Where and what CBT packages are available?
- What type of equipment is required? What standard of equipment is necessary?
- Is this equipment available in the organization or are some purchases necessary?
- What arrangements have to be made for the use of the equipment?
- If the approach is via the Internet, is this available in the organization?
- Are there any restrictions on the use of e-mail in the organization?
- Can the package work efficiently on an intranet or internal network?
- What is the testing pedigree of the package?
- To what extent are supporting materials provided by the package supplier or does the learner have to obtain some?
- Are there specific licensing requirements if the package is run on more than one computer?
- Is it possible to try or test out the package before purchase? Are samples available? If not, why not? (Be careful of suppliers who cannot/will not enable this pre-purchase investigation.)

There are an increasingly large number of Web sites all over the world on to which the Internet user can log. The majority appear to be principally in the US, with a smaller number in the UK. Many of these sites are located in universities, although an increasing number are being offered by commercial providers. The majority comprise pages of textual information obtainable by logging-on to the site, with a range of assorted explanatory graphics – diagrams, photographs, charts, icons and animations, and perhaps (although as yet limited) video scenarios. Some of the programs provide links with other sources of information, enable speedy jumping from one part of the program to another, use e-mails as a means of providing instantaneous contact with the learners and are interactive, eg with question-answer inserts.

One of the problems that faces the planner who is considering the use of CBT via the Internet is locating the most suitable source. There is no problem of browsing the Web to identify sites, but which one to use? Years of traditional types of training and development have enabled the build up of a substantial amount of intelligence about the effectiveness of certain programmes and their providers, but such intelligence is in its early days as far as the Web is concerned. However, more and more organizations are using this facility and it is a reasonably simple task to make contact with these (through, for example, trainer information exchange forums such as UKHRD and, in the US, TRDEV-L. To subscribe (free) to UKHRD, send an e-mail addressed to majordemo@ukhrd.com; leave 'subject' blank and enter message 'subscribe to network'; and for TRDEV-L, visit the Web site http:www.train.ed.psu.edu/TRDEVL. The trainers are able to offer firsthand comments on these vehicles and this is ideal until a universal intelligence is formed.

The other major problem for planners once they have: a) decided that Internet available CBT is the approach to take; and b) identified some possible sources of the training, is to obtain the agreement of the organization to follow this path. The arguments of reduced time away from work, multiple use among a number of learners, easy availability for several learners via an intranet, etc may be outvoted by a simple factor – cost. The Internet programs are costly in themselves, in spite of research showing their cost efficiency, although there is not as yet any reliable indicator to the cost- and value-effective charges. As an example, Colin Steed (1999) described an online curriculum delivery site, *Peritas Online*, which offers a range of several hundred classroom-based courses with 31 online courses:

- Networking;
- Soft skills;
- UNIX;
- PC applications;
- PC technical (MCSE/MCSD).

The course durations range from two to six weeks and the costs from £75 to £420 (1998/9 prices) plus VAT. All the information necessary to make a decision can be obtained in advance from the Web site, prior to signing up for a course. At the start of the course the learner is sent specifically designed open learning materials, information about how contact by e-mail can be made, and issued with a personal password to enter the relevant 'classroom'. Support is available in the 'classroom' eight hours a day and the learners are encouraged to use the 'classroom' as often as necessary. Assignments are given and e-mailed back for marking and assessment. Although not mentioned in any descriptions there is an addition to the course costs in terms of the phone charges which, if the learner is online for any time, can mount up substantially. This latter factor is probably why Web-based training has taken off more in the US than in the UK, the former having much more user-friendly telephone charges.

CBT is not always a better substitute for other forms of training nor is it necessarily any less expensive – frequently it is more expensive in direct cash terms. The type of learning must take high consideration as, like any 'prescriptive' form of training, learning soft skills such as interviewing, etc cannot be effectively learned by CBT – at some time, sooner rather than later, personal interventions become essential. Workplace psychology, management and personal commitment can all be factors working against the acceptance of CBT, as they are in many other forms of training, traditional or non-traditional. But CBT, whether through the Internet or by more local methods, is here to stay, has its place in effective self-learning and self-development, and where several learners require a learning approach is a force to be considered.

PART THREE

Planning and Designing Off-the-job Training and Development

The chapters in this part will consider in detail the various aspects that need to be taken into account when planning and designing off-the-job training programmes or approaches.

7

Off-the-job Training Approaches – I

This chapter will describe:

- the method of planning for and designing processes for off-the-job training;
- the range of training formats and structures available;
- methods of sequencing programme material;
- the suggested format for a design blueprint;
- some of the principal methods used in off-the-job training and development – input sessions; buzz groups; syndicates; discussions; demonstrations, and question and answer sessions. Other methods will be described in Chapter 8.

In the previous three chapters we considered some of the on-the-job methods available for satisfying the training and development needs identified in a TNIA and the range of planning options available to satisfy these needs. In these cases the planning may be initiated by a formal or central 'planner', but the real planning might fall on a trainer, a line manager or subject expert. There is no doubt that on-the-job methods have increased in number and effectiveness in recent years, particularly in the technological area, but many research activities show that some form of off-the-job training event is still an important aspect of training and development. There are, however, many ineffective approaches to this training and development and it falls to the planner to make every programme as effective as possible, through using all the modern means available. The days of the simple 'stand up and talk' event are (or should be) long gone, but significant planning is essential if the variety of approaches are to be welded into an impactive and effective programme.

THE OFF-THE-JOB PLANNING PROCESS

In Chapter 4 we considered a process for planning the basics of on-the-job training. The following performs the same function for the basics of off-the-job training and development programmes.

1. List the agreed objectives for the training programme – these will be available from the preceding TNIA or may have to be determined at this stage.
2. Consider the learning population and as many of the influences that you can identify that these individuals will have on the programme design.
3. Against each objective list the possible ways in which these might best be met.
4. Decide whether the learning will be best achieved by an on-the-job or off-the-job programme form and whether these approaches might be combined in some way.
5. Consider the possible training accommodation needed and as many of the effects that you can identify that this resource will have on the course design and practice.
6. Confirm whether you are restricted to containing the programme within a certain period of time or whether it will be allowed the time required for effective completion.
7. Confirm from any available previous information when the programme is required to start and by which date it has to be completed, or obtain this information.
8. Consider material design.

OBJECTIVES AND THE LEARNING POPULATION

These were considered fully in Chapter 4 and the process for off-the-job training will follow very similar patterns to those for on-the-job training. Additional comments related to off-the-job training are:

- How many people will need to be covered by the programme? This will obviously have an effect on how many events or courses must be included.
- The age range of the learning groups can have an effect on the design or practice of the events. If the groups can be selected so that similar groups are formed – if indeed this is the most effective method of mixing learners – a group of young, active learners will

probably react to a different approach than a group of older, less active, and perhaps more contemplative people. However, you have to be careful about making assumptions about age or sex differences and their learning processes. In practice, you are most likely to be presented with a completely heterogeneous group, and the overall principle of training design should be followed – make the programme as varied as possible to ensure that it will appeal to all the participants at as many stages as possible. But remember the phrase that you can satisfy some of the people some of the time, but not all the people all the time (sometimes not even some of the people some of the time).

- Learning styles should be taken into account as far as possible, as described earlier, but again if the groups are heterogeneous (similar to the population as a whole), you must try to make the programme attractive and useful to all by varied approaches.
- As with on-the-job training, the location of the learning groups will have a significant effect on planning. When the learners are distributed nationally or internationally, rather than on one site, the decision has to be made as to whether the training should be provided centrally, involving the additional costs of bringing the learners to the centre, or whether the trainers should be the ones who should travel to the learners, perhaps to convenient selected centres. This will also be a significant factor in the final decision about whether off- or on-the-job training will be more effective and/or economical.
- One of the problems encountered in on-the-job training is the availability of the training programme when required. With on-the-job programmes this is less of a problem than with off-the-job training, when either a suitable training course is not available when needed (either by individuals or groups) or, although a training event is available, the learners cannot be released at that time. Unless these problems can be resolved you should seek other ways of satisfying the needs – eg open learning packages or other on-the-job approaches.

TRAINING ACCOMMODATION

The effects of where the training is to be held cannot be ignored at any stage of the design and presentation of training programmes. If the organization has a central training centre or college and there are no problems of bringing learners into this centre then the possible problems are dealt with by the administration departments. It can be assumed in such cases that the centre possesses all the necessary resources in types of accommodation to avoid problems of design that revolve around these matters.

But if there is no centre and training accommodation has to be found elsewhere design must consider any effects that restrictions imposed in these locations may place on the programme. For example, if the programme requires a considerable amount of experiential activity during an event, resulting in the need for large areas of space or a substantial number of rooms, the choice of a suitable location is critical, and one must be sought or the programme modified to take account of the constraints.

The role of the initial planner will be to ensure that the type of accommodation to be used is suitable, and to give guidelines to the trainer on the essential elements required in practice. Few locations are ideal and the training practitioner will usually be called upon to make on-the-spot decisions about various aspects and any modifications to the original plan.

A number of commercial sources offer information and help about the availability and booking of accommodation suitable for the particular purposes. A very useful publication (Kaye Thorne, 1998) not only offers valuable advice on choosing training venues but gives a lot of reference information about actual venues and venue advisory services in the UK, USA and Australia.

Many purpose-built conference and training centres exist and most of these are very suitable, not only in terms of the accommodation offered but also the facilities they provide. The same can be said of a number of hotels, but care must obviously be taken in selecting a hotel as a training venue because, after all, their principal function is guest service rather than training.

Questions to consider when choosing a suitable training venue include:

- What type of learner will be attending the event? What level are they at in the organization(s) they represent? Is there a mixed level of participants?
- Is there a 'best' location in the country that will be suitable for all or the majority? Is this defined by travel resources or by the existence of a company training centre?
- Is there a preferred type of location – country, town, etc?
- What training accommodation is required? How many training rooms are needed of what nature? Does the main room need to have any especial characteristics? Can the main room double as a syndicate or small group room?

- Will the training rooms allocated be exclusive to the training course? Can equipment and other materials be left overnight? What are the security measures?
- What audio-visual/technological equipment is needed? What audio-visual/technological equipment is available at the venue? Is a technician available for any assistance required? Are there power facilities for brought-in equipment?
- If outdoor activities are to be included in the programme, what facilities are at or near the venue – gardens, fields, woods, streams, shopping centres, libraries, etc, depending on needs?
- Does the training programme have any other special requirements that may or may not be provided at/by the venue?
- What leisure facilities are provided at or near the venue?
- If the programme is residential, what accommodation is available – number of bedrooms, suites, standards, services, etc.
- What type of travel arrangements need to be made for participants not travelling to the venue by car?
- What are the overall, inclusive costs, and does the budget cover these for the number of people involved?

ADVANTAGES AND DISADVANTAGES OF OFF-THE-JOB TRAINING

The factors that will help the planner to make one of the basic decisions – whether in fact off-the job training is the most appropriate – will include considerations of the advantages of direct training events:

- Groups of people with similar needs can be brought together for learning events in the most economical and cost/value-effective manner.
- A wide variety of learning methods, including many of those discussed for on-the-job training, can be included.
- Views, opinions and information can be shared with the other people in the group, who may come from the same or different parts of the same organization, or from a range of organizations, and who can bring a wide range of experience or knowledge to the discussions.
- New concepts and techniques can be presented to a large number of people in the shortest possible time.
- Opportunities exist for the learners to clarify and practise aspects of the learning that they do not understand or on which they require additional information.

Disadvantages include:

- Individuals have different learning skills and speeds, but this means that the group is usually forced to progress at a compromise rate.
- The different learning preferences of individuals or groups of individuals cannot always be taken into account.
- Not all the learners will be starting at the same knowledge or skill level and there is the risk that the ones starting at the lowest levels, if account is not taken of this, will be lost from the start. If the starting point is too low, unless the particular learners are brought in to help the learning process, they will lose their initial interest, which may not be regained.
- Not all the learners will be attending the event with similar motivation levels and, in fact, some may be resisting learning because they did not want to come or because of some of the other learning barriers discussed in Chapter 2.

TIME

There are several aspects of time that are significant in the planning of a training course or programme away from the job.

The first is the possible conflict between a constraint imposed on the time available for a programme or the events within a programme. This constraint might be imposed without consideration of the needs demonstrated by the TNIA – 'You have *x* days in which to run a training event' instead of '*x* days are needed to run the training event'. In such cases substantial restrictions are placed upon the design of the programme. Irrespective of the total needs identified, decisions must be made about priorities and which of the needs must be included in the programme. Early prioritization of the objectives will help in this instance, whether this is based on importance of the subject or on the widespread nature of the deficiencies. Whichever base for the constraint exists, it is incumbent on the designer with senior manager support (for example, the training manager or senior line managers) to try to reverse such a decision. The alternative approach would be for the designer to take the identified needs and the minimum priorities from these needs, and propose and fight for a length of time sufficient to mount an effective programme.

In many cases, if the designers or their representatives are effective negotiators, a compromise will normally result – not quite sufficient time to make the training programme a fully effective one, but time not so constrained to make it almost a non-event.

Starting and finishing dates

From the point of view of the planner and designer these can be critical factors, involving planning to include the target population, weighing the priority of the new programme against the demands of existing ones, and the availability of the potential learners. Given that if the demand for the provision of training originated at a senior level it was usually wanted yesterday this is a good argument for the training manager to be involved in decisions on training at an early stage, thus avoiding a dictat appearing demanding unreasonable or impossible action.

If any training demand is unreasonable and would make a mockery of the proposed training it should be challenged in the most appropriate way. The strongest argument that can be offered is that if the request is unreasonable, but is complied with, the resulting programme might be less than effective and as a result the organization's money will not have been wisely spent. The end result of an improvement in the business must always be behind the provision of training and development.

The design of not only a complete training programme, but the planning of individual events and sessions are very time-consuming activities for which sufficient time is almost invariably not afforded (or so the designers often claim!). There can be no doubt that when a programme has to be constructed from nothing there is a lot of work, and consequently time, involved. It is impossible to even hazard a guess at the time involved as planning and design are not usually a continuous process, with the designer working without interruption. On the smaller scale, some researchers suggest that a single session needs planning and production time of between 6 and 10 times that which will be allocated to the session itself. Of course this time will vary considerably, depending on the complexity of the subject, the availability of material and training aids (or their production time), the experience of the trainer, and so on.

A TRAINING PROGRAMME PLANNNING GUIDE

This represents a two-stage process for the planner: 1) guidelines for the design of the training programme; 2) guidelines for the training practitioners to help in putting the programme into practice.

Training programme design

Once the major factors described earlier in this chapter have been resolved the planner and designer will need to:

- decide on the nature of the training approaches (see following material for a summary of these);
- plan the sequence of the sessions for a logical learning progression designed to meet the programme objectives;
- prepare a programme outline plan showing the sequence of sessions and general comments on their proposed format;
- discuss the proposed plan with the training practitioners, the training manager and, if possible, with representatives of the learning population and their line manager, and agree the final plan;
- complete a final, agreed outline and part-detailed programme from which the training practitioners can produce detailed session plans;
- pass the agreed, final plan to the training practitioners who will be responsible for the individual session.

Guideline document for the training practitioners

This document, which can be described as a training blueprint, follows on from the final item of the preceding section. It gives the training practitioners the basis of the training programme and enables the planner to check that the major steps have been taken. The document will contain, as a minimum:

- a statement of the aims and objectives of the programme, expressed in measurable terms;
- details of the agreed timetable in terms of achievement period and maximum time allowed for the programme itself;
- information about the potential learning population; a summary of the training needs identified and analysed; the learners' existing knowledge and skills levels; differences in status and organizational origins that may affect the programme;
- a checklist of the recommended training methods to ensure that the trainers are themselves skilled in these practices;
- guidance on the flexibility that will be allowed to the trainers to use alternative approaches appropriate to the various sessions;

- the detailed, agreed outline programme design showing the proposed sessions, their aims, objectives and methods, and timing, including advice on training aids that would be useful;
- final agreement of the programme design with the training practitioners involved;
- considered evaluation methods and agreement with the trainers and others involved for the processing of these evaluations;
- agreement and arrangements for reviews to be held with the planners and trainers following the first conducted event, to consider achievement of success and validation of the training;
- discussion with the trainers on the written reports about the training and its evaluation that will need to be produced and agreement with the training and management administration for these actions.

KNOWLEDGE OF TRAINING FORMATS

In order to satisfy all the factors included in the design guide and the programme blueprint, the planners must be aware of the various training formats that are available for off-the-job training and development programmes.

Training courses

A 'training course' is a coverall term used to describe an event attended by a group of learners who are to learn or revise knowledge, skills, attitudes and techniques as a group rather than in an individual manner. It can be arranged internally for the staff of an organization, publicly for mixed groups from a range of organizations, or a mixed group from a number of small organizations. The latter can be organized for those companies that may not have sufficient staff or free resource time to hold their own training courses or send the staff on public courses, may not be able do so for financial reasons, or may prefer not to do so. This approach is becoming more popular as more smaller firms are developing, and is usually organized by an external consultant or the training department of a larger employer in the area or sector.

Training courses can have durations ranging from half a day to several weeks or months; the latter have discrete events usually separated by several weeks in which learning is practised in work conditions or projects agreed at the preceding event are carried out, to be reported on at the next event.

Courses can consist of:

- a mix of peers from the same organization;
- a mix of peers from different organizations;
- a mix of different hierarchical levels from the same or different organizations;
- stranger, cousin or home groups;

and can be structured, unstructured, semi-structured; or formal or informal.

The style and techniques of the course 'leaders' can be:

- tutors or teachers using more formal techniques;
- trainers with a wide range of adult learning techniques to offer;
- facilitators who use more informal, non-directive approaches.

The training course, of virtually any nature, usually consists of a series of 'sessions', which may be input sessions, discussions, activities or any of the other learning methods in a mix that has been agreed is the most suitable for the particular learning requirements.

Workshops

This is a widely misused title, with some organizations describing ordinary training courses and even publishing activity collections as workshops. They are usually more development events than training, with a group of people coming together to consider a specific subject or a number of related topics or themes. They are definitely learning events, however, and involve substantial participation by the learners with little or no trainer input or guest expert sessions. Any inputs are short and intended to set the scene for the participants to 'workshop' the subject; they can be arranged by the trainer or facilitator or may be requested by the group – this latter will usually be during the life of the workshop as the participants meet problems. The workshop participants, who may be all from the same work area, from various parts of the same organization, or from different organizations with the same or different disciplines, often decide themselves how the workshop will be run within the principal subject area and what the terminal objectives will be.

The workshop process is for the participants to investigate, analyse, consider, make proposals about and reach action decisions about the workshop subject. This subject can of course be any topic within an organization, eg 'How can we extend the existing market for our products?'; 'What do we want to/need to do to make our management training more effective?'; and learning subjects such as 'What is it and how can we include NLP in our training and development?' and 'We need to revise and improve the evaluation of our training'. The emphasis of the workshop process is on practical work rather than relatively passive learning. Within the specific context of this book, a relevant workshop is one consisting of a team of planners/designers, trainers, line managers etc, meeting to thrash out the details of new aspects of training. The normal end of workshop result is for the participants to return to work with actual work problems solved, training programmes designed, training materials produced or designed, or with new methods of approaching their problems etc.

Conferences

Conferences are not always recognized as training events, either by the organizers or the participants, but the basic aim of any conference is that those participating leave with a greater awareness than they had when they arrived. This may be the new expectations of the chief executive, a changed marketing approach, the introduction of new products and so on. The format is commonly a series of lectures by company or external experts on the topics to be covered, frequently supported by 'sidelined' small group discussions or workshops. The biggest danger is that the organization's annual conference degenerates into being seen as a social event or even a company's thank-you to its staff for their year's work rather than a learning occasion. Consequently the planner must be very aware of the aims of the conference and adjust the planning accordingly.

Seminars

These can be described as mini-conferences as they follow a similar format of a series of lectures by experts in the topic of the seminar. However they are usually smaller in size as it is necessary for the lectures to be highly interactive. The lectures are frequently followed by mini-workshops in which the topic is discussed in depth and decisions made for action or otherwise. A seminar is often described as a symposium, and it is difficult to differentiate between these, but the purpose of both is to disseminate, discuss and refine views and information and consequently they are learning events, usually at the professional level.

OFF-THE-JOB TRAINING METHODS

The choice of training methods that can be considered by the planner falls into three basic structures – structured, semi-structured and unstructured events, although the last-named is frequently a misnomer as the event has been planned to be unstructured. Most off-the-job training events of whatever format involve a group of learners who take part in sessions either as the full group, in pairs or in small groups (often known as 'syndicates'). The methods available for these groups include:

- trainer presentations/lectures/input sessions (or similar descriptions of activities of this nature);
- buzz groups;
- syndicates, small group work or breakout groups;
- discussions;
- demonstrations;
- question and answer sessions;
- case studies and simulations;
- role plays;
- activities – including icebreakers, games and group tasking;
- videos;
- computer assisted training (CAT) or computer-based training (CBT);
- brainstorming.

Many of these approaches and techniques can be, and commonly are combined to make more varied, interesting and impactive events and sessions – this is particularly the case with trainer presentations or input sessions.

The methods are described briefly here so that the programme designer might have an overall appreciation of what might be included in a programme, but there are a number of books that give fuller details (for example my *Techniques of Training*, 1995, 3rd edn, Gower).

Trainer presentations

These are 'tell' events in which the trainer gives what can sometimes be described as a lecture or, less didactically, an input session. By their very nature they are passive events as far as the audience is concerned and the concept is that they will learn by listening and taking in the words of this expert speaker! In many ways it is the easiest form of training approach to use as the trainer has complete control of content, manner of expression and timing, but there is considerable doubt about the extent to which it contributes to real learning.

Very few learning events include presentations consisting solely of the speaker talking for the whole period, with no variations. A more effective trainer presentation or input session can be achieved by the inclusion of appropriate training aids, breaks in the lecture flow with the use of buzz groups, discussions, videos, computer program inserts, and activities. There will be some rare occasions when the straight lecture will the most appropriate approach – usually when there is no opportunity to use other approaches – but even the most didactic lecture is usually relieved to some extent by the use of overhead transparencies or 35mm slides.

Planning for input sessions must take into account the communication barriers and in particular the 'attention/listening/learning span' of an audience (see Chapter 2). Planning for sessions of this nature should therefore include, at or about the 20-minute period, some form of break in the pattern, whether this is an actual break or a change in the presentation format – for example a video, a discussion, a computer program etc. This change can be repeated at further intervals during the session, although there will be an optimum length of time for the session as a whole – about 15 minutes or so for a straight presentation, longer for a multiple style approach.

If there is to be a multiple style approach the 15- to 20-minute maximum need not be adhered to, although any one session should desirably last no longer than 45 minutes to an hour. The exact length will depend on the nature of the various component parts of the session, the complexity of the subject and the likely motivation of the learners. Initial design might suggest a session that could follow a pattern of:

A brief introduction to the subject	up to 5 minutes
Oral presentation supported by visual aids	up to 20 minutes but preferably 15
An activity related to the subject to give the learners the opportunity to practise what has been learned	15 to 20 minutes
A feedback session on the activity	about 15–20 minutes
A summary of the session and the lessons learned	up to 10 minutes
Total time for the session	about 65 minutes

In this example time for the constituent parts has been cut to the bone, and considers a relatively simple subject content. Even so the approximate time required is just over an hour – effective training takes time, and it is better to reduce the amount of learning material to ensure its effectiveness than to try to cram too much into a constrained period. But the essential is to have a varied production with frequent change of interest and preferably involving learner activity.

Buzz groups

An effective interrupting technique during an input session is when the trainer, preferably before the decreasing attention watershed, poses a question to the learning group or, having made a statement, asks them to consider this. Frequently it is not convenient or desirable for the group to leave the room to do this, so the technique known as a 'buzz group' is introduced. The learning group is asked to break up into smaller groups – say, in a group of 12 learners, into four groups of three learners each – by moving their chairs into these sub-groups and discussing as requested. The 'buzz' becomes evident as up to 12 voices can be heard in the room!

Usually buzz groups last for only short periods – 5 or 10 minutes – and can be particularly effective early in the course when individuals may not be keen to speak out in public. In this case, a spokesperson is elected to speak eventually for each group when the full group is reconvened, giving, neutrally, the sub-groups' views or responses.

Buzz groups can be introduced at almost any stage in a session or programme, the timing being planned or not, although instant buzzes can throw the timing of the session out.

Syndicates

A syndicate in training is sometimes referred to as a task sub-group or a breakout group. Usually the full learning group, either during a presentation or at the end of it, is divided into smaller sub-groups and given a task to complete. The syndicates are allocated separate rooms where they can work in private before returning at the end of the allotted time to the main group to what is referred to as a plenary or review/feedback session.

The task given to the syndicate can be a problem-solving, decision-making one; a views and opinions gathering exercise; or a management or other skill exercise, game or activity. A specific time in which to complete the task is usually allocated and, in meeting or leadership training events, a group leader is selected or the group is asked to elect a leader.

When the syndicates return to the full group a review and feedback session is held during which the observations of the observers (if any) are given to the participants, followed by a general discussion on the activity and the lessons learned. Recall of the events during the syndicates, often a problem, can be helped by preceding the review session with the learner leaders and members completing questionnaires designed to identify events during the activity. The recalled information can then be used in the ensuing discussion.

Syndicate activities can be lengthy affairs, the time required depending on the nature, complexity and requirements of the task, and this timing must be planned carefully, including (what is often forgotten) time for the syndicates to be briefed, to disperse to their rooms and then to return to the main room at the end of the exercise. Plenary sessions can also be lengthy affairs, particularly when a number of syndicates and observers are involved, with a lot of people wanting to have a say.

One method of reducing the time necessary for this report-back event is, when each syndicate has had an observer or observers, for each syndicate's observer to review simultaneously the activity with each group. When this syndicate-specific feedback has been given a much shorter plenary session can then be held to discuss common problems and points that have emerged in each group.

Discussions

Discussions have a similarly wide use as syndicates, and of course syndicates can be used as discussion groups. They are particularly useful in varying a bare, not very effective input session, and involve the open or syndicated discussion of topics relevant to the learning event.

Discussions can be either pre-planned or spontaneous and can be held as separate session events or as integral parts of sessions. Pre-planned discussions can be separate sessions in which the learners are asked to discuss, usually in small groups, the appropriate topic. The objective of the session can be simply to allow the learners to air their views, or can aim to have a specific terminal result or decision. This type of discussion can also be planned to take place during an input session, at a pre-planned time, the topic obviously being directly related to that of the session.

Apart from the in-session, planned discussion, more informal, spontaneous discussions can arise during a session. These can be important learning events, but the same caveat of time usage must be applied as with the unplanned buzz groups.

The discussions, planned or unplanned, can be led by the trainer, who should be a skilled discussion leader, or the group can be given the responsibility for controlling its own discussion, with a selected or elected leader from the group.

Discussions can often, in terms of time control, be unknown quantities – the subject matter for one group may be an uninteresting or a strange topic, whereas with another group it may be of riveting interest and one of which they have substantial knowledge. These opposite aspects will have an effect on the interest in and depth of the discussions, and consequently on the time needed.

Inexperienced trainers or those inexperienced in discussion leading tend to shy away from including discussions in their session plans because of these unknown quantities and their uncertainty about their ability to control the situation.

Discussions that are planned as specific events during, or as a session, require more preparation than they are usually afforded and should be viewed by the planner as being almost as substantial as input sessions. A number of pitfalls can occur with discussions and these are usually the result of the discussion being unplanned or badly planned. Even spontaneous discussions will normally be controlled, albeit covertly, by the trainer, who must be skilled in discussion leading or controlling. Discussions form part of almost every activity in a training course and consequently are a 'must' for inclusion by trainers in their 'training toolkit'.

Demonstrations

Demonstrations are the Tell and Show parts of the Tell – Show – Do approach and are most frequently found in sessions that are concerned with learning the knowledge and/or skills of operating some object, piece of machinery or equipment, or performing an office procedure. In a group situation a typical demonstration practice would be for the trainer to describe, perhaps with overhead projector transparencies, the object, its use and its operation. This description would then, wherever possible, be backed up by the object being shown to the group and operated in the correct manner by the trainer. In some cases, for example large pieces of machinery or other immovable objects, the trainer may have to take the group to where the object is located: otherwise drawings and particularly photographs will need to be used. The final stage is for the learners themselves to practise using the object, initially under close supervision by the trainer or supporting skilled operators.

Question and answer sessions

This can be a difficult and dangerous approach, particularly where questions are asked in an inappropriate way, or a series of questions becomes an interrogation. But in so many training situations it is essential that questions are posed to obtain information, views, opinions and feelings and the skilled trainer must be capable of using them effectively.

Questioning techniques are dealt with extensively in the training literature and guidance is usually contained on the use of, and advantages and disadvantages of using particular types of question:

- closed questions in which only simple answers are received;
- leading questions that restrict the range of responses;
- multiple questions that frequently result in the response being to the part of the question the questioner felt was least important.

The questioning trainer is recommended to use wherever possible:

OPEN QUESTIONS THAT WILL GIVE THE RESPONDERS THE OPPORTUNITY OF EXPRESSING THEMSELVES FULLY.

Other 'question and answer' traps are when the trainer tries to obtain the views of all the learners in a group and questions each of them. It becomes only too easy, even when questioning starts at one point in the group and the trainer has the intention of moving along the line so that everybody is approached, for hiccups to occur and the original line of questioning to be sidetracked or a discussion arise half-way round the group. As a result, one or more members may not be questioned and they may think that you are not interested in their views – so from that point they do not give their views easily or voluntarily. The planner and trainer must agree on a specific strategy since, as with so many active parts of a session, time can simply run out.

8

Off-the-job Training Approaches – 2

This chapter will describe:

- further principal methods used in off-the-job training and development – case studies and simulations; role plays; activities; brainstorming; videos; CAT, CBT and CD-i.

CASE STUDIES AND SIMULATIONS

Case studies

Case studies and simulations have been mentioned earlier and can be significant aids to learning, either as complete learning events or, more usually, as activities linked to other parts of the training. In the latter case the common use of these activities is to follow an input session or series of linked sessions with a case study that, as a real-life example, or as an artificially constructed study, contains the opportunity for the learners to practise the learning points that have been covered. They are similar to syndicate problem-solving activities in that the learners are given a statement of information that contains a problem they are required to solve.

Case studies of a complex nature are very suitable for inclusion at the end of a training event, for example on group leadership, the study requiring the learners to practise all the aspects of leadership that have been covered and may have been practised individually in syndicate groups. A major case study such as this can require a substantial period of time to perform and frequently an even longer period for the subsequent review and feedback session.

Simulations

Simulations are usually studies involving the allocation of almost real-life roles, the use of computers and the completion of reports, holding meetings and numerous cases of problem-solving and decision-making. Individuals are given, or select from within their group, the roles of managing director or chief executive, financial director, sales and marketing director, production director, personnel and training director and so on. The group is given a set time in which to solve a number of problems or otherwise exist as a company with the objective of making a profit over a sum given to them at the start. Many variations of this type of simulation are possible and the time allocated can be varied extensively. Consequently planning for simulations will certainly have to be done during the programme planning phase and may represent a complete learning programme.

A substantial amount of the planning time for a case study or simulation is taken up in writing the case or modifying an existing one to suit the particular circumstances, possibly involving visits to workplaces to observe functions and interview job-holders, in addition to collecting and collating reports, critical incident reviews etc. This information is then included in the complete simulation as written briefs, reports, minutes etc and computer program data – so that everything necessary for the effective performance of the activity is available for the learners.

Preparation must include the printing and recording of the information and data referred to above and, if observers are to be used, observational aid instruments for these learners. Similarly, many cases and simulations require a number of rooms and a variety of equipment – typewriters, paper, computers, calculators etc – and plans must be made for these to be available.

The pre-allocation of the time required is the most difficult part of the planning activity, particularly if a case is being used for the first time. This is one occasion where a dummy run with a guinea-pig group can be most worthwhile, not only to iron out problems, but to assess the time required. As with the majority of training and development events, a review and feedback session must be planned. This session will obviously be a substantial one. An approach that has been used successfully is to delay the review session – although not for too long – asking the participants to spend the intervening time reflecting on the event, identifying incidents on which they would want to comment, and planning what they want to say. The review can be a separate occasion, say the following week, half a day or even a day, depending on the complexity of the case being allocated to the event.

ROLE PLAYS

Role plays, like simulations and case studies, are important parts of a training programme, linked closely with the sessions in the programme. Substantial planning is necessary to ensure that the role situations are as close to real life as possible and that they reflect closely the learning of the preceding sessions. Role plays are usually associated with interview training, one learner taking the part of the interviewer, the other the part of the interviewee, but roles can be allocated in syndicate groups, case studies and simulations.

The cases can be developed from real-life cases that have occurred in the learners' organizations (names and places being changed to protect the originators of the cases), or the learners can be asked to provide details of cases of which they are aware or in which they have been involved. The latter case is particularly valuable as it gives an individual the opportunity, having learned new techniques, to 'repeat' the interview, avoiding any mistakes of the original one. A useful twist is to have the case 'owner' act as the interviewee, thus giving a view from the other side of the fence.

Variations

A number of planned variations are possible with role plays, depending on the circumstances within the programme, including:

- reverse role play, where the original interviewer in real life becomes the interviewee;
- ghosting or doubling in which, at stages during an interview, or if the interviewer seems to be losing their way, the trainer or another learner stands behind the interviewer and carries on the interview for a period until the original interviewer is ready to continue;
- empty-chair role playing, in which the problem-owner starts by describing the problem as they see it to an empty chair placed opposite them, and discussing all aspects of the problem and raising solutions.

The planner must also decide whether a training group is to be divided into smaller groups to practise the role plays, or whether role plays should take place in front of the rest of the group (as, for example in presentation skills training). The former approach saves time, with multiple events taking place simultaneously, but the latter, although more expensive in time, offers a wider range of review feedback.

Review and feedback

A particularly important aspect of role plays, for which substantial amounts of time have to be built into the programme, is the detailed review and feedback of the performance. These can be longer than the actual role plays and can be performed profitably with the role playing pair and their observer, a final roundup of learning taking place in a plenary session.

Observing role plays

Planning for role plays, and the methods of feedback, also includes the area of observation, a particularly key area in role play activities. The options, many of which will depend on the time available, include, eg:

- role plays by two learners in front of the whole group, observation for eventual feedback being made by the learning group and the trainer;
- role plays by the full learning group simultaneously in pairs with no observers, reliance being placed on the learners noting their own processes, giving feedback to each other and reporting in plenary;
- in triads, the third member acting as the observer and eventual giver of feedback to the role players within the triad, with a final report in plenary;
- either of the above approaches, but also using CCTV to record the interview, the CCTV being supplemented on occasions by an observer.

The most effective and time-saving approach is for the review to take place immediately following the event, the interviewer and interviewee's observer giving the feedback and conducting a review discussion with them. Again this can be occurring simultaneously with every role play event that has been taking place, the trainer(s) moving round the groups to ensure that all is going well. At the end of the reviews the full group can reconvene for a plenary session at which a discussion can take place on the points that have arisen in the sub-group reviews. Obviously, if these reviews are to be worthwhile, they can use up a substantial amount of time and this must be planned for in the session preparation.

The use of CCTV, although highly desirable, introduces significant, additional time requirements and complicated processes if more than one role play is taking place at the same time.

Action summary

Planning and preparation for role playing sessions can be summarized as requiring:

- consideration of the type of role playing to be used – pairs, triads, whole group etc;
- consideration of the type of role playing to be used – straightforward, reverse, ghosting, empty chair etc, or introducing these as and when circumstances demand;
- role briefs for the participants – these should be sufficiently detailed to enable the role player to understand the role and the situation, but not too detailed as to confuse or require over-concentration on the situation rather than the skills required;
- consideration of the use of observers and how feedback reviews will be held.

ACTIVITIES

'Activities' is the term I use for a range of practical training events that are variously described as 'games' or 'exercises,' and which can have a variety of uses, ranging from buzz group discussions, syndicate events to problem-solve, icebreaker events, group introduction events, and even the more specific case studies and simulations. Many take place during a programme having been linked with a preceding input session, giving the learners the opportunity to practise in the safe atmosphere of the training course what they have attempted to learn. This practice, in addition to increasing their skills, also gives them the opportunity to assess the learning issues prior to deciding whether to implement them at work.

Activities, of whatever nature, can require time periods ranging from five minutes to several hours, and part of the session planning to include an activity must be to identify the most effective activity for the objectives involved that can be completed in the least time.

Activity restraints

Many trainers do not use activities as much as would be useful to their programmes and the learners. This restriction may often be because:

- activities lead the programme format away from the 'safe' atmosphere of the lecture or other trainer presentation;

- the trainer has not previously run activities and may be hesitant about entering an unknown world;
- the feedback and review session can be a daunting process for trainers with little or no experience in this;
- the designer or trainer is not aware of relevant and suitable activities;
- there is concern about the time necessary for the activity and its review;
- the trainer is afraid that the learners may not 'play the game' or will treat it simply as a game.

Many of these fears and concerns can be resolved relatively easily. The final 'fear' in the list above is a common one, but in my experience and that of many trainers with whom I have had contact, it rarely happens, or if it does it takes place in the very early stages: as the activity progresses the learners soon settle down and become immersed in the task.

A useful learning and planning experience for the trainer is, before including an activity in a programme, to take part in the activity and thus gain firsthand experience of it. Even activities that appear to be childish games if presented effectively can become serious and valuable learning experiences. I have experienced more than once a group of older, senior managers crawling around the training room floor with Lego bricks, completely immersed in building a mast or bridge and not seeing anything unusual or childish in this.

Choosing activities

I have used activities to a very substantial extent in my training career and have researched them extensively so I have the reverse problem to the trainer who doesn't know where to obtain a suitable activity – I know of the availability of so many activities that it is a problem searching the mass for the one I want! At one time the number of training activities was quite limited and new trainers simply inherited sets from their predecessors. Some trainers with creative minds either modified existing activities or created new ones, usually because of the learner demands for organization/task/role relationship of the activities. This creation of activities has become almost a separate part of the publishing industry and the published collections now offer more than 7,000 activities.

The planner has the initial problem of how to choose from so many activities:

- Which and how many collections should you obtain?

- Where are these collections?
- How can you find the type of activity you seek easily?
- Which parallel activity should you use if the basic one is not suitable?

Many of the earlier activity collections were general ones containing activities in a wide range of application. More recently, more specifically directed collections have been made available – activities for time management, counselling, discipline interviewing, team building and so on. This has eased the problem, but it cannot be entirely resolved until a complete descriptive index of all published activities has been prepared – an almost impossible task. However publishers such as Echelon, Gower, Kogan Page, McGraw-Hill, Fenman and others do offer collections of this nature.

The collections also offer a solution to some of the other concerns raised:

- full descriptions of the activity are given, indicating the relevant situations in which to use them, and in many cases suggesting a range of alternative situations;
- in most cases the time and resources necessary for the activity are detailed;
- full guidance is given about how to set up, introduce and run the activity;
- guidelines are given in many cases about how to review the activity, detailing many of the relevant questions to ask.

Knowing that there are so many individual activities in a large number of collections creates a particular problem for the planner, who has to find the most suitable activity or set of activities for specific training purposes. Is there any way of finding a suitable activity other than either buying a number of collections or studying a set of library collections that seem to cover the area involved? Up to about two years ago the answer would have been 'no', but recently a number of publishers have taken action to resolve what was becoming an increasing and major problem. Two major publishers of activity collections – Echelon and Gower – have introduced Web sites that contain searchable databases. From a wide range of search criteria visitors to the sites can identify individual activities published in the collections and purchase these online as single or multiple units, the Echelon activities being sent by e-mail, the Gower purchases by snail-mail. The publishers concerned at the present time can be found on:

Gower – *www.gowertraining.co.uk* selecting the 'GAIA' section of the home page
Echelon – *www.learningmatters.com*

Selection on both these sites is by using the search facilities for the type of activity sought and thumbnail descriptions of all the activities involved can be displayed. At the time of writing, the Echelon site contains about 1,000 activities and the Gower one almost 3,000 activities. Echelon also offers, on request, a free browser CD-ROM for those seekers who either do not have access to or do not wish to use the Internet. This facility will eventually be available from Gower.

Technological advances

The online availability of activities was preceded by an interactive CD-ROM, 'The Complete Games Trainers Play' produced by McGraw-Hill in 1996, which put into digital form the four traditionally published books of activity collections by John W Newstrom and Edward E Scannell – *Games Trainers Play, More Games Trainers Play, Still More Games Trainers Play*, and *Even More Games Trainers Play.* Over 400 activities have been included on the one CD-ROM, the subjects being grouped in sections including conference leadership; climate setting and icebreakers; presentation tools; methods; motivation; self-concept. A consistent format is followed throughout – title; objective; procedure (including any information or graphic material the participants will require); discussion questions; materials required; approximate time required; and (where available) the original source of the activity.

This CD-ROM is remarkably easy to use, with simple reference buttons and menu items: installation is straightforward and there is a very useful set of search, bookmarking, text annotating and object importing facilities. Immediate movement to a particular activity is possible from the comprehensive contents list by means of a simple mouse click, and all the features can be printed. The activities can even be saved in a word processing application – Microsoft Word, WordPerfect and WordPad are all supported.

This is an excellent medium for viewing a large number of activities and making selected ones easily available, but the obvious limitation is in the number and range of activities contained in the four collections.

Another, more recent development of the digital theme appeared in Spring 1999 with the book *Team Development Games for Trainers* which, in addition to being published traditionally, was made available digitally by Gower, providing a total of 59 games that can be purchased as a single collection or in smaller collections. The digital publication of books is another area of technology that is developing rapidly and certainly has an important role to play in making activities easily available.

Action summary

Because 'activities' have many practical similarities to role plays described earlier in this chapter, planning action can follow the same stages as those for role plays. The essential features are:

- selecting the appropriate activity for the learning area and participant level;
- allowing sufficient time for the activity (including 'passage' time between rooms);
- allowing ample time for the review and feedback of the activity process and results – whether in immediate full plenary, in the practising small groups then plenary, with or without observers or self-analysis;
- ensuring that a final summary is produced of the key learning points intended to be brought out and actually emergent in the activity.

A full discussion of activities, their use in training and development and descriptions of the types of activities that are available that can be found in several published books (eg Rae, 1999).

BRAINSTORMING

The final 'traditional' form of training to be considered, and which can be included in training and development programmes and sessions, utilizes the technique that has the overall description and aim of creativity, with a practical application in brainstorming. Brainstorming can be included in trainer input sessions, discussions, activities and so on, and although utilizing free and generous thought applications it follows a strict discipline, consequently not presenting too much of a time challenge to planners.

Brainstorming is a creative technique that can be used during input sessions, discussions, activities, case studies and the like whenever the generation of a lot of ideas is required. The principle behind brainstorming is that participants allow their minds to freewheel and make suggestions for the subject, some of which will be old and tried, others completely new, yet others apparently rather silly and still others completely unworkable. I say 'apparently rather silly' as, when they are looked at, some may turn out to be the most effective solution or suggestion. After all who would have thought logically about a bouncing bomb to destroy a German dam? Why did a wine press give Gutenberg the idea of a printing press?

The brainstorm follows a strict pattern of a leader introducing the topic, inviting suggestions, controlling interruptions or explanations (which are not allowed), encouraging further suggestions and summarizing, at intervals, the suggestions made as the brainstorm proceeds. A recorder records *every suggestion* made, however apparently silly or unworkable, and helps the leader in the interim and final summaries. The participants are encouraged to come up with as many suggestions, ideas and proposals as they can, without describing them or accepting disagreement or argument from others.

At the end of the brainstorm (after a predetermined time or when ideas dry up completely) the list of suggestions is analysed (by the same or a different group) into:

- previously used or suggested and rejected ideas – circumstances may have changed and what was once a non-acceptable idea might now be realistic;
- attractive and possibly workable ideas, particularly if they are completely new and novel, but not over the top;
- unusual ideas that may work – who knows;
- obviously unworkable ideas, rejected only when it is absolutely certain that they would not work (at that time).

From the analysis a final selection of the best solution or solutions is made for submission to the person who has raised the question.

VIDEOS

Videos and their uses were covered extensively in Chapter 6 when their use in both on-the-job training and self-development were being considered. Obviously they can be equally valuable when included in an off-the-job training programme to support the other forms of training input. It is difficult to envisage complete training programmes being conducted with a series of videos, although some video producers have offered these. More usually the video on a single topic – eg time management, counselling interviews, effective questioning etc – is included in a trainer's input session and is valuable as an attention refresher, giving a different or similar viewpoint to that being presented, or as an introduction to a discussion or other activity.

Too frequently when a video is being used the trainer presents it with little or no explanation other than 'Now you're going to see a video on *x*'. After seeing the video the learners are asked if they enjoyed it and if they have any comments – usually there is little or no response – not surprising!

This ineffective approach can be improved considerably by planning the session to include the video – a small increase in time but a significant increase in learning. This plan includes:

- giving a more effective introduction, including;
  - comments on the reasons why the video is being included;
  - a brief summary of the video content;
  - guidance on what the viewers should be looking for in the video;
- showing the video – either straight through without stopping or interrupting it on one or more occasions;
- issuing a questionnaire seeking comments on the key learning points of the video after it has been shown;
- leading a discussion on the information that the learners have extracted from the video, the views they have on this information, and how they might apply the lessons on their return to work.

Videos and interactive videos can be accommodated in traditional training sessions as:

- an introduction to the subject at the start of the session;
- a summary of the subject at the end of the session;
- an interim review of the learning material at a critical stage in the session;
- presentation of a model or concept in which the session presenter is not an expert (whereas the video presenter is such an expert);
- a trigger for discussion.

CAT, CBT AND CD-i

Computers, interactive CDs and the Internet have been discussed in the earlier chapters on on-the-job and self-development training as, in the main, they are used on an individual basis rather than in an off-the-job, group situation. This is not to say that their use in the latter is not possible, rather that they are more suited to individual working. Interactive CDs can be introduced during a training event in the same way that the introduction of videos and trigger videos was suggested.

Computer-assisted training (CAT) is the more usual way in which computer programs are used to support the more traditional programmes. Where, for example, the training event is focused on the use of computers or software applications, the computers and the applications themselves are essential elements of the training. The problems arise if there is only one computer available and the group is larger than four people, but this can be circumvented by a number of slave computers linked to the trainer's main computer in a closed, mini-network. The trainer can display material to be seen by all the participants, or in practice activities the individuals can work at their own stations, their results being eventually available to the trainer and the remainder of the group.

The computer programs used in the group process can be based on commercially produced software, eg Microsoft Excel – the computer spreadsheet application, or Microsoft Access – an application for producing databases; on programs custom-made by commercial organizations to the specifications of the user; or programs produced by programmers in the organization itself. Use of insert programs such as these not only enables expert support for the rest of the training, but adds up-to-date variety to the event.

PLANNING THE TRAINING PROGRAMME – SUMMARY

Suggested formats for planning the different stages of the training programme were shown in Chapter 7 and are summarized here now that the various training methods available have been described:

1. List the agreed objectives for the training programme – these will be available from the preceding TNIA or may have to be determined at this stage.
2. Consider the learning population and as many of the influences that you can identify that these individuals will have on the programme design.
3. Against each objective list the possible ways in which these might best be met.
4. Decide whether the learning will be best achieved by an on-the-job or off-the-job programme form and whether these approaches might be combined in some way.

5. Consider the possible training accommodation needed and as many of the effects that you can identify that this resource will have on the course design and practice.
6. Confirm whether you are restricted to containing the programme within a certain period of time or whether it will be allowed the time required for effective completion.
7. Confirm from any available previous information when the programme is required to start and by which date it has to be completed, or obtain this information.
8. Decide on the nature of the training approaches (see following material for a summary of these).
9. Plan the sequence of the sessions for a logical learning progression designed to meet the programme objectives.
10. Prepare a programme outline plan showing the sequence of sessions and general comments on their proposed format.
11. Discuss the proposed plan with the training practitioners, the training manager and, if possible, with representatives of the learning population and their line manager, and agree the final plan.
12. Complete a final, agreed outline and part-detailed programme from which the training practitioners can produce detailed session plans.
13. Pass the agreed, final plan to the training practitioners who will be responsible for the individual sessions.

9

Planning the Training Sessions

This chapter will describe:

- techniques for planning, designing and constructing the individual training sessions in the overall programme.

In this book, and particularly in this chapter, 'session' is used to describe a singular, bounded period of time on a training course in which the trainer presents some form of activity. This format includes not only an 'input session' in which the trainer presents a subject, but also multiple activity sessions, practical activities or syndicate working etc. The material available to the trainer to plan and design a 'session' has been described principally in Chapters 7 and 8, but some aspects of the on-the-job training described in earlier chapters can also be utilized in off-the-job, group training.

If there has been a prior, separate programme planning process, the practitioner will have agreed an outline plan with the planner in which suggestions will have been made for particular forms of approaches suitable for the type of programme and the other factors involved. But the practitioners must play a very active part in the final design of the sessions as they will be responsible for offering them, using particularly their own styles of presentation and process control.

THE STAGES IN DESIGNING A LEARNING SESSION

Practitioners must ask themselves the following questions to lead them to a model for designing the sessions:

1. What do the learners need to learn from the session? (Their objectives.)
2. What do you (and the earlier planner) feel should be included in the session? (Your objectives.)
3. What are the priorities in the material that has to be presented in the sessions? (Must knows, should knows, could knows.)
4. How much time has been allocated or what time is available for the session?
5. Which training method or approach will be most appropriate for each session?
6. What sequence should the sessions follow?
7. What training aids do you need for the session?
8. Should you produce a session plan and what form should it take?
9. What form of brief is going to be most appropriate for the session?

1. What do the learners need to learn from the session? (Their objectives)

The basis of the response to this question will be found in the TNIA report, which reflects the views, knowledge, skills and attitudes of the learners when the TNIA was being developed. This, however, reflects the overall objectives of the target population, and within this population there will be a range of personal objectives based on individual levels of knowledge and skills. If there is a very wide range in these needs problems can develop for the trainer – at what level should the trainer aim the learning material; how fast should the sessions move etc? If the level is aimed at the participant with the least knowledge and skills or one who is a slow learner, the more skilled and faster learners will soon become frustrated. If the aim is at the highest points, the lower skill members will lose interest as they are left behind. If there are no ways to select reasonably homogeneous groups the trainer is left with these problems, the only answer possible in most cases is to try to strike a happy medium. One attempt to help the lower level participants can be for them to take part in pre-course open learning material prepared by the trainer, in order to try to have all participants at more or less the same level at the start of the session.

The luxury of knowing the abilities of the potential individual learners is not frequently available to the trainer, who must build into early sessions an attempt to determine these ability levels or requirements. Usually this can only be done, because of time constraints, if linked with the normal introductory activities.

The simplest way is to ask the participants, during their self-introductions or other introductory approaches, to describe their personal objectives – these might be discussed if there is time. This will at least give the trainer some information on what the level might be, or the chance to observe 'problem' learners carefully for their reactions and learning. It may then be possible for some individual coaching, say in the evening on a residential course.

One very successful joint introductory/personal objective statement activity is the 'Who am I?' chart. Once the starting activities of the event are completed, the learners are given an outline chart, similar to the one shown in Figure 9.1, for completion and use as an introduction.

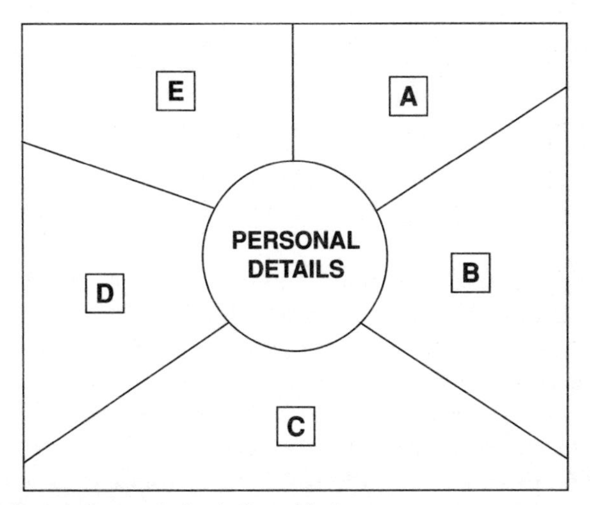

A = Problems they are encountering in the subject area
B = Their personal strengths
C = How supportive is the boss of their learning
D = Concerns they have about the event
E = Personal objectives

Figure 9.1 *A 'Who am I?' chart*

2. *What do you (and the earlier planner) feel should be included in the session? (Your objectives)*

These objectives are included in the overall objectives for the programme, which are based on the TNIA results and agreed between the planner and the practitioner. Some of the material may be so extensive that it will need to be spread over several sessions but, whether this is so or not, each session must have specific objectives set for it so that success or otherwise can be assessed in the evaluation process. These objectives, as with any objectives, should be written down to avoid 'mental adjustment' after the event, and the learning group should also be made aware of them – in a handout or on a posted flipchart available from the start of the session.

3. *What are the priorities in the material that has to be presented in the sessions? (Must knows, should knows, could knows)*

Within the objectives for the session the material itself, the organization's culture or express wishes, the learners' line managers and the time available will define the priorities for the material to be presented during the session. Some of these priorities can be decided on by the planner/trainer, but probably the major constraint to offering all the desired material will be time. Every trainer knows that time constraints are their biggest enemy and even the most carefully worked out session can face barriers of insufficient time to put over the necessary material. It is rarely a case of having too much time available!

The respective priorities can be expressed by three simple indicators, into which all the session's material can be divided prior to the session. These are the **must knows**, the **should knows** and the **could knows**.

The *must knows* are items that, if they are not included would cause the session to be a failure and not to achieve its objectives. These are the essential items that *must* be covered during the session, and the rest of the session must be built around them.

The *should knows* are the items that, although not essential, would help the learners considerably in understanding and practising the subject of the session. Every attempt must be made to allocate time for them, but during the session some of them can be omitted. It is therefore a useful practice to prioritize the *should knows* to help in the ongoing decisions about what to omit.

The *could knows* represent material or activities that, if omitted, would not appreciably affect the learning of the group. Of course it would be interesting and useful to include them, but they and only they, will be the first items to be omitted if time is pressing; their inclusion would have to be at the expense of the *must* and *should knows*.

4. *How much time has been allocated or what time is available for the session?*

The allocation of time for sessions etc in a programme is one of the most difficult areas in event design. There are a number of factors working both for and against effective allocation. The practitioner trainers themselves will have favourite sessions and will try hard to have the maximum amount of time allocated to these, often irrespective of the subject's importance. The TNIA may have shown a wide range of associated topics that should be included in one programme to make it coherent – however, to include them all may mean that each session cannot have its optimum time allocated. Some sessions in a programme may have higher priorities than others and will demand a greater time allocation. The approach to these and other problems can be the application of the *must, should* and *could* priority factors, and reference back to the overall planner may be necessary.

One essential action for the session practitioner is that, when the timing has been agreed, adherence must be complete if the programme contains a series of sessions, each with specific time allocations. Extension of one session beyond its time can not only have an effect on the following session but a cumulative effect, until one session is curtailed to bring the process back on line. Obviously, in the more informal types of programmes, exact timing is not *as* relevant, but there must be some adherence to timing.

5. Which training method or approach will be most appropriate for each session?

Although the choice of training method may be influened by many factors – time available, type of session objectives, trainer skills, organization cultural requirements etc – the overriding criterion must be that the method used must be the (or one of several) most appropriate for learning in that particular session subject. Most of the possible approaches have already been described in previous chapters and even these brief descriptions should suggest the most appropriate approaches. Reference to publications with more extended descriptions and guidance should be made for final decisions. Figure 9.2 summarizes the approaches and strategies against the areas of most likely usefulness.

6. What sequence should the sessions follow?

The sequencing of material in a session will in most cases follow a logical progression, the progress depending on the type of material being presented for learning. The options for sequencing include:

- *From the known to the unknown* This is the most common sequence for learning, being a logical progression from the start of the session with material with which the learners are familiar (and therefore comfortable), through newer material.
- *From the simple to the complex* Launching into a session of new material with the complex aspects of the subject will certainly 'turn off' the slower, less experienced learners. Start with the simpler concepts and move progressively to the complex ones,

LEARNING EXPERIENCE	POSSIBLE USES
Activity – (or exercise, game, practical or experiential activity) an activity in gathering information, problem-solving, task performance etc.	Practical group work to develop or reinforce learning or practise skills, attitudes and behaviours.
Brainstorming – wide ranging creative discussion to obtain ideas for problem solutions.	Creativity. New ideas. Problem-solving. Decision making. Group and team training.
Buzz groups – groups of two to six people discussing subject for a short time.	Safe environment for expression of views and neutral feedback in group or team without needing to leave the training room.
Case studies – real or manufactured complex problems to be analysed in detail to produce solutions.	Group problem solving with application of principles.
CAT – computer programs inserted or added to other forms of group training.	As change of pace and expertise, self-development within groups or on an individual basis.
CBT – Use of computer programs from software or the Internet to enable, particularly, knowledge learning.	Usually for self-development on an individual basis or in work groups linked by an intranet.
Controlled discussions – subjects are discussed under general control of trainer or elected/selected leader from the group.	Promotion of wider understanding and expression of points of view within a group. Use of discussion techniques. Behaviour observation.
Demonstrations – trainer or expert performs an operation, skill or service with learners watching.	Practical skill training using real objects or situations to show the operation etc.
Instructional talk/input session – a trainer presentation of a subject in terms of knowledge, information and details, and using a variety of training aids.	The basic strategy of a group training event.
Lecture – a (usually) uninterrupted talk to larger audience.	Provision of information at conference or symposium.
Open learning – (programmed learning, distance learning, learning packages etc). Text or multi-media packages with sets of information, questions or tasks.	Individual learning, self-development situations. Mixed pace groups. Valuable for regular training need satisfaction of small number of staff and/or geographically dispersed staff. Stand alone, with or without support.
Projects – an exercise in gathering information, performing a task or producing material.	On- or off-the-job small or larger group activities to develop or consolidate and extend learning and encourage co-operative activity.

Figure 9.2 *Training strategies and their uses*

LEARNING EXPERIENCE	POSSIBLE USES
Question and answer – a series of appropriate questions from the trainer to the learning group.	To check understanding and encourage interaction and thought at all levels.
Reading – of a book, article or handout, in the training situation or away from it.	To prepare for learning, to reinforce course or other forms of learning, or as individual self-development.
Role plays – learners given roles, real or artificial in a group, paired one-to-one or triads, to carry out situation cases.	Reinforcement of learning, practising skills, awareness through feedback, attitude change.
Seminars – a group of people with similar interests who discuss a group or series of related topics.	Updating of knowledge with presentations by subject experts to encourage critical thinking and discussion.
Simulations – the duplication of real situations with complex problems, or a game activity with participants taking on roles or positions.	Simulation of an activity that cannot be practised directly, in problem-solving and team development.
Syndicates – learners form small groups from the full group and meet separately to consider and solve problems, perform tasks etc. The sub-group views are then presented to the full group.	Used in group learning events when it is desirable/necessary to obtain different views or approaches by small groups. Useful for observation of small group behaviour, leadership and membership, and problem-solving and decision-making.
Video (linear) – a video that is shown straight through or stopped at intervals for discussion.	Support for other training approaches, change of pace and presentation, expert input, dealing with emotive issues, presenting situations not ordinarily possible on the event.
Video (trigger) – a video consisting of short scenarios after which questions are raised for discussion of each scenario.	Guiding discussion on best practices, encouraging discussing and expression of views, values and ideas. Reinforcing prior learning.

Figure 9.2 *Training strategies and their uses (continued)*

ensuring along the way that the relevant learning has been achieved.

- *Logical stepping* Most learning material can be broken down into logical steps (see the tea-making activity in Chapter 5). If these steps are followed, with learning checks along the way, achievement is much more likely than with a disconnected approach.
- *Interesting to more serious* If relevant, start with a fun item, or at least light material, before moving on to the heavier aspects.

However, be careful not to emphasize the fun part too much or it may become difficult to move on.

- *Dependency* The session material may relate directly to or depend on the material in a preceding session and this must be taken into account to ensure continuity (and unintended overlap).
- *Knowledge to doing* Where the session material is completely new to the learners the sequence will usually be an input of knowledge and information, followed by a period of practice and feedback.
- *Doing to knowledge to doing* Where the learners have *some* knowledge or skills in the subject a practical activity at the start of the session can identify the level of knowledge and skills. This would be followed by input material to extend the knowledge level, to be reinforced by a further, more demanding activity requiring use of the knowledge and skills presented.

Although the practitioner must be aware of the problems of time, it must be remembered that sessions are rarely fixed and inflexible plans. Many factors can emerge while the session is progressing that suggest the original plan has to be modified on the spot by the trainer. The *must knows* etc can be useful in this context, ie deciding to omit and/or add material. The experience of the planner will suggest sessions where this is most likely to happen and contingency plans can be formulated.

7. What training aids do you need for the session?

Decisions on this planning aspect will depend on and link with the next stage, but consideration should be given to the nature of the most suitable aid(s); their use in the session; the time that using them will add to the session; and the time and resources needed for their production. Training aids will always add time to a session, but this will be strongly outweighed by their value in assisting the learning process for many of the learners.

8. Should you produce a session plan and what form should it take?

A session plan is essential in the planning process and is in two stages: 1) producing an outline session plan when decisions have been made as to what will be included; and 2) a brief for use during the session itself. The 'brief' is known by a number of descriptions – 'session notes', 'script' and so on. I prefer 'brief' to 'script' as it describes more accurately an effective form. 'Script' suggests a layout using the session material verbatim and notes that will either be memorized and repeated parrot fashion or read from the sheets. Both these latter methods are highly ineffective ones for presenting a session.

Whichever method you use, the essential feature is that you write down something that will reinforce your thoughts and act as a reminder during the session – you may never need to refer to it when you know the session well, but it is always advisable to have it to hand in case of emergencies.

The general plan follows the more general planning outline, but concentrated on the session itself. Some trainers prefer to incorporate it in the brief, having it act as an introductory note to the brief itself. When the trainer is very familiar with the session this introductory outline may be all the reminder that he or she needs. An example session plan is shown in Figure 9.3.

SESSION PLAN FOR INITIAL PRESENTATION SKILLS SESSION

		Approximate time
1.	Introduce the session and describe the session objectives. Seek information on the group's experience of presenting.	10 minutes
2.	Present input session, concentrating on skill attributes of the presentation of a session. Include attention span and barriers to communication.	35 minutes
3.	During the input, when barriers are to be introduced, form buzz groups to identify possible barriers. Take feedback, discuss and return to buzz groups to identify possible ways of breaking down barriers. Take feedback.	(15 minutes)
4.	Learning group members present their pre-course prepared 10-minute presentations – two groups of four learners. Required 4 × 10 minutes and 4 × 10 minutes review and feedback of each presentation plus discontinuity time = 80 plus 20 minutes.	1 hour 40 minutes
5.	Final review session in plenary.	15 minutes
	Total session time	2 hours 40 minutes (allow 2 hours 45 minutes)

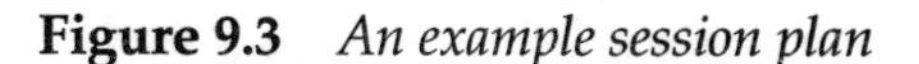

Figure 9.3 *An example session plan*

9. *What form of brief is going to be most appropriate for the session?*

The different types of brief and the timing they require are described in the sections that follow.

TIMING

Whichever form of brief you are going to use, it will be necessary to have some indication of time during the session related to the parts of the brief. Two timing approaches can be used, both of which can also be used in the full brief. The first, as used in the initial outline, shown in Figure 9.3, indicates the time to be taken for each part of the session; the second will have beside item 1 the actual time the session starts, alongside item 2 the actual time that part of the session should start, and so on. The principal argument against the second approach is that it is inflexible and is very sensitive to a variety of time delays – it has the advantage that a glance at the outline should show how far into the session you are, rather than your having to calculate that you have taken the correct time (or not) for the items to that stage.

DETAILED SESSION PLANNING

As mentioned earlier, the production of a session brief and having it at the session is strongly recommended, even if it is not actually used. In some cases two documents are necessary, one on which the planning is entered, the other being used during the session. To satisfy the various preferences of different trainers these briefs can take several forms:

- the traditional text or vertical method format;
- the headline format;
- OHP slides as briefs;
- the horizontal plan format;
- patterned notes.

Some of these briefs can be used directly as in-session briefs, others need to be modified or converted for this purpose.

THE TRADITIONAL TEXT OR VERTICAL METHOD FORMAT

This form of 'brief' is a full-text script in which what is to be said is written down in full, word for word, as if it were a report or essay to be read out on some occasion. The principal difference from the report etc would be the use of the 'spoken' form rather than the 'written' form – for example, when we are speaking we generally say 'can't', whereas it is usually written as 'cannot'. The full script is useful in the preparation and planning stage as it ensures that everything is included, but it is rarely used as the actual session brief. Even speakers who do use it, reading from it substantially, present parts without reading directly. It is also difficult to refind your place if you have to diverge for some reason from the plot. Various strategies can be used to help the document to become a more living 'brief' or planning document from which other forms of brief can be constructed.

Division into paragraphs and sub-paragraphs

Text forms can be read more easily, and hence are more easily understood and referred to if the script is divided into paragraphs and sub-paragraphs as it would be in a report, or as in a book, with headlines for each main section.

This is not just for the sake of grammatical accuracy, but to make each section of the text more individual and clearer visually. Grammatically a paragraph contains material relating to one subject and this rule, if followed, signposts the reader/user from one aspect to another, rather than their having to search within a multi-subject paragraph for the various ideas.

The layout should have plenty of 'white space' – broad and variable borders; substantial line spaces between paragraphs and sub-paragraphs – and different colours can be used for alternate paragraphs or sections. Particularly if the script is produced on a computer or modern typewriter, different fonts and sizes of fonts can aid this clarity.

Underlining for emphasis

It is necessary when using a script of this nature to make the separate parts obviously separate and visually impactive. Underlining words, phrases, sentences and even paragraphs with single underlining or, for more emphasis, double underlining can help in this. Even more impact is possible if **bold printing** is linked with the underlining. *Italic printing* is frequently used in published books instead of bold – there are various views on this, so make up your own mind by printing something in each format, either as a standard or for use on different occasions.

Colours for emphasis

Colours can be used for separate parts of the text to isolate these from each other, but they can also be used as another form of impact or emphasis; for example, some red lettering in a section printed in blue will stand out effectively. Avoid yellows or pastel shades as these tend to be lost.

If the script is handwritten coloured pens or highlighters can be used, or blocks shaded to make them stand out as diffferent sections.

Framing for emphasis or isolation

Adding a frame or boxed border, particularly if combined with some of the previously described emphasizers, can add further impact.

The frame or border, in addition to containing words or graphic images, can also contain a degree of shading for more impact or to separate it from another box.

Broad margins

It can be helpful to leave broader than normal borders at both margins of the text, again for impact, but also so that notes can be added – questions to be raised, necessary amendments as the session proceeds, and any stage directions. As many of these notes will be scribbled a broad margin is helpful – the margins used here are 1 inch (2.5 cm) from the standard margin.

Stage directions

It is a useful practice to annotate the script (in the broad margins) with notes, possibly in a different colour to the script, action notes or 'stage directions'. These can indicate when to use an OHP slide, issue a handout or questionnaire, ask a question to start a discussion, and so on. These directions can also include the timings to be followed during the session (see page 165).

None of these effects – boxes, underlining etc – should be overdone or they may become the norm for the document and cease to have impact.

This full-text method is useful as a first stage of planning and preparing a brief. Once the script has been produced most trainers convert it into a more usable form, but the script has served its purpose in reinforcing the material in the trainer's mind.

THE HEADLINE METHOD

The headline method is a simplified and abbreviated form of the full-script approach and, by cutting out much of the text itself, produces a much shorter, clearer and more easily referenced brief.

The method can be summarized as:

- *List the headlines on A4 sheets.* The important topics or key ideas of the subject are identified first, then listed as the main subject headings. These can be written down as they are thought of, to be put in order when all the headlines have been identified.
- *Enter inter-heading summary notes.* Under each heading, ordered in a logical manner, brief summary notes about the topic are entered. These notes should be sufficiently brief for quick and easy reference, containing all the significant key points. If it is felt that the notes are too long they can always be edited at a later stage.
- *Complete the working brief, with impact techniques.* The summary notes can finally be annotated or marked for maximum impact and ease of reference, as described in the section above on the traditional script method – upper and lower case lettering; different fonts and effects; different colours for each heading and perhaps in some of the summaries themselves; underlining; boxes; marginal stage directions and so on.

The headline method is probably the one used by the majority of trainers to produce at least the basic material summary that, if a substantial document, is reduced to a working session brief. The summaries are examined carefully and reduced to as few words or phrases as are necessary to remind the trainer what to cover. Consequently, the stages of preparation for a working headline brief can be:

1. Construct a full, traditional planning script with all the material included in detail. (This stage can be omitted depending on circumstances.)
2. Contract the full text or the material to headlines followed by summarized notes related to the headlines.

3. Contract further to headlines followed by key words and phrases relating to the headlines.

One of the suggestions made earlier that is very relevant for the working headline brief is to leave broad margins for annotation. This can be specific instructions at progressive stages – 'Show OHP slide 1 and start discussion'; 'Ask question *x* at this stage'; 'Put into buzz groups here for 8 minutes to discuss *x*'; etc. These stage directions can be written or marked in a prominent colour to direct attention to them.

Trainers will have personal preferences about how the brief is constructed physically, the two major options being A4 sheets or large index cards. A useful tip for both the traditional and headline methods is: if there is more than one A4 sheet or index card, number each one clearly. This will solve any problems if the papers are dropped or get out of order. However, if it is at all possible, the session headline brief should be restricted to one sheet of paper – this may be too abbreviated for inexperienced trainers or if the material is new, but eventually the number of sheets should be reduced. This reduction will be more difficult with index cards if the writing is to be made sufficiently large to be seen easily during the session. Sheets can be handwritten or computer produced, cards will normally be handwritten, the effects produced by coloured pens or highlighters.

Large print or handwriting will help the trainer to follow the brief without it being too obvious that it is being looked at during the session. However, you should not worry about whether or not the learners see you looking at the brief – in my experience in most cases they don't even notice or, if they do, they will not be concerned, perhaps even being assured that you have a concern for accuracy and effectiveness. It is unusual to remember everything – text and stage directions – in an extended and complex session. Be accurate and confident and refer to your brief whenever necessary. The aim is to produce a brief that contains all the key word reminders and is in a format that is sufficiently clear to enable you to refer to it whether you are seated or standing.

The proposed life of the brief and the session to which it refers can affect the way in which it is presented. If the session is a one-off the brief can be produced to last only that one session, but this short life should not preclude completeness and clarity. Briefs that are intended for use on more than one occasion or over a long period can be converted into more permanent forms. Some organizations with printing/publishing departments offer the equivalent of commercially produced, permanent briefs. This can be dangerous, as training sessions are rarely static and a system for updating should be included.

If the brief is produced in the permanent form referred to above the best approach I have found is to include the session briefs, produced on a good laser printer from computer files, in an A4 ringbinder, each session being tagged for easy identification, or perhaps printed on different coloured paper. OHP masters, activity briefs and handouts can also be filed with the relevant session. When amendment is necessary revision notes can be entered in the margins and the appropriate new pages printed from the edited computer file.

The introduction of computers has eased brief construction and maintenance considerably and a large number of session and programme plans and briefs can be retained in a small space – eg on floppy or zip disks.

OHP SLIDES AS BRIEFS

A number of experienced trainers (and some inexperienced ones who are not aware of the dangers) decide not to use a brief as described in the previous sections, but use their set of OHP slides as the brief. As each successive slide is presented, the trainer talks about the slide and it acts as a trigger of what to talk about. Notes are added to the frame at the side of the transparency from which comments can be made, but the only 'brief' may be a list of the slides to be shown and their main messages. If you have a large number of slides and you are familiar with the subject and the session content, this approach can be acceptable, although if taken to too great an extent the session can suffer from a surfeit of slides.

There are a number of problems with this approach, with some of which the experienced trainer can cope, although some may be outside their control. If the trainer is not careful it will become obvious that he/she is talking 'to' the slides and the learners stop listening, only reading the slides. This type of session can also be rather boring and monotonous.

The principal danger, however, is that if something happens to the electricity supply the slides cannot be presented. Similarly, the projection bulb may 'blow' and, unless a spare is carried or is part of the projector, projection is impossible. Trainers I know who have relied on OHP slides as their 'briefs', when training away from their own location have even fallen victim to there being no projector on which to show their slides!

My advice is that, unless you are *very* familiar with your material and could cope with the projector failure, if you are going to talk to your set of slides always have a written brief available, either to use or as fallback support.

A technological variant of sessions using OHP slides is a computer slide program, such as Microsoft PowerPoint. Here the OHP slides are reproduced as a series of graphic slides that can be sorted into a continuous slide-supported talk, using the computer (usually with a large projection screen) as the source projector. The slides can have notes (only visible to the presenter) appended or a written brief can be with the presenter, who usually stands at the computer controls. The benefits of this approach include the small size of a floppy or zip disk (the means of inserting the program), which can be carried in the pocket. It does, of course, mean that a computer must be available at the training site, but this doesn't have to have the PowerPoint program installed – the disk 'slide show' can contain its own portable program.

The same problems described for the OHP slide approach apply to the computer slide program, although for one problem a portable answer is possible. It is not unknown for airlines to lose a traveller's possessions. I know of one trainer who was going abroad to fulfil a training consultancy and who carried all his visual aid material on floppy disks in his luggage – this did not arrive with him! Fortunately, he carried as hand luggage his briefcase containing a set of OHP slides, which he was able to use until his luggage turned up.

HORIZONTAL PLANNING

A very useful method of planning and using a training brief is known as 'horizontal planning'. This, as its name suggests, differs from the traditional or vertical format method in that the planning layout is horizontal. It is not only a planning approach but can also be used for the practical brief. In addition to breaking away from the traditional formats of a vertical script or headlines brief, it can almost always be presented on one sheet of paper, albeit in the planning stage of A3 size. The translation to the working brief, however, can usually be to a sheet of A4 paper or a large index card.

Planning stages

The horizontal planning approach is in four stages.

Stage 1

The first stage has many similarities with the start of the headline approach, with the first thoughts on the key headlines being entered on the sheet of paper. However, the paper is placed in the landscape position, ie with the longer sides horizontal rather than vertically. The key words or phrases are entered, spaced out across the sheet. They need not be in a logical order or the order in which they will be used in the session – this aspect can be edited and other headings can be added later in the process.

An example of this stage of the method can be in the planning of a session on presentation skills:

ADULT LEARNING	BARRIERS TO COMMUNICATION	PRESENTATION STAGES	SKILLS etc

Stage 2

In this second stage each subject heading is considered and words or short phrases written below the heading describing the content of that heading. Again, additional ones can be added as the later entries trigger thoughts that lead to entries in the earlier sections.

ADULT LEARNING	BARRIERS TO COMMUNICATION	PRESENTATION STAGES	SKILLS etc
Learning styles – Kolb and Honey/Mumford LSQ etc	Listeners The trainer Means of modifying etc	Introductory – aims and objectives Content Questioning etc Main body Summary Conclusion Discussion etc	Verbal – use of voice etc Non-verbal – appearance, manner etc

These initial subject areas under the key headings will themselves usually need to be broken down into greater detail to ensure full understanding (this detail of course will be abbreviated when the practical use sheet is being prepared). If there is a lot of material it may be necessary at this stage to use a separate sheet for each heading, the sheets being amalgamated when the material is being abbreviated.

Stage 3

Once all the subheadings have been entered under the main, key headings, the material can be prioritized as described previously:

must, should and *could knows,* the various entries being annotated M, S or C as appropriate, or material that would exceed the time being deleted.

When the content to be included has been assessed in this way the stage directions (in abbreviated form) can be added with coloured pens, arrow-linked items and the other impact techniques mentioned that are appropriate to this format. Only a minimum of this material should be added, to avoid a diminution of clarity, but an effective brief should be maintained.

Stage 4

Now the planning document can be made into a fair copy, any reorganization, additions or omissions being included and the assessed stage directions clearly marked. This document, if possible contained on one A4, landscape format sheet, is the brief you will take with you into the session and use in the same way as the other brief formats, but with a simpler and more logical outlook, in which the complete session with useful triggers can be taken in at one glance. The sheet enables any part of the material to be located speedily and editing usually involves only a little writing.

PATTERNED NOTES PLANNING

The system of patterned notes, mind maps or spidergrams, pioneered by Tony Buzan and described in Chapter 6, can be applied successfully to planning sessions and producing 'scripts'. The method avoids a mass of words that can be unclear and can contain a session brief on one sheet of paper for easy reference.

Like the headline and horizontal planning methods, the technique seeks initially the identification of the subject key words or phrases, which are entered on the mind map. The key words radiate from the central point and act as triggers to the memory, enabling fuller details of the sub-topic to be recalled. To help this recall, sub-branches radiate from these main key lines and give, again in abbreviated form, further information on the sub-topic.

The mind map is essentially an individual production, as each person's mind works in a different way and reacts to different stimuli, one person's mind map being unintelligible to another. I prefer key phrases rather than single words on both the main and sub-branches, starting my rotating pattern at about 11 o'clock and progressing in a clockwise direction.

In a similar way to the headline and script methods, all the impact features described earlier can be used on the mind map, and a useful treatment is to make each main branch and key word/phrase a different, distinctive colour to make identification easier. Some key words/phrases might be boxed, the shape of the box mirroring the key word. For example, a branch relating to an OHP might be enclosed in a box shaped like an OHP. Linked ideas and back/forward references can be joined by two-way arrows, and recognized or personal symbols can be used as shorthand reminders – * !! ? > # @ ☎ 🖳 🗐 etc. Almost anything can be used in an individual pattern as long as it is meaningful to the producer and enables recall of the material.

The planning mind map can be converted easily into a session brief, requiring simply a cleaning up and clarifying process, although users must be very familiar with the technique and the mind map they have produced, otherwise it can be very confusing.

Briefs or scripts, whether for planning or practical purposes, are individual documents and usually only make complete sense to the person who produced the document. The use of another's brief is not to be recommended except in emergencies. A new trainer's personal brief should be be constructed from an existing one but in the new trainer's own style.

10

Planning Activity Sessions

This chapter will describe:

- techniques for planning, designing and constructing individual training sessions other than input sessions.

The use of practical activities in training demonstrates one of the most important developmental milestones in the history of training and development, moving training sessions on significantly from the more passive input type of session. The introduction of practical activities and all the following related aspects, we can now see clearly is described very succinctly by the various learning styles and the learning cycle – doing, reflecting, analysing and planning. The use of these learning stages has been shown to enhance learning and the 'activity' is at the heart of this cycle, in fact usually the trigger for the learning process.

Activities go under the name of activities, games, exercises, experiential activities, practical events, small group events, and so on, but have as a basis a practical action – problem-solving, decision-making, behaving, discussing, interview and role playing practice – usually in sub-groups, triads or pairs from the main training group, followed by a review and feedback discussion of what happened and what resulted.

PLANNING QUESTIONS

The principal questions to be asked in planning for activities are:

- What are the learning objectives for the session for which an activity is being considered?
- What would be the most effective approach to achieve these objectives?

- If this effective approach is, or would contain, a practical activity, are the objectives likely to be achieved by this approach?
- What is the existing level of knowledge, skill and experience of the learners?
- What is known of the experience of the learners in taking part in training activities?
- What is the consequent learning gap that will need to be filled?
- To what extent will the activity fill the learning gap?
- Why do I want to use an activity? Am I sure it is not just because I like practical activities myself? Is the activity necessary or just desirable?
- What advantages are there in using or not using an activity?
- Is time a relevant factor in my choice of an activity?
- How many activities? What form of activity?
- When should I include the activity?
- Can the activity I am considering be completed successfully in the time available?
- How much time is available?
- To what extent have I a selection of activities available, a range of knowledge of activities or do I know where to look for them?
- Have I all the resources available to run the activity?
- What constraints – staffing, material resources, money, attitudes etc – exist?
- To what extent can I resolve the problems caused by these constraints?
- What consideration have I given to what form of observation, if any, I want or need?
- What consideration have I given to what form of review I want/need to use?

Some of these questions are self-explanatory and may seem unnecessary, but they are all worth asking, as it is only too easy to decide to include an activity without ensuring that it is the most appropriate approach and the activity chosen is the most relevant one for the purpose. The most significant of these questions are those relating to: Why an activity? How many activities? Which activity?

Why?

The reason for including an activity must be because this form of learning support is the most appropriate for the learning to be achieved in either or both of: 1) the type of material; 2) the learning preferences and styles of the learners. Activities should not be included because they are 'easy options' for the trainer (many turn out to be far from this!), because the trainer feels he/she is short of material for an input session, or because the trainer likes including activities. The objectives of the activity must be relevant, even though the activity itself, superficially, may not appear to be directly related to the subject. Some of the relevant reasons for including an activity are:

- to consolidate, through practice, learning from other parts of the programme, eg input sessions, discussion, video assessment;
- to introduce learning points by letting the learners try out an activity then analyse the learning successes or failures and why these occurred;
- to introduce, in a realistic way, an activity to lighten a 'heavy' programme or change the mental direction of the learners, for example with a relevant or irrelevant activity, an icebreaker or session shaker;
- to introduce during an evening session on a residential course an enjoyable and attractive learning form when the more traditional approach might not be well received.

How many?

Following the introduction of the concept of learning through activities, many trainers went overboard in including lots of activities in their programmes, which quickly became known as the 'game shows'. In these programmes activities tended to follow one another, often with minimal or even no feedback and review session. Quite soon it was realized that people learnt as little from just games as they did from just input sessions and that a balance had to be reached.

Many sessions benefit from the input etc being completed and reinforced by a following, supportive activity in which the learners can practise the learning. But if this happens too frequently, say after every input session, there is a danger that the learners will react with 'Oh no, not another game!' whether this is spoken or unspoken.

Planning for activities should take into account the learning preferences of the members of the group. The strong reflectors and theorists are less likely to accept activities, or too many of these unless there is ample opportunity for discussion, review, feedback and analysis of the results. The activitists and pragmatists will enjoy the activities (provided, in the case of the pragmatists, that they have a work relationship), but will not be too keen on extended post-activity discussion.

The principle for activity inclusion should follow those for programmes as a whole – in general, no undue emphasis on one particular approach, but a balanced mix of input etc and activity to satisfy all types of learners.

Which and what form of activity and where from?

The answers to these questions are far reaching and too extensive for complete coverage in this planning guide – readers are referred to the several books published on the subject (eg my *Using Activities in Training and Development*, 1999, 2nd edn, Kogan Page) and to the numerous collections of published activities. There are, however, two predominating sources of activities – internally produced and externally available ones.

Internally produced activities

These are the activities 'invented' by an organization's trainers and are characterized by their direct relevance to the actual work of the organization or use of case studies drawn from the organization. This avoids the common complaint by learners that the activities are too artificial, although artificial activities can be well constructed to ensure that all the relevant key learning points are included. The work-based activity will be well received by the learners, who will be easily able to relate to the situations, and even more so if they are introduced by the learners themselves. These can be suggested to the trainer by the learner, the trainer modifying an existing activity from the suggestion, producing a 'new' activity from the information, or even impromptu activities raised during the course by comments from a learner. This last-named type of activity is the most lifelike as it is based on what is in the minds of the learners at the time. It may, however, not cover all the points the trainer would wish, so the feedback and review session must be carefully directed to ensure that the maximum learning is attained.

Work-based activities must be kept up to date – organizational policies and practices change and the credibility of an activity can be reduced if these factors are not taken into account on an ongoing basis.

Externally available activities

There will be (many?) occasions when an internally produced practical activity is not available or suitable for a specific purpose, does not include all the required learning points, or is simply not relevant. You must then look to commercial sources for suitable activities, seeking the best from the wealth available. Herein lies a minefield of problems.

The questions to which you must seek answers about available programmes include all the general questions concerning activities and their use described earlier in this chapter, but additionally:

- Am I quite sure what type of activity I am seeking?
- Where should I look for the activity?
- I remember seeing an activity I would like to use, but where did I see it?
- Have I recourse to all the collections of likely resources?
- Are there other collections that may contain the activity for which I am searching?
- How can I find the particular activity from the mass of activities that seem to have been published?

TYPES OF ACTIVITY

Somewhere in the published collections of training games, exercises and activities will be found examples of activities for almost every specific type of training event and those for more general use. The latter fall into the categories of introductory activities where the course participants introduce themselves or each other, the basis and form of introduction activity being chosen from a wide range. Other general activities include icebreakers, which are usually short, impactive activities held either after the introductions to bridge the gap between that stage and the main body of the course, or as breaks from the possibly serious business of learning.

Similar to the icebreakers are the energizers, which have the particular uses of bridging the change between two major aspects of the course, or simply again as light relief from the serious side of the training. At the other end of the programme from the introductions are the activities that are concerned with validation, evaluation, action planning and saying 'goodbye'. Many of these activities are short but have a value that considerably outweighs their size; they can be risk items, where emotions and behaviours can be extreme.

The more specific activities are usually directly related to the subject of the learning, although not necessarily work oriented the lessons to be drawn from them are very much related to the learning and work situation. Activities abound for such subjects as problem-solving, decision-making, creativity, behavioural skills, communication, team development, interviewing skills, to name but a few. As suggested earlier they can be either directly related to the work situation or related to the subject by dint of the lessons to be drawn from the activity and extrapolated to the work environment. An example of the former in problem-solving might be a work problem that is selected from examples brought to the event by the learners. Small groups, furnished with as much information as possible and with the problem-owner available to offer more information, consider the situation and suggest possible solutions to the problem. A similar, follow-on activity could eventually be the same group considering the possible solutions, proposing a decision and its implementation.

The classical example of the non-work type of activity is the one that requires sub-groups to work with sets of Lego building bricks to construct masts, bridges, cranes, weather satellites etc. This type of activity has a general application, but care must be taken to discuss the application to the working environment of the principles raised. Activities of this nature can be used to observe and draw lessons from group and individual behaviours, planning of a task or project, leadership skills, and the setting and achieving of realistic aims. Other activities require general problem-solving skills, negotiation, selection and so on.

THE FINAL CHOICE

Unless you have a readily available personal collection of activities that you use in your training, you will need to: 1) identify a source of relevant activities; and 2) select the most appropriate activity from that source. This sounds easier than it really is because, for example, if you are seeking a general, problem-solving/decision-making activity there are at least 50 published collections containing more than 1,500 such activities!

For a number of years the desirability of some form of database that contained information about *all* the activities that had been published, by all publishers in both the UK and the US was sought and suggested by training practitioners who used activities extensively. Because of the tremendous range of published activities, this is now obviously a monumental task that would require many man-hours to construct, but recently some smaller steps towards this have been taken. A small number of publishers of activity collections have developed databases of their own material and made these available in a number of ways.

RESOURCE ACTIVITY LISTING

The first thing that will be of help in trying to choose the most appropriate activity for a specific purpose is an awareness of the major sources of activity collections. A representative selection of the activities and similar resources that are available in the UK, produced by the principal activity collection publishers – Echelon, Fenman, Gower, Kogan Page, McGraw-Hill and Melrose – is included as an Appendix in my *Using Activities in Training and Development* (1999, 2nd edn, Kogan Page), which contains an offer of an update to readers.

This list identifies 185 resources with 7,164 activities, lets you know where activities can be found and, from the titles of the collections etc, gives some indication of the types of activity included in any particular collection. But this still leaves the potential user with a lot of material in which the desired activity may be lurking. It is doubtful whether even substantial learning resource libraries will contain *all* the collections, so it can happen that the ideal activity may be in a collection that is not held. In addition, of course, examining many activities in many collections can be an extensive and time-consuming exercise. This is the principal reason why activity users have long sought a simple source from which to select their desired activities. Some of the advances being introduced at the present time by several publishers are aimed at making this more possible.

TECHNOLOGICAL ADVANCES

Developing from an interactive CD-ROM, *The Complete Games Trainers Play*, produced by McGraw-Hill in 1996 and containing over 400 activities, interest and application in making training activities more readily available than in traditional publications have increased. A CD-ROM is an excellent medium for concentrating a large number of activities and making selected ones easily available, but the obvious limitation is in the number and range of activities in the original source.

Activities on the Internet

The introduction, development and increasing usage of the Internet has opened up many exciting avenues, including giving help in the activity selection process. Developments are occurring with such speed that the information given here will almost certainly be out of date by the time the book is published, although the sources mentioned will certainly stand, changes being supplements to these approaches. The two principal Internet users in this way in the UK are currently Echelon and Gower.

The Echelon learning library

One of these innovations was the opening, during the winter of 1998/9, of an interactive Web site on the Internet by a comparatively small, new publishing house – Echelon. The site contains details of the activities in collections published by Echelon, with approximately 1,000 activities available to view first on the Web site as 'Thumbnails' and then available to buy online, either as single or multiple units, through a simple procedure. The site is www.learningmatters.com.

Not everybody has a computer or the facility to visit the Internet, so Echelon has produced the database on CD-ROM as a browser disk and is developing the facility for users to produce their own library of references from the CD information.

The GAIA project

A suggestion that I made to Gower Publishing some years ago resulted in 1998 in *The GAIA (Gower Activities Index and Abstracts) Project*, which contains details and abstracts of all the activities published by Gower.

This index, containing summaries and abstracts of more than 2,000 activities, is available on the Internet on www.gowertraining.co.uk and, like the Echelon product, will enable users to purchase complete collections, or only the activities they require, having identified these from the database index. Other aspects of choice support are also planned, including: a) the translation of the printed collections into a digitalized form on CD-ROMs; and b) the full GAIA abstract index on a CD-ROM, so that the choice of activity will also be available to those practitioners not using the Internet.

The Training Zone

This Internet site is not a source of activities as such, but is the provider of a wealth of information to the training practitioner, including reference to other sources of activities. A weekly e-mail newsletter is published that contains training and development news but, more importantly, links to other sites where resources created by smaller producers can be downloaded or obtained. This site can be visited at www.trainingzone.co.uk.

Other Internet sites

In addition to the Web sites described above, there are some (and the number is increasing) that belong to individuals or consultancy companies where training activities are offered either as freeware or for purchase. An example of such a UK site is at www.users.globalnet.co.uk, but the majority are found in the US (see below).

US sites

As if we didn't have enough material available in the UK, there is an equal if not greater amount available in the USA, much of which again is available on the Internet, so the Atlantic Ocean is producing no problem.

Typical of such US sites is Thiagi, Inc., reachable on the Internet via www.thiagi.com, a producer and distributor of a wide range of activities. The Web site includes indexes to the range available, papers on activities and their uses, and examples of the activities, in full detail, that they have available.

Other significant US providers of activities include the major producer, Pfeiffer, which parallels in size the activity collections of Gower in the UK, and HRD Press, Inc., among others, the latter publishing more than 100 collections.

Free or purchasable activities are also available from a large number of locations on the Internet, from private individuals and commercial or semi-commercial organizations. An example of such sources is to be found at www.squarewheels.com, this being an unusual example of the many sites.

USING THE RESOURCE COLLECTIONS

The activities included in the various resource collections, whether or not on the Internet, vary in their format from publisher to publisher, but in general give the information necessary for any trainer to introduce the activity in their programme. The more experienced trainers need to read only some of this information and can 'play tunes' on the activity to suit their particular needs with the many possible variations and customizations. The basic format usually includes:

- the title of the activity (often descriptive of the content, but many are more cryptic);
- a general description of the activity and suggestions for its uses;
- any pre-course work necessary;

- methods of use – these are usually detailed notes that can be followed by a trainer (whatever their level of experience), suggesting divisions of the learning group into sub-groups where necessary; use of the activity briefs and handouts etc;
- sections giving suggestions on the timing of the activity in a programme; the most effective range of participants; the time required; and resources necessary other than the ones usually available in the training room;
- suggestions for the process and content of the feedback session that must, almost invariably, follow the practical part of the activity;
- suggestions for some of the variations possible;
- handouts, participants' briefs and OHP masters.

With these notes, descriptions and comments, and with all the physical resources either described or provided, a 'strange' activity can be introduced with every chance of success. Commonly, matrices are provided with each collection of activities to show at a glance the areas of learning into which the activity falls, the activities grouped in time required, the linking of various activities and so on.

PLANNING THE INTRODUCTION OF AN ACTIVITY

Once it has been decided to include an activity in the session, or as a session, and you have decided on a particular activity or activities, part of the planning action is how the activity will be introduced. The principal stages include:

- familiarizing yourself with the activity and, if possible, taking part in one yourself, either on someone else's event or by setting up your own dummy-run with colleagues or 'guinea pigs';
- either ensuring that you have suitable participant briefs, instruction sheets and working sheets available or producing your own;
- checking that all the resources necessary for the activity are, or will be, available, including syndicate rooms and CCTV (if used) and that all relevant materials are in each of the rooms;
- deciding whether the activity will be for the learning group as one group or whether you will divide it into a number of smaller groups and, if so, how the small groups will be decided on;
- checking any safety factors necessary, particularly where physical action forms part of the activity, or the activity takes place out of doors;

- confirming the activity duration requirements;
- preparing the introductory, verbal description of the activity to be given to the learners;
- deciding the observation strategy;
- deciding how the activity is to be reviewed and feedback given.

OBSERVATION AND REVIEW

The last two aspects in the preparation list are not only particularly important but are also hungry eaters of time. Sufficient time must be built into the activity time for review of the activity, feedback to the participants of their skills and behaviours, and identification and discussion of the learning points. In many cases, to give this part of the activity sufficient time to do it justice, it will probably need to be as long, if not longer than the activity itself, although in practice the review time will have to be cut back.

Observation

Considerable attention must be paid in the planning process to observation during the activity, an important aspect in the feedback. The choices include:

- observation by the participants themselves with no external intervention;
- observation and feedback by the trainer(s);
- observation by participants taken from the learning group;
- the 'fishbowl' method of observation;
- remote observation and CCTV.

Review and feedback

Similarly, the methods of reviewing will need to be considered and decisions made, depending on the time available:

- self-feedback by the participants, preferably assisted by a self-awareness questionnaire/checklist;
- full group feedback by the trainer and/or member-observers;
- sub-group feedback by member-observers followed by full group plenary;
- self-criticism from video recordings.

Detailed advice and guidance on the methods that can be used for the observation and review of activities can be found in a sister book by this author in this series, *Using Activities in Training and Development* (1999, 2nd edn, Kogan Page). Such methods will need to be incorporated in the overall planning of an activity and include observation and feedback:

- by the participants themselves within the activity;
- by participants withdrawn from the activity;
- by the trainer(s);
- fishbowl observation;
- remote observation, including CCTV.

The various processes for planning and designing programmes and sessions have covered the principal approaches and their use will have enabled you to see clearly what is available and what can be done. If you have followed the process to this stage and completed as many of the planning processes and documentation that appeal to you, and which you feel you need or are apparently required, you will have planned most of the aspects of your training and development programme and session content and be able to see the way ahead completely. The remaining item in the process, considered in the next chapter, concerns the very important subject of planning for the evaluation of the programme.

PART FOUR

Planning the Evaluation of Training and Development

This part will consider in detail the various aspects that need to be taken into account when planning and designing the validation and evaluation of training programmes or approaches.

11

Planning the Evaluation of Training and Development Programmes

EVALUATION AND VALIDATION

The terms 'evaluation', 'validation' and 'assessment' are used in various ways by different writers, users of the processes and the producers of the several process models. I use the terminology defined some years ago by the then Ministry of Labour, in which:

- *Evaluation* is the assessment approach that considers the complete training/learning process and is principally concerned with measuring the effects and impact of the training/learning on the individual's practice at work and on the business – the 'bottom line'. It answers the questions related to the implementation at work of the learning linked with expenditure on the training in terms of whether it was cost and value effective.
- *Validation* concentrates primarily on the training programme itself and the immediate effects on the learners. Has the programme satisfied its objectives and those of the learners? Are the learners returning to work having changed from their level prior to the training, ie have they changed in an effective manner? In order to achieve the programme and learner results, was the programme designed and performed effectively?

Validation and evaluation of training are extensive subjects, about which much has been published over the years, probably more than is actually practised!

The reasons for this latter comment are our old enemies 'time' and 'resources', and although many organizations, when questioned about their evaluation practices, say that they perform these, when their practices are examined many fall short of real evaluation.

There can be a problem in persuading both organizations and training professionals of the value and benefits of time invested in evaluation. A 1997 training survey by the Industrial Society suggested that, whilst 84 per cent of organizations distribute 'happy sheets' (end-of-course 'reactionnaires' to obtain participants' feelings about the training) a much lower proportion actively do anything else to test in objective terms the effectiveness of their training effort.

REACTIONNAIRES

The most common form of 'evaluation', more correctly described as validation, is using what are derogatively (and often rightly) described as end-of-course 'happy sheets'. These end-of-course reactionnaires have a valuable place, but not as egoistic justification of the trainers and the course, as is too often the case.

Reactionnaires are most effective when they are designed to obtain specific reactions to particular, physical aspects of the training course. One example of this is when a training location is used for the first time, when a reactionnaire can ask participants at the end of the programme for their views on the location – catering, accommodation, facilities and so on. It will be useful to repeat this exercise after two or three events to obtain a representative view because of the subjectivity of the responses that will be obtained – my opinion of the bedroom I was allocated for instance, may vary considerably from those of some other participants.

Other effective uses of reactionnaires can be when new programmes have been introduced and, in addition to validating the learning, the designers and practitioners are looking for the views of the 'customers' and their reactions to the course. A typical reactionnaire of this nature is illustrated later in this chapter (see Figures 11.3 and 11.4).

Evaluation is too important to be treated in what is often a cavalier fashion and is far more extensive than a simple questionnaire, starting long before the end of the programme and extending far beyond it. I would contend that evaluation is so important in the training and development process, particularly the stages following the training programme, that if it is not performed effectively then there is doubt as to whether running the programme is even worth doing. Without the information provided by the evaluation processes there is no 'evidence' of the success or otherwise of the training and learning, so if the training is to be shown to lead to individual and business improvement, there can be no concrete denial that the training is being performed for training's sake only.

PLANNING EVALUATION

Because evaluation covers the whole training process it must be considered early in the design and planning process, and planning as well as practice must start long before the training event takes place.

Reasons for evaluation

Planners must be aware of the reasons for evaluation so that they can ensure it is included in the total training process. Evaluation:

- can justify the investment in the training;
- ensures that the training is seen to make a change in the working practices of the individual and the organization;
- evaluates the training investment in terms of costs versus value (bottom line) benefits;
- ensures that valid responses to challenges about the training are possible;
- provides the instruments from which concrete evidence can be produced to enable senior management to be aware of the effectiveness of the training programmes;
- enables assessment of the planning and design of the training programmes;
- ensures that the training programmes are achieving their objectives;
- demonstrates whether the learners are achieving their objectives;
- helps the learners to appreciate what they have learned, what they have to do with this learning and provides a mechanism for achieving practice;
- helps to suggest improvements to the training programmes;
- helps the trainers to assess their own achievement and provides evidence for their managers also to do this;
- at its most effective involves more people than just the trainer and the learner;
- supports the practical implementation of learning by the learners when they return to work.

Reasons given for not evaluating

These are manifold and very revealing of the attitudes of many people, trainers and managers alike, to evaluation. They include:

- 'You can only *know* when a course has been successful or not.'
- 'You don't need to have all those pieces of paper to know how successful you have been.'
- 'Evaluation only works for practical training.'
- 'Evaluation is somebody else's responsibility.'
- 'Nobody has ever asked me to do it.'
- 'The client didn't raise the question of evaluation or didn't want to pay for the extra work involved.'
- 'What more do you want? I hand out a questionnaire at the end of the course!'
- 'It would take up so much time that I wouldn't have any time to train.'
- 'The difficulty of isolating the effects of training from other variables means that it is often impossible to prove the direct impact of training.'

From this very negative list, the only response that may have any substance is the last one, but even that represents restricted thinking in which the process of evaluation is not controlled effectively. A broader, more realistic approach to the responsibilities involved in evaluation will give an effective response to this complaint.

WHO UNDERTAKES EVALUATION?

If the trainer is the only one on whom the burden of evaluation falls it is not surprising that all the problems shown above are raised. The purpose of a trainer (including the planner and the designer) is to provide training opportunities that will help the participants to learn. To do this they must be aware of the real evidence showing that they are succeeding, but because of all the constraints other people must also be involved as the trainer alone cannot do this, nor is he or she always the right person. Traditionally many people in an organization consider the trainer responsible for any evaluation that might be performed, but they are only one element in the training quintet that should exist, each with responsibilities that include evaluation at different stages. The concept of the Training Quintet was raised in Chapter 1 and Figure 1.1 showing the quintet is repeated here as Figure 11.1.

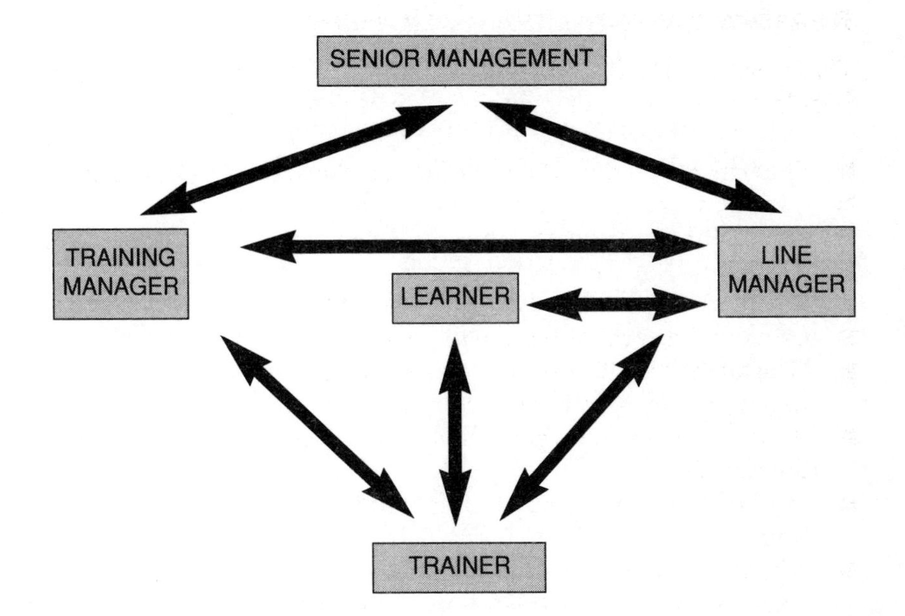

Figure 11.1 *The training quintet*

In addition to responsibilities in training, members of the quintet also have specific responsibilities in the area of evaluation.

Senior management

The senior management group must be involved and demonstrate their involvement in the evaluation of the training and development programmes in their organization at the earliest stage; and their involvement should be encouraged by others in the quintet. Senior management should:

- state clearly and authoritatively that evaluation should be included in all training and development programmes, and that evaluation should be performed as agreed and in an effective manner;
- state clearly and authoritatively the responsibilities for evaluation;
- require agreed evaluation analyses and review these regularly.

These responsibilities are much more than the bland statements of support that are more commonly given – if even those occur.

The training manager

The training manager is responsible (principally as a controller), for evaluation practices related to the training and development programme, and also performs certain aspects of the evaluation process. These responsibilities include:

- control of evaluation strategy and practice;
- assistance with evaluation practices, especially when a more neutral assessor than the trainer is required;
- close examination of the evaluation results and their analysis, and discussion of these;
- collation of a series of evaluation analyses representing the training department's range of work;
- presentation of analysed results to senior management;
- representing training and development when evaluation is considered (or should be considered) at senior management meetings.

The trainer

The trainer is the kingpin of the evaluation process, particularly those areas devoted to the actual training. If the ideal evaluation world does not exist in the organization trainers may be called upon or want to perform other parts of the process, but they must remember that this additional involvement may have to be at the expense of other (usually training) activities. Their particular responsibilities include:

- Designing and implementing validation approaches ('validation' is defined here as the assessment of the effectiveness of the actual training events).
- Designing measures for the evaluation of implementation of learning aspects and supporting these activities where necessary. This latter aspect is not a prime responsibility, but may become so if there is a failure of others to fulfil their responsibilities.
- Supporting line managers in their briefing and debriefing roles (not necessarily directly, but in terms of guiding them about what to do and how to do it).
- Supporting line managers in their post-training evaluation roles (again not necessarily being directly involved, but providing guidance, advice and education so that the line managers can fulfil their responsibilities).
- Providing analyses of evaluation (or at least validation of the training programme) for the training and development programmes for which they are responsible.

In many cases, for a variety of reasons, line managers fail to fulfil their responsibilities and it must be a prime responsibility of the trainer, who has an overall interest in evaluation, to ensure that in some way line managers are educated in the responsibilities of their roles.

The line manager

Traditionally the line manager has looked on the responsibility for both training and evaluation as the training department's alone. But line managers *must* have an input, even if only because *their* staff are involved in the training, and a large proportion of the training costs are attributable to *their* budgets. Trainers can visit the learners at work after the training programme (if they have the time to do this) to look at the learners' implementation of their learning, but only the line manager is in a position to: a) observe effectively *in situ* the implementation of the learning on a continuous basis; and b) evaluate the cost and value effectiveness of the training that led to the learning and whether the business (*their business*) has benefited. Ideally the line manager should have a role in:

- the design of the evaluation process with the training department – essential, as this brings line managers in at the start and they are a very interested party in the end result of the training;
- pre-programme briefing sessions with the members of their staff;
- post-programme debriefing sessions with members of staff on their return from the training event;
- agreement with the learners for the implementation of their learning and action plans, and interim reviews as necessary;
- involvement in, if not sole operation of, medium and/or longer-term evaluation as an assessment of business improvement.

The learner

Last, but not least, although usually omitted when evaluation is being designed and introduced, is the learner who must be involved as much as possible – after all it is the learner who is relied on for accurate and honest reporting and comments on the evaluation process. In the same way as line managers, the training planner and practitioner should try to involve learners at all stages of the planning and design of the evaluation of the training in which they will be involved. Their input will be very valuable and may suggest different approaches for the trainer/training to take at an early rather than later stage, say after the training. Part of the educative activities of the trainer will be to interest learners in the evaluation and let them know the results.

PLANNING THE EVALUATION PROCESS

Evaluation planning should begin during the planning and design of the training programme and the general questions that should be asked at the start of the process should include:

- Which level of evaluation is to be attempted?
- Which aspects of the training need to be evaluated?
- How should the evaluation methods to be used be chosen?
- Which are the areas of evaluation responsibility for the trainer and others in the organization?
- To what extent will the evaluation be costed as part of the overall training?
- If the trainer is an external consultant, how will the evaluation required be costed to the consultancy? Will it be funded separately or will the consultant be expected to include it in his/her costs (or even exclude it as a payment)?

Following clarification of these factors, 12 stages in the complete evaluation process can be identified, 11 of which fall within the parameters of this book. (The 12th is the TNIA, the start of training and hence evaluation; without TNIA there is no evidence that training is required. Evaluation demonstrates that the results and objectives of the TNIA have been achieved.) Within these parameters the 12-stage process is:

1. Training Needs Identification and Analysis.
2. Design the evaluation process.
3. Perform pre-course testing or assessment of existing knowledge, skills and attitudes. (If stage 3 is not followed these activities should be performed at the start of the training, either through tests or observation of practical sessions.)
4. Line manager holds pre-training briefing with the learner.
5. Interim validation of the progress of learning.
6. End of programme testing or other assessment of levels achieved by the learners.
7. End of programme validation and reaction review.
8. Learner action planning at end of programme.
9. Line manager post-programme debriefing and arrangements for implementation of action plan and any other learning.
10. Medium-term follow-up evaluation of implementation of learning.
11. Longer-term follow-up evaluation of implementation of learning

and final assessment of cost and value effectiveness of the training.
12. Assessment of the evaluation and report on achievement of objectives.

OTHER EVALUATION MODELS

A substantial number of evaluation models have preceded the one I describe above, many variations on a theme and some too complex and extended to ever be put into practice by professional trainers (as opposed to research workers). I have encountered one model that I feel is a practical, applicable model that does not appear to be too complex to frighten the would-be evaluator. This is the Kirkpatrick model that developed from a series of articles written in 1959 in the American Society of Training and Development (ASTD) journal *Training and Development*. However, when examined closely, within its four apparently simple levels, there is a high degree of complexity that matches or exceeds my 12-stage evaluation model.

The model's four levels of evaluation are:

- Level 1 Reactions;
- Level 2 Learning;
- Level 3 Behaviour;
- Level 4 Results.

Level 1 measures the participants' attitudes and reactions to the training. These must be in the main highly subjective views (often reflected in the happy sheet) and it is doubtful whether they can seriously be considered as indicating the value of the training as there is little specific emphasis on learning.

Level 2 is concerned with the learning achieved and considers the use of questionnaires, the involvement of line managers pre- and post training and testing the longer-term retention of the learning. This correlates well with most of the factors of my 12-stage model, but concentrates solely on the learning of skills, leaving the change in behaviour due to the learning to the next level.

Level 3 considers the impact of the training on the behaviour of the learners; and

Level 4 is the evaluation of results level that concentrates on the correlation between the training and the 'bottom line' and is principally concerned with post-training assessment of the relationship between what has been learnt, its implementation and its effects on the actual work.

The details of validation and evaluation can really only be described at length, space for which is not available here. The reader is again referred to the many books on the subject, some of which are listed in the Recommended and Further Reading section at the end of this book and which includes, for example, my *Using Evaluation in Training and Development* (Kogan Page, 1999). In these books the detailed, staged approach to validation and evaluation is described and many suggested instruments of questionnaires, reactionnaires and action plan documents are illustrated.

Specifically for the planner, once the extent of the evaluation has been decided, an assessment must be made of the time and resource required for it, particularly that relating directly to the validation of the training programme itself – start of course assessment, interim validation measures, end of course validation questionnaires, reactionnaires and action planning. Depending on the fulfilment of responsibilities by the other members of the quintet, it may be necessary to assess the time/cost for the trainer in activities outside the actual training programme.

A LIMITED EVALUATION PLAN

In an attempt to introduce an effective evaluation system into organizations I have developed over the years a four-stage plan that provides a reasonably acceptable evaluation system that utilizes minimal resource time, particularly that of the line manager.

I do not claim that this model is better than or even approaches in effectiveness the full evaluation model described above, which whenever possible should be followed to its fullest extent. But if it is a choice between attempting this modified approach or having nothing effective done at all, then I would recommend taking the restricted, modified action described.

Four problems seem to be most evident when evaluation is being discussed with and within an organization:

1. Who does it?
2. Who pays for it?
3. Full evaluation uses a lot of resources – people, time and money.
4. Line management is loath to spend resource time on evaluation.

These problems arise more particularly when an external consultant is providing the training and raises the question of evaluation. Jean Harris of Garner Harris Association identifies two major arguments:

1) we haven't got the time to do it ourselves; and 2) we haven't got the budget to pay an external consultant to do it.

Very few organizations follow the full cycle described earlier, and there is no doubt that it is quite expensive in terms of resource. However, too many organizations 'evaluate' at the opposite pole, sometimes all that happens to happy sheets is that they are put in a file and never referred to again.

Surely there is something effective in between these two poles? I have introduced, and used for some years a four-stage approach, as both an internal trainer and external consultant, that appears to be attractive to a number of companies since it satisfies the four problems raised at the start of this section – it does not require too much time resource from the organization and little payment additional to the learners' and line managers' normal salaries is necessary. Even the on-cost for the latter's time, the only additional payments, is small, amounting to an initial half hour per learner, then eventually a further hour. Surely even busy line managers can afford an hour and a half over about three months, particularly when the results demonstrate whether the training for which they are paying from their budgets is both cost and value effective.

If an effective evaluation approach is followed, then both the external consultant and the internal trainer are also more satisfied with the end results of their training programmes and will be more committed to the value of the learning, knowing that their efforts are being recognized and there is an assurance that the learning achieved by the participants is being implemented under controlled conditions.

The four-stage evaluation process

The model I suggest:

- demonstrates whether the event has achieved its objectives and those of the learners;
- ensures that the learners return to work committed to implementing their learning;
- encourages (ensures that?) the line manager becomes involved in the learning and its evaluation, with the consequent benefits, and enables them to assess the cost and value effectiveness of their expenditure.

There is of course nothing to stop the trainer/consultant following other parts of the 12-stage model without reducing training time and content and without requiring additional funding by the organization. For example, it is beneficial in evaluation to know where the learners are 'coming from' – this information can be obtained by the completion of questionnaires or tests, or from observation of activities that are part of the training programme, before attending or at the start of the event. It is also natural and practical to include some interim evaluation measures during the event in a similar way to that introduced at the start of the programme. But the principal evaluation etc starts at the end of the training event.

Another essential in the process is that as much time as possible is given to all the stages – this will obviously be within the control of the trainer/consultant during the training event, but line managers should be encouraged to be generous with time when they are performing their part of the process.

Stage 1

This takes place in the final stages of the learning event and time must be built into the programme to enable the learners to complete the questionnaire without being rushed or encouraged to treat it superficially. The non-reliance on scoring systems supports the latter aspect. From the completed questionnaire the trainers will be able to assess the success of their event from the items included in the responses and will help the learners to progress to the following stage.

If the practitioner can allow time and/or feels that completion of a reactionnaire will be of use this can be added, but it is less essential than the learning questionnaire. The reactionnaire, as suggested earlier, should be designed to answer specific questions.

Recommended questionnaire

Figure 11.2 shows a recommended form of end of event learning questionnaire. It does include a limited scoring approach so that some 'statistical' analysis can be produced, but the emphasis is on seeking as much textual information as possible from the learners to the two open questions. It is from these responses that the consultant can assess the extent of the learning and hence the success and achievement of the event. The questionnaire is shown here with reduced space, but the actual questionnaire should allow lots of space for the responses.

Appropriate form of reactionnaire

As suggested earlier the reactionnaire can be a useful addition, particularly when a new or modified programme has been introduced and

Please consider the learning programme that you have attended and complete the following, being completely honest in your assessments and answering the questions as fully as possible.

PART ONE: LEARNING

To what extent do you feel you have learnt from the programme? (Please ring the number that you feel most closely represents your views.)

Learnt a lot 6 5 4 3 2 1 Learnt nothing

If you have rated 6, 5 or 4, please describe: a) what you have learnt; and b) what you intend to do with this learning on your return to work.

↕

(Ample space)

If you have rated 3, 2 or 1, please state as fully as possible the reasons why you gave this rating.

↕

(Ample space)

PART TWO: CONFIRMATION OF LEARNING

To what extent do you feel you have had previous learning (perhaps some you have forgotten) confirmed in a useful manner?

Confirmed a lot 6 5 4 3 2 1 Confirmed little

If you have rated 6, 5 or 4, please describe: a) what has been confirmed; and b) what you intend to do with this learning on your return to work.

↕

(Ample space)

If you have rated 3, 2 or 1, please state as fully as possible the reasons why you gave this rating.

↕

(Ample space)

Figure 11.2 *End of event learning questionnaire*

maximum information (for use by the trainer initially) about the reaction of learners to the programme is required. The questions suggested in Figures 11.3 and 11.4 can be changed to obtain responses on specific aspects about which views are desired – for example, comments on the length of the course, type of content and accommodation. But it must be remembered that this reactionnaire does not represent evaluation.

For every item place an 'X' in the scoring box that most closely represents how you feel about the programme. Also, please comment briefly on each item about your reasons for giving this score, particularly if your ratings are 3, 2 or 1.

	6	5	4	3	2	1	
Stimulating Please comment briefly why you have given this rating	☐	☐	☐	☐	☐	☐	Boring
Useful for my work Please comment briefly why you have given this rating	☐	☐	☐	☐	☐	☐	Useless
Relevant to my work Please comment briefly why you have given this rating	☐	☐	☐	☐	☐	☐	Irrelevant
Good discussions Please comment briefly why you have given this rating	☐	☐	☐	☐	☐	☐	Limited discussions
Flexible structure Please comment briefly why you have given this rating	☐	☐	☐	☐	☐	☐	Rigid structure
Well conducted Please comment briefly why you have given this rating	☐	☐	☐	☐	☐	☐	Poorly conducted
Demanding Please comment briefly why you have given this rating	☐	☐	☐	☐	☐	☐	Undemanding
Challenging Please comment briefly why you have given this rating	☐	☐	☐	☐	☐	☐	Patronizing
Well spaced out Please comment briefly why you have given this rating	☐	☐	☐	☐	☐	☐	Too condensed
Good use of time Please comment briefly why you have given this rating	☐	☐	☐	☐	☐	☐	Poor use of time
Good level of activity Please comment briefly why you have given this rating	☐	☐	☐	☐	☐	☐	Poor level of activity
My objectives achieved Please comment briefly why you have given this rating	☐	☐	☐	☐	☐	☐	My objectives not achieved

I would recommend the programme to my colleagues YES ☐ NO ☐

Any other comments:

Figure 11.3 *End of event reactionnaire (1)*

As with the learning questionnaire, ample space should be left for textual responses in addition to the scoring. It should be noted that the wording seeking textual responses is not the frequent, too general 'please comment' which frequently results in no responses. Instead a more definite request is made, detailing the type of response required. The written request can be reinforced by the trainer/consultant when the reactionnaire is being introduced.

Figure 11.4 suggests an alternative reactionnaire that excludes the use of scoring scales, a feature which many people either consider of little value (it is too easy for a 'tick' to be placed, sometimes at random), or they believe implicitly, but erroneously, in the results because they are 'mathematically based'.

1. **Which parts of the event did you find the most useful?**
2. **Which parts of the event did you find the least useful?**
3. **Are there any parts you would have omitted? If so, which parts and why?**
4. **Is there anything you would have liked to have seen added to the event? What should have been removed to make room for it?**
5. **Which of your personal objectives were satisfied?**
6. **Which of your personal objectives were not satisfied?**
7. **Have you any other comments you wish to make?**

Figure 11.4 *End of event reactionnaire (2)*

Stage 2

Stage 2 links closely with stage 1 as the action is taken immediately following completion of the end of event learning questionnaire. The learning questionnaire, among other things, identifies the learning that the participant in the event has taken particularly to heart and has started a commitment to the implementation of the learning. This second stage reinforces this commitment and asks the learner to produce a specific action plan, showing the learnt items that they intend to implement on their return to work.

One area of discussion concerns the number of action items that should be included in the action plan. Many 'authorities' suggest three as a maximum, on the grounds that if more are listed there is less chance of them being implemented. I do not go along with this, principally from my own experience, considering that if a learner identifies, say, six items and is asked to plan only three, he/she may gain the impression that the other three aren't important and thus forget them. It is all very well to say that they should implement the first three then plan and implement another three. My experience is that the likelihood of the second three taking place reduces with the time taken to get round to them. If the learner has identified, say, eight items of learning, and has taken the trouble to list these in the learning questionnaire, they should be encouraged to plan action, at that time, for all these learnt items.

Figure 11.5 suggests a straightforward format for an action plan that can be completed by the learners and taken with them on their return to work. If the consultant/trainer is to be involved in the later stages of evaluation they should retain a copy of this plan, but basically the relationship for the action plan is between the learner and their line manager.

ACTION PLANNED:	TO BE STARTED BY AND COMPLETED BY:	HOW TO IMPLEMENT – RESOURCES, ETC:

Figure 11.5 *An Action Plan format*

Post-training evaluation measures

Stages 3 and 4 take place after the training and the responsibility for undertaking this part of the evaluation process lies firmly with the line manager. He/she is the only one with intimate contact with the learner, in a position to observe and assess them, and also to assess whether the expenditure of the training costs from *their* budget in respect of *their* staff has been cost and value effective. Consequently, irrespective of it being their responsibility, it is in their own interests to be committed to fulfilling this responsibility.

This is the area where the evaluation process usually comes to a halt, for the reasons quoted earlier and a number of others. It is incumbent on the trainer/consultant to obtain the commitment for evaluation from the organization's senior management and hence the line management and ensure that steps are taken to educate the latter in their responsibilities. Not an easy job, but one that must be tackled. Most practitioners find that using the cost and value effectiveness approach of the training for which the line management are paying is likely to have the most effect. The reference is to the bottom line – in this case well-trained staff by organization-assessed effective training at an acceptable cost.

Stage 3

This stage takes place immediately after, or as soon after the training event as possible. The line manager and the learner are the ones involved, the trainer/consultant only taking part if invited to do so and if fees have been agreed or the practitioner is otherwise willing to take on this activity.

The basis of the stage is a meeting between the line manager and the learner, preferably within a week of the end of the training programme, the learner's action plan being the working document. At the meeting the participants discuss the learning, the actions proposed and any requirements resulting from these proposals. The meeting terminates with an agreement that:

- the learner will keep the manager informed of implementation progress;
- the manager will observe the learner's implementation whenever possible;
- interim meetings will be arranged, as required, to discuss the progress of the implementation.

Figure 11.6 is a checklist of questions and points that should be considered at this post-training, debriefing meeting.

Stage 4

This is the final stage of this limited evaluation process and again concerns the learner and the line manager, the training practitioner only becoming involved if invited to do so or if prior arrangements have been made for such involvement.

During the three to six months following the post-training debriefing meeting between the learner and the line manager, the learner should have been implementing the learning to which they had committed themselves in the action plan. The line manager, in addition to ensuring that any necessary interim meetings were held,

The questions that should be considered at the post-training debriefing meeting between the learner and his or her line manager should include:

1. **How effective was the training programme as far as the learner was personally concerned? Did this differ from the views of others?**
2. **How effective were the trainers? Approachable, logical, clear in their presentations, good use of visual aids, not too hurried etc?**
3. **How appropriate was the training material as far as the learner was concerned?**
4. **How up to date was the material?**
5. **Were the programme objectives achieved? If not, why not?**
6. **Were the learner's personal objectives achieved? If not, why not?**
7. **What did the learner learn as new material, have usefully confirmed or be timeously reminded of?**
8. **A full discussion of the learner's action plan:**
   - **What is planned to be done? How is it to be implemented?**
   - **When and over what period? What resources are required?**
   - **Does the learner want the line manager to help in any way?**
9. **Any other aspects not covered by the above.**
10. **A date arranged, between three and six months hence, to discuss a final implementation review. The availability of interim reviews should also be discussed and agreed.**
11. **The line manager should discuss with the relevant trainers any feedback from the learner about which it is felt they should be made aware.**

Figure 11.6 *Guidelines for the post-training debriefing meeting*

should have been observing the learner in the implementation processes that had been agreed.

At between three and six months a final or major interim review meeting should be arranged, to look at: a) what has happened in that period; and b) what needs to be done in the future. At this meeting the longer-term, lasting value of the learning can be assessed: the real assessment of any learning and training processes. Figure 11.7 suggests guidelines for this longer-term evaluation meeting.

The questions listed in Figure 11.7, and any other relevant ones, will have ensured that action to implement the learning has been or will be taken and, apart from any later review to consider actions that have followed this review, the assessment of the learning is complete.

The line manager, looking to the training of other members of staff, might wish to extend the discussion past the guidelines listed above and consider with the learners their views of the training process they underwent, with the hindsight that time and learning implementation has given them.

Questions can include:

1. Which parts of the event were found to be the most useful?

2. Which parts of the event were found to be the least useful?
3. Are there any parts that should have been omitted? If so, which parts and why?
4. Is there anything that should have been added to the event? What should have been removed to make room for it?
5. Which personal objectives were satisfied?
6. Which personal objectives were not satisfied?
7. Any other comments?

The questions that can be usefully considered and discussed between the learner and the line manager at the 3 to 6 months review meeting include :

1. **Which items of the action plan have been implemented so far?**
2. **What degree of success has been achieved in respect of these items?**
3. **To what factors or reasons is the success in implementing these items attributed?**
4. **Which items of the action plan have not yet been implemented?**
5. **Which of these items have been tried but couldn't be implemented?**
6. **Why did this occur?**
7. **Which items have not yet been attempted?**
8. **Why have these not yet been attempted?**
9. **What plans does the learner have to:**
   - **attempt to rectify unsuccessful items?**
   - **implement the as yet unattempted items?**
10. **Are there any additional plans? If so, obtain similar comments or full details.**
11. **What needs, other than the action implementation discussed, does the learner have that the line manager can ensure are satisfied?**

Figure 11.7 *Guidelines for the longer-term review meeting*

Any appropriate comments can then be passed by the line manager to the trainer/consultant or the organization's training manager.

This process will help line managers who are interested in and committed to the training and development of their staff and also their own self-development. One aspect of this will be how they have managed the post-training evaluation, as seen through the eyes of the learner. So, part of the final review process, although principally to confirm the implementation of the learning, can also be used to ask the learner questions that seek responses about their views on how the follow-up procedure and its outcomes have been processed and managed – was it what they wanted and expected or would they have preferred some other type of approach or some other person?

I believe an evaluation system such as that described will be attractive to consultants, trainers, senior managers, line managers and learners alike, and will go a long way to achieving effective training and learning evaluation. To do less is hardly worth the title of evaluation.

Whichever method or approach is used, the planner must take into account that there will be a time cost. One particular emphasis must be on the inclusion in the programme for time at different stages for validation approaches, and certainly for the end of course learning questionnaire and action planning. If the course finishes at lunchtime on the final day most of the morning being usefully allocated to this. On longer programmes the simple action plan process can be improved by pairing the participants to discuss their plans and make mutual suggestions for improvements. This, of course, requires even more essential time, but it is well worth it, as is any time devoted to validation and evaluation.

PLANNING CONCLUSION

I hope the reader has found the practical advice given for planning training and development sessions and programmes of use and has not been put off by the apparent complexity of the techniques and approaches. I have tried to keep them as straightforward and readily practical as possible, but whatever time is spent on planning, whether in business or not, this time is well spent, any event being less than effective without it. There are strong arguments for having a training programme planner in an organization, whether to plan and develop the programmes before passing them over to the course/session planner/practitioners, perform the full process hand in hand with the practitioner, or as a consultant, internal or external, to the practitioner/planner. It is essential for any training planner to have an extensive knowledge of training practices and techniques, usually more wide ranging than the practitioners themselves, and the 'external' location of such a planner ensures that views and guidance are made from a neutral standpoint.

Recommended and Further Reading

Publications relating to all areas of training and development are now abundant, quite a different situation from when I wrote my first book, *The Skills of Training*, in 1983 – which I did precisely because of this very lack of training advice books. The following list contains books to which I have referred in the text, and others, the majority of which I have used and can recommend. But there are many more and, like activities, it is difficult at times to find the one you want. Obtain catalogues and book lists from the principal publishers and use personally recommended books. Another source is the *Training Journal*, which publishes in the monthly issue reviews and announcements of recent books, videos and other resources, principally with a training and development connection. The Internet now has online bookshops where information can be sought and publications purchased (eg www.Amazon.co.uk and www.uk.bol.com). Gower publishes an *Interactive Directory of Training Resources* on PC disks that give instant reference to 6,200 CD-ROMs, CD-is, computer-based training products, open learning programmes, training videos, activity manuals and books in over 200 topics from 140 publishers and producers. The major publishers also have Web sites where online catalogues can searched and in many cases books ordered online.

Activities

Elgood, Chris (1993), *Handbook of Management Games*, 5th edn, Gower.

Elgood, Chris (1996), *Using Management Games*, 2nd edn, Gower.

Jones, Ken (1993), *Imaginative Events*, **1** and **2**, McGraw-Hill.

Jones, Ken (1997), *Games and Simulations Made Easy*, Kogan Page.

Ments, Morry van (1999), *The Effective Use of Role Play*, 2nd edn, Kogan Page.

Rae, Leslie (1999), *Using Activities in Training and Development*, 2nd edn, Kogan Page.
Russell, Tim (1998), *Effective Feedback Skills*, 2nd edn, Kogan Page.

Coaching, etc

Alred, Geoff, Garvey, Bob and Smith, Richard (1998), *The Mentoring Pocketbook*, Management Pocketbooks.
Atherton, Tony (1999), *How to be Better at Delegation and Coaching*, Kogan Page.
Buckley, Roger and Caple, Jim (1996), *One-to-One Training and Coaching Skills*, 2nd edn, Kogan Page.
Fleming, Ian and Taylor, Allan J D (1998), *The Coaching Pocketbook*, Management Pocketbooks.
Jerome, P J (1995), *Coaching Through Effective Feedback*, Kogan Page.
Parsloe, Eric and Wray, Monika (2000), *Coaching and Mentoring*, Kogan Page.
Salisbury, Frank (1994), *Developing Managers as Coaches: A trainer's guide*, McGraw-Hill.

Computer, Internet and Web training

Crainer, S (1995), *The Complete Computer Trainer*, McGraw-Hill.
Greer, T (1998), *Understanding Intranets*, Microsoft Press.
McConnell, D (2000), *Implementing Computer-supported Co-operative Learning*, 2nd edn, Kogan Page.
McDowell, Steve and Race, Phil (1998), *500 Computing Tips*, Kogan Page.
Steed, Colin (1999), *Web-based Training*, Gower.
Tucker, B (1997), *Handbook of Technology-based Training*, Gower.
Wynn, Peter (1994), Computer-based training, in *Handbook of Training and Development*, 2nd edn, ed John Prior, Gower.

General training techniques

Adair, John (1986), *Effective Teambuilding*, Gower.
Bailey, Diane (1998), *The Training Handbook*, Gee (also now on CD-ROM).
Buckley, Roger and Caple, Jim (2000), *The Theory and Practice of Training*, 4th edn, Kogan Page.
Buzan, Tony (1984), *Use Your Head*, BBC Publications/Ariel.
Buzan, Tony (1986), *Use Your Memory*, BBC Publications.
Cotton, Julie (1995), *The Theory of Learners*, Kogan Page.

Cotton, Julie (1995), *The Theory of Learning*, Kogan Page.
Cotton, Julie (1995), *The Theory of Learning Strategies*, Kogan Page.
Davis, John (1992), *How to Write a Training Manual*, Gower.
Forsyth, Patrick (1992), *Running an Effective Training Session*, Gower.
Landale, Anthony (ed) (1999), *Handbook of Training and Development*, Gower.
Margerison, C J, McCann, D J and Davies, R V (1986), The Margerison and McCann team management resource: theory and applications, *International Journal of Manpower*, **7** (2).
Rae, Leslie (1988), *The Skills of Interviewing*, Gower.
Rae, Leslie (1992), *Guide to In-company Training Methods*, Gower.
Rae, Leslie (1995), *Techniques of Training*, 3rd edn, Gower.
Rae, Leslie (1998), *Using People Skills in Training and Development*, Kogan Page.
Rae, Leslie (1998), *Using Training Aids in Training and Development*, Kogan Page.
Rickards, Tudor (1988), *Creativity at Work*, Gower.
Robson, Mike (1988), *Quality Circles: A practical guide*, 2nd edn, Gower.
Siddons, Suzy (1997), *Delivering Training*, IPD.
Thorne, Kaye (1988), *Training Places*, Kogan Page.
Tilling, Mike (1999), *The Induction Organiser*, Gower.
Tilling, Mike (1999), *The Learning Organiser*, Gower.
Townsend, John (1996), *The Trainer's Pocketbook*, 8th edn, Management Pocketbooks.

Learning

Honey, Peter and Mumford, Alan (1992), *Manual of Learning Styles*, Honey.
Honey, Peter and Mumford, Alan (1996), *How to Manage Your Learning Environment*, Honey.
Kolb, David (1984), *Experiential Learning*, Prentice-Hall.

Planning Training Programmes

Bailey, Diane and Sproston, Clare (1993), *Choosing and Using Consultants*, Gower.
Bourner, Tom, Martin, Vivien and Race, Phil (1993), *Workshops That Work: 100 ideas to make your training events more effective*, McGraw-Hill.
Cartey, Ron (1996), *Inspirational Training*, Gower.
Fletcher, Shirley (1997), *Designing Competence-based Training*, 2nd edn, Kogan Page.

Harrison, Nigel (1995), *Practical Instructional Design for Open Learning Materials*, McGraw-Hill.
Hottos, S (1993), *CD-i Designers Guide*, McGraw-Hill.
Leatherman, Dick (1990), *Designing Training Programmes*, Gower.
Mager, Robert F (1984), *Preparing Instructional Objectives*, Pitman.
Mager, Robert F (1988), *Making Instruction Work*, Lake Books.
Pinnington, Ashley (1992), *Using Video in Training and Education*, McGraw-Hill.
Pont, Tony (1996), *Developing Effective Training Skills: A practical guide to designing and delivering group training*, McGraw-Hill.
Rae, Leslie (1994), *How to Design and Introduce Trainer Development Programmes*, Kogan Page.
Rae, Leslie (1994), *The Trainer Development Programme*, Kogan Page.
Truelove, Steve (1997), *Training in Practice*, Blackwell Business.

Training needs analysis and evaluation

Bartram, Sharon and Gibson, Brenda (1994), *Training Needs Analysis*, Gower.
Bartram, Sharon and Gibson, Brenda (1999), *Evaluating Training*, Gower.
Bramley, Peter (1996), *Evaluating Training*, IPD.
Craig, Malcolm (1994), *Analysing Learning Needs*, Gower.
Kirkpatrick, Donald L (1996), *Evaluating Training Programs: The four levels*, Berret-Koehler.
Petersen, Robyn (1998), *Training Needs Assessment*, 2nd edn, Kogan Page.
Rae, Leslie (1997), *How to Measure Training Effectiveness*, 3rd edn, Gower.
Rae, Leslie (1999), *Using Evaluation in Training and Development*, Kogan Page.
Reay, David (1995), *Evaluating Training*, Kogan Page.

Index

action learning 104–05
activity planning 176–87
activity resources 182–85
  observation of activities 186–87
  planning the introduction 185–86
  planning questions 176–80
  reviewing activities 186–87
  technological advances 182–84
    Echelon learning library 183
    GAIA project 183
    Internet 182–83
    Learning Zone 183
    US sites 184
  types of activity 180–81
alternative learning model 24
alternative on-the-job training approaches 101–24
  action learning 104–05
  books 106–08
    patterned note-taking 107–08, 174–75
  computer assisted training (CAT) programs 115
  computer based training programs 115–16
  job rotation 103–04
  multimedia open learning packages 112–15
  open learning packages 108–12
  quality circles 102
  secondments 102–03
  self-learning packages 108
  support groups 105–06
  Web and Internet based training 116–18
areas of responsibility 9–14

barriers to learning 33–42
  attributable to trainer 39–41
  environmental factors 41–42

coaching 72–82
  benefits 74–75
  disadvantages 75
  practice (stages) 75–82
  uses 72–73
computer assisted training (CAT) 115
computer based training (CBT) 115–24
  benefits 118–19
  disadvantages 119–20
  trainer attitudes 120–21
  use of planning 121–24

delegation 97–99
  barriers 97–99
  process 99

establishing training priorities 54
evaluation planning 191–210
  definitions 191–92
  limited evaluation plan 200–210
    post-training evaluation 206–10
    process 201–06
      action plan 205–06
      appropriate reactionnaire 202–05
      recommended questionnaire 202–03
  process planning 198–99
    Kirkpatrick model 199–200
    other evaluation models 199–200
    twelve stage model 198–99
  reactionnaires 192–93
  reasons 193–94
  who undertakes evaluation 194–97

learning 22–44
  alternative learning model 24
  barriers to learning 33–39
    attributable to trainers 39–41
    environmental barriers 41–42
  learning attention span 42–43
  Learning Cycle (Kolb) 22–24
  Learning Style Questionnaire (Honey and Mumford) 24–29
  learning styles and effects on learning 30–31
  sensory learning 31–33
Learning Cycle (Kolb) 22–24
learning session 157–65
  designing stages 157
    learner objectives 158–59
    material priorities 160
    method 161
    sequence 161–64
    session plan 164–65
    time 160–61, 166

trainer objectives 159
training aids 164
summary of approaches and strategies 162–63
Learning Style Questionnaire (Honey and Mumford) 24–29

mentoring 90–91
multimedia open learning training packages 112–15
audio cassettes 112
audio-visual packages 112–13
trigger video 114
video and interactive video 113–15

off-the-job training 127–56
advantages 131
conferences 137
disadvantages 132
objectives 128–29
planning process 128
seminars 137
time 132–33
training accommodation 129–37
training formats 135–37
training methods 138–56
training programme planning guide 133–35
workshops 136–37
off-the-job training formats 135–37
conferences 137
seminars 137
training courses 135–36
workshops 136
off-the-job training methods 138–56
activities 148–52
action summary 152
choosing 149–51
restraints 148–49
technological advances 151–52
brainstorming 152–53
buzz groups 140
case studies 144
CAT, CBT and CD-i 154–55
demonstrations 142
discussions 141–42
planning 155–56
question and answer sessions 143
role plays 146–48
action summaries 148
observing 147
review and feedback 147
videos 153–54
simulations 145
trainer presentations 138–40
one-to-one instruction 83–89
criteria 84
cycle 84–85
designing 88–89
planning 85–88
on-the-job training 63–97
consideration of target population 64–67
level of starting knowledge 66–67
location 67
training 67
planning stages 63
programme material 68–71
competences 68–71
references to agreed objectives 63
types of approaches 71–91
coaching 72–82
delegation 94–99
GAFO 71
mentoring 90–91
one-to-one instruction 83–89
project management 89–90
team development 91–97
open learning 108–12
planning 110–11
text-based 111–12

patterned note-taking 107–08, 174–75
pre-course questionnaire 15
project management 89–90

quality circles 106

sensory learning 31–35
session planning methods 166–75
headline method 169–71
horizontal planning 172–74
OHP slides as briefs 171–72
patterned notes 174–75
traditional text format 166–69
vertical text format 166–69
SMART 46
start of course 15–18
identifying key needs of learners 16–17
T-Chart 16–17
'What do you want?' activity 18
'Who am I?' activity 17–18
support groups 105–06

team development 91–97
four stages 93–95
team roles 95–97
training approaches 54
training cycle 7–8
training objectives 45–59
action plan 56
advantages 50
clarification 52–54
disadvantages 50–51
practical application 52, 57–59
during and at end of programme 59
prior to programme 57–58
start of programme 58–59
SMART 46–49
training quintet 9–14, 194–97
learner 13–15, 197
learner workshops 14
other learner approaches 14–15
line manager 11–12, 197
senior management 9–10, 195
trainer 13–14, 196–97
training manager 10–11, 196

Web- and Internet-based training 116–24